GLOBAL
GENDER ISSUES

DILEMMAS IN WORLD POLITICS

Series Editor

George A. Lopez, University of Notre Dame

Dilemmas in World Politics offers teachers and students of international relations a series of quality books on critical issues, trends, and regions in international politics. Each text examines a "real world" dilemma and is structured to cover the historical, theoretical, practical, and projected dimensions of its subject.

EDITORIAL BOARD

GLOBAL GENDER ISSUES

■ ■ ■

SECOND EDITION

V. Spike Peterson
University of Arizona

Anne Sisson Runyan
Wright State University

Westview Press

A Member of the Perseus Books Group

Dilemmas in World Politics Series

Cover photos: *(left)* UNHCR/S. Errington; *(center top)* Anne Sisson Runyan; *(center bottom)* Gary Massoni/AFSC; *(right)* Amnesty International

Copyright © 1999 by V. Spike Peterson and Anne Sisson Runyan

Published in 1999 in the United States of America by Westview Press, 5500 Central Avenue, Boulder, Colorado 80301-2877, and in the United Kingdom by Westview Press, 12 Hid's Copse Road, Cumnor Hill, Oxford OX2 9JJ

Library of Congress Cataloging-in-Publication Data
Peterson, V. Spike
   Global gender issues / V. Spike Peterson and Anne Sisson Runyan. —
2nd ed.
      p. cm. — (Dilemmas in world politics)
   Includes bibliographical references and index.
   ISBN 0-8133-6852-9 (pbk.)
      1. Women in politics. 2. World politics—20th century.
I. Runyan, Anne Sisson. II. Title. III. Series.
HQ1236.P45 1999
305.42—dc21   98-39827
                                                                        CIP

The paper used in this publication meets the requirements of the American National Standard for Permanence of Paper for Printed Library Materials Z39.48-1984.

10   9   8   7   6   5   4   3   2   1

To our sisters,
for all that we share

□ □ □

Contents

1 Introduction: The Gender of World Politics   1

How Lenses Work, 1
Why Global? 3
Why Gender? 5
Why Issues? 13
The Immediacy and Import of Global Gender Issues, 14
Notes About This Text, 15
Mapping the Book, 17
Notes, 18

2 Gender as a Lens on World Politics   21

Denaturalizing Gender, 29
The Social Construction of Gender and Gender Hierarchy, 33
The Gendered Who, What, and How of World Politics, 48
Gendered Divisions of World Politics, 51
Conclusion, 61
Notes, 65

3 Gendered Divisions of Power   69

Women as State Actors, 70
How and Why Are These Women Rendered Invisible? 78
Why So Few? 83
How Do Women Get to the Top? 94
What Are the Gender Consequences of Women in Power? 95
What Makes Actors/Agents Powerful? Who Gets Attention?
   For What? 97

□ □ □

Tables and Illustrations

Acknowledgments
to the Second Edition

Contrary to common assumptions and our expectations, a second edition can be more difficult than the first. In this case, we faced the challenge of both documenting how the world has radically changed and reflecting how the field of gender and international relations has substantially grown since the early 1990s. When our first edition appeared, the Cold War had barely subsided and the process of globalization or global restructuring was only beginning to be analyzed. There were also few book-length treatments of gender and world politics available. Unfortunately, the few hopeful signs that the world was changing for the better in the early 1990s dissipated quickly. Encouragingly, however, the reassertions of oppressive world-politics-as-usual have been met by the broadening and deepening of local, national, and transnational women's and other gender-aware social movements committed to political, economic, social, cultural, and ecological justice. Feminist challenges to the study of international-relations-as-usual have also proliferated, within as well as outside of the discipline. We take particular pleasure in noting the extensive book and journal literature produced by members of the now ten-year-old Feminist Theory and Gender Studies section of the International Studies Association.

It is these women and men, struggling in progressive social movements and doing critical work in academe, whom we especially thank for continuing to build supportive, caring, and joyous communities that enlarge the space for feminist transformations of the international relations field and world politics more generally. We cannot do justice to the breadth and complexity of their work, but we do acknowledge how crucial these communities of activists, scholars, teachers, and friends are to our well-being and that of the planet.

Thanks also go to the many teachers around the world who have used the first edition of our book to introduce the study of gender and international relations to students in their undergraduate and graduate courses. It is for them and for their (and our) many students—who are the future of feminist international relations thought and feminist world politics practice—that we prepared this second edition. We can only hope it will continue to serve this important purpose and its readers well.

In addition, we wish to thank the many people who suggested changes to and provided new materials for this second edition. They include Marianne Marchand, Sandra Whitworth (and her students), Margaret Leahy, Laura Parisi, Cynthia Enloe, and several anonymous reviewers. We could not address all of their insightful comments without producing an entirely new book, but we have accommodated many of their suggestions and are grateful for the time and energy they invested. Many thanks, too, go to the numerous artists, cartoonists, and photographers whose images of gender injustice and women's struggles enliven the pages of this book.

We also acknowledge Westview Press for seeing the need for and encouraging us to produce a second edition. Thanks in particular go to the series editor, George Lopez; the Westview editorial staff in New York, including Leo Wiegman, Adina Popescu, and Kwon Chong; and Jane Raese and Kristin Milavec as well as other Westview production staff members in Boulder. Special thanks go to Christine Arden for competent and insightful copyediting. We all weathered the storms of ownership and staffing changes at Westview and look forward to its continued commitment to publishing progressive texts on world politics.

More personally, Anne is indebted to her support staff at Wright State University, including Joanne Ballmann for her extraordinary manuscript production skills and many kindnesses; Women's Studies secretary Pamela Mondini and Women's Studies student assistant Jacqueline Ingram for their help with correspondence, research, and photocopying; and graphic artist Bruce Stiver for the production of charts and graphs. Anne is also grateful for the faculty development grant and other travel and research funds that were provided by Wright State University's College of Liberal Arts to subsidize the preparation of the manuscript.

Anne further thanks family, friends, and colleagues nearby and far away for nurturing and nourishing her feminist ideals and work. Although her sister, Malinda, did not live to see the first edition and her father passed away during the preparation of the second, they live on in her commitments to social justice, which they shared. Her mother, whom she now can take care of, continues to teach her and her remaining sisters to remember. To her husband, Albert Adrian Kanters, she owes her deepest gratitude for his loving support of her work and her life for so long. And to Spike goes love and sisterhood always.

Spike is indebted to a number of overlapping communities. Closest to her heart, because they provide affirmation, sustenance, and partnership-in-partying, are close friends: especially rosie, eva, paula, and jane. A wider circle of feminists in Tucson, family in Illinois, and friends around the world constitute a community of support and inspiration for which Spike expresses deep gratitude and affection. Students make a different difference. Their questions, insights, challenges, contributions, and, often, friendship make academe a place worth being. Friends among the Feminist Theory and Gender Studies section comprise another special community. Their personal support, solidarity of spirit, and professional interventions in the field of international relations make it, too, a place worth being. Less concrete but equally crucial, the scholarship and activism of feminists around the world are sources of inspiration to Spike. Being critical of domination takes courage; doing it with love in your heart *and* in your strategies takes much more. Spike honors and thanks the loving radicals who combine these traits, and especially the many who face dire consequences for doing so.

Finally, Spike is still learning to decipher Anne's handwriting—and still learning from her how to love better. But the best part is how they laugh together.

V. Spike Peterson
Anne Sisson Runyan

□ □ □

Acknowledgments
to the First Edition

Venturing into new terrain requires vision as well as commitment. Our thanks go first to George Lopez, the series editor, for recognizing the importance of gender as a dilemma in world politics. Jennifer Knerr's professional guidance and personal warmth were invaluable for keeping not only our efforts but also our enthusiasm on track. Of the many other people at Westview who eased our task, and editorial board members who supported our project, we thank especially Marian Safran, Libby Barstow, Deborah Gerner, and Karen Mingst. From start to finish, the farsightedness and expertise of Lev Gonick and Mary Ann Tetreault have enhanced this project and its product.

Exploring new terrain requires bold spirits and reliable support systems. Among the bold spirits, we thank our foremothers, who took great risks to clear new paths, and our feminist colleagues, who also take risks in order to pursue and expand those paths. Our support system is the global community of feminists who refuse to separate theory and practice. Of the countless women and men who make up this community, we thank especially our friends in the Feminist Theory and Gender Studies section of the International Studies Association, who have given us invaluable support, encouragement—and permission to party. In particular, because the integrity of their energy makes such an important difference, we acknowledge our appreciation of Simona Sharoni, Theresa Scionti, and Judy Logan.

More personally, Anne thanks her secretary, Jackie Brisson, and her student assistants, Michele Sylvestri and Mary Burns, for their tremendous assistance with research, photocopying, mailings, and tracking down addresses and phone numbers (mostly of illustration copyright holders, many of whom were very gracious and helpful). It was, indeed, an all-women struggle at SUNY–Potsdam that brought Anne's part of the book to fruition. She also thanks her husband, Al Kanters, who, as always, lovingly cared for her basic needs throughout this project. It is the reproductive work of men like him that makes the productive work of women possible. She is also grateful to family members, friends, and colleagues, close by and far away, who have so strongly supported her feminist ideals and her feminist work. Finally, she offers her heartfelt appreciation to Spike, who has been not only an intellectual partner but a dear friend and true "sister."

Spike leaned heavily on the research assistance and emotional support so effectively rendered by graduate students Stacey Mayhall, Jacqui True, and Anwara Begum. Words only begin to convey how the community generated during the states seminar has enhanced Spike's quality of life. She is indebted to this group especially—and students more generally— because they not only make the hard work worthwhile but also keep her mentally and physically dancing. "It doesn't get any better than this." Her deepest thanks, as ever, go to family and friends whose love, affirmation, and inspiration keep her going—and growing; to those whose ways of being, loving, and knowing offer a lighted path: thanks especially to beryl, eva, rosie, and ozone. Finally, she wants to let Anne know that the best part of this project, like their friendship, was/is learning to love better, for which Anne gets the credit.

V. Spike Peterson
Anne Sisson Runyan

Acronyms

AAFSW	Association of American Foreign Service Women
AAWORD	African Association of Women for Research and Development
AFL-CIO	American Federation of Labor and Congress of Industrial Organizations
AIDS	acquired immune deficiency syndrome
Alt-WID	Alternative Women in Development (United States)
AMNLAE	Luisa Amanda Espinosa Nicaraguan Women's Association
AMPRONAC	Association of Nicaraguan Women Confronting the Nation's Problems
B-WAC	Brooklyn Welfare Action Council
CDS	Sandinista Defense Committees
CEDAW	Convention on the Elimination of All Forms of Discrimination Against Women
CEO	chief executive officer
COSATU	Congress of South African Trade Unions
CRIAW	Canadian Research Institute for the Advancement of Women
DAWN	Development Alternatives with Women for a New Era
DSWA	Diplomatic Service Wives Association (Great Britain)
ECE	Economic Commission for Europe
EPS	Sandinista People's Army
EPZ	export-processing zone
EU	European Union
FDI	foreign direct investment
FLS	Forward Looking Strategies for the Advancement of Women
FSLN	Sandinista National Liberation Front
FTZ	free trade zone
GABRIELA	General Assembly Binding Women for Reform, Integrity, Equality, Leadership, and Action

GAD	gender and development
GATT	General Agreement on Tariffs and Trade
GDP	gross domestic product
GNP	gross national product
ICFTU	International Confederation of Free Trade Unions
ICJ	International Court of Justice
IFI	international financial institution
IGO	intergovernmental organization
ILGWU	International Ladies Garment Workers Union
ILO	International Labor Organization
IMF	International Monetary Fund
IPU	Inter-Parliamentary Union
IR	international relations
ISIS/WICCE	Women's International Information and Communication Service
MNC	multinational corporation
MPS	Sandinista Popular Militias
NAC	National Action Committee on the Status of Women (Canada)
NAFTA	North American Free Trade Agreement
NATO	North Atlantic Treaty Organization
NGO	nongovernmental organization
OPEC	Organization of Petroleum Exporting Countries
PR	proportional representation
SAP	structural adjustment program
SEWA	Self-Employed Women's Association (India)
SID-WID	Society for International Development/Women in Development Programme (Europe)
TNC	transnational corporation
TRIPs	Trade-Related Intellectual Property Rights
TUC	Trade Union Congress (United Kingdom)
UK	United Kingdom
UN	United Nations
UNCED	United Nations Conference on Environment and Development
UNDAW	United Nations Division for the Advancement of Women
UNDP	United Nations Development Programme
UNED	United Nations Environment Programme
UNESCO	United Nations Educational, Scientific, and Cultural Organization
UNFPA	United Nations Fund for Population Activities
UNHCR	United Nations High Commission for Refugees

UNICEF	United Nations Children's Fund
UNIFEM	United Nations Development Fund for Women
UNSNA	United Nations System of National Accounts
US	United States
USAID	United States Agency for International Development
WAND	Women and Development Unit (Caribbean)
WAO	Women's Action Organization (United States)
WED	women, environment, and development
WEDO	Women, Environment and Development Organization in the United States
WFP	World Food Programme
WHO	World Health Organization
WID	women in development
WIDE	Women in Development Europe
WILPF	Women's International League for Peace and Freedom
WPP	Woman's Peace Party (United States)
WTO	World Trade Organization

GLOBAL
GENDER ISSUES

ONE

□ □ □

Introduction:
The Gender of World Politics

In this text, we explore how world politics looks when viewed through a **gender-sensitive lens.** This lens enables us to "see" how the world is shaped by gendered concepts, practices, and institutions. To introduce the text—and establish its significance to international relations (IR)—we first consider the metaphor of lenses: How do lenses focus our vision and filter what we "know"? How does this focusing and filtering shape our lived experience—what we think of as "reality"—and our understanding of it? We then take each of the terms in our title, *Global Gender Issues,* and answer the questions: Why global? Why gender? Why issues? We also clarify why global gender issues, which have not traditionally been a focus of analysis, are important to the study of world politics *now.* Finally, we identify some assumptions made in this text and outline the chapters to follow.

HOW LENSES WORK

Whenever we study a topic, we do so through a lens that necessarily focuses our attention in particular ways. By filtering or "ordering" what we look at, each lens enables us to see some things in greater detail or more accurately or in better relation to certain other things. But this is unavoidably at the expense of seeing other things that are rendered out of focus—filtered out—by each particular lens.

According to Paul Viotti and Mark Kauppi, various theoretical perspectives, or "images," of international politics contain certain assumptions and lead us "to ask certain questions, seek certain types of answers, and use certain methodological tools."[1] For example, different images act as

1

lenses and shape our assumptions about who the significant actors are (individuals? states? multinational corporations?), what their attributes are (rationality? self-interest? power?), how social processes are categorized (politics? cooperation? dependence?), and what outcomes are desirable (peace? national security? global equity?).

The images or lenses we use have important consequences because they structure what we look for and are able to "see." In Patrick Morgan's words, "Our conception of [IR acts as a] map for directing our attention and distributing our efforts, and using the wrong map can lead us into a swamp instead of taking us to higher ground."[2]

What we look for depends a great deal on how we make sense of, or "order," our experience. We learn our ordering systems in a variety of contexts. From infancy on, we are taught to make distinctions enabling us to perform appropriately within a particular culture. As college students, we are taught the distinctions appropriate to particular disciplines (psychology, anthropology, political science) and particular schools of thought within them (realism, behavioralism, liberalism, structuralism). No matter in which context we learned them, the categories and ordering frameworks shape the lenses through which we look at, think about, and make sense of the world around us. At the same time, the lenses we adopt shape our experience of the world itself because they shape what we do and how and why we do it. For example, a political science lens focuses our attention on particular categories and events (the meaning of power, democracy, or elections) in ways that variously influence our behavior (questioning authority, protesting abuse of power, or participating in electoral campaigns).

By filtering our ways of thinking about and ordering experience, the categories and images we rely on shape how we behave and thus the world we live in: They have concrete consequences. We observe this readily in the case of self-fulfilling prophecies: If we *expect* hostility, our own behavior (acting superior, displaying power) may elicit responses (defensive posturing, aggression) that we then interpret as "confirming" our expectations. It is in this sense that we refer to lenses and "realities" as interactive, interdependent, or mutually constituted. Lenses shape who we are, what we think, and what actions we take, thus shaping the world we live in. At the same time, the world we live in ("reality") shapes which lenses are available to us, what we see through them, and the likelihood of our using them in particular contexts.

In general, as long as our lenses and images seem to "work," we keep them and build on them. Lenses simplify our thinking. Like maps, they "frame" our choices and exploration, enabling us to take advantage of knowledge already gained and to move more effectively toward our objectives. The more useful they appear to be, the more we are inclined to take them for granted and to resist making major changes in them. We forget that our particular ordering or meaning system is a choice among many alternatives. Instead, we tend to believe we are seeing "reality" as it "is" rather than as our culture or discipline or image interprets or "maps" reality. It is difficult and sometimes uncomfortable to reflect critically on our assumptions, to question their accuracy or desirability, and to explore the implications of shifting our vantage point by adopting a different lens.

Of course, the world we live in and therefore our experiences are constantly changing; we have to continuously modify our images, mental maps, and ordering systems as well. The required shift in lens may be minor: from liking one type of music to liking another, from being a high school student in a small town to being a college student in an urban environment. Or the shift may be more pronounced: from casual dating to parenting, from the freedom of student lifestyles to the assumption of full-time job responsibilities, from Newtonian to quantum physics, from East-West rivalry to post–Cold War complexities. Societal shifts are dramatic, as we experience and respond to systemic transformations such as economic restructuring, environmental degradation, or the effects of war.

To function effectively as students and scholars of world politics, we must modify our thinking in line with historical developments. That is, as "reality" changes, our ways of understanding or ordering need to change as well. This is especially the case to the extent that outdated worldviews or lenses place us in danger, distort our understanding, or lead us away from our objectives. Indeed, as both early explorers and urban drivers know, outdated maps are inadequate, and potentially disastrous, guides.

WHY GLOBAL?

In textbooks on world politics, the history of international relations has two interrelated dimensions. On the one hand, actual world events are identified as the "substance"—the *what*—of IR. Examples include: the formation of European states since the Peace of Westphalia, the wars between nation-states that shift boundaries and shape international power dynamics, and the economic and technological developments that affect interactions between states. On the other hand, the history of IR refers to the development of the academic discipline itself—that is, to *how* we study or think about the "what" of IR. This second dimension is about what framework, image, or lens is used to make sense of the events and institutions that we are studying. Typically, textbooks present images of IR or schools of thought as they have appeared in the historical development of the discipline (e.g., idealism, realism, pluralism). In short, our ways of thinking about IR are shaped by our perception of "real world" events.

Developments in the discipline of IR exemplify this interaction of changing events and frameworks. The "what" of IR after World War II included East-West blocs, bipolar economic and military rivalry, expanded militarization, and a U.S.-based capitalist world economy. The dominant IR lens, realism, made sense of these events by identifying states, acting as unitary and rational decision-makers in pursuit of the national interest, as the primary units of analysis. The national interest was defined as national security (maintaining state sovereignty), which could be achieved most effectively by manipulations of power (understood as material attributes enabling military success).

In contrast, the "what" of IR in the 1970s included increasingly powerful multinational, or transnational, corporations (MNCs or TNCs), many new Third World states, a U.S. defeat in Vietnam, energy issues raised by the power of the Organization of Petroleum Exporting Countries (OPEC), and transformations in the global economic system. As international relations responded to and shaped these historical developments, the images of IR were altered and expanded. International relations analysts increasingly recognized the significance of nonstate and interstate actors as well as the complexity of states as actors. They asked new questions about whether states were unitary decision-makers and focused more on the multiple actors and agencies determining foreign policy. The U.S. defeat in Vietnam confirmed that military power alone could not ensure victory. Analysts questioned existing categories and frameworks. Previous images were adjusted and new images emerged to make better sense of changes taking place on the stage of world politics.

As images and frameworks were adjusted, different issues, actors, and processes gained visibility. Domestic bureaucratic politics were revealed as significant factors in foreign policy decision-making. The role of misperceptions in decision-making by national leaders became a focus of inquiry. Increased Third World voices in the General Assembly of the United Nations (UN) focused attention on the relationships between prosperity of the North and underdevelopment of the South. Regimes analysis explored how states in fact cooperate even without reference to governmental structures.

The world at the turn of the century confirms the need to rethink categories and frameworks as we pursue new understandings that "match" new world politics. For example, both decentralization (marked by subnationalist movements) and centralization processes (exemplified by the European Union) challenge conventional accounts of sovereign states. The demise of the former Soviet Union disrupts decades of East-West analysis. Crises of nuclear proliferation, economic maldevelopment, transborder epidemics, and environmental degradation cannot be addressed by state-centric decision-making. And in response to global crises, social movements around the world demand more than the absence of war: People are raising deeper questions about the nature of power, the abuse of human rights, the human costs of global inequities, and the meaning of a just world order.

Consistent with trends in IR thinking that recognize the limitations of state-centric analyses, the use of the term *global* in our title points not simply to the actions of states or between states but to how those actions are embedded in a global context marked by international but also sub-, trans-, and supranational processes. The global focus does not exclude states or minimize their political power, but it does include more than interstate actions. As current events suggest, it is not only state power but also transnational political, military, economic, and social processes that are the "what" of today's "real world." To study this "what" effectively requires a global lens.

WHY GENDER?

The data regarding how men and women are situated differently within global processes reveals, starkly, the extent of gender inequality. In 1997 the United Nations Development Programme (UNDP) unequivocally concluded that "no society treats its women as well as its men."[3] In 1981 it was reported to the UN Committee on the Status of Women that women composed one-half of the world's population and performed two-thirds of the world's work hours, yet were everywhere poorer in resources and poorly represented in elite positions of decision-making power.[4] Little has changed, as shown in Figure 1.1. Although systematic inequalities between men and women are made vividly clear through these statistics, the important question in this text is how such inequalities are relevant to the study of world politics.

Unlike **sex** (understood as the biological distinction between males and females), **gender** refers to socially learned behavior and expectations that distinguish between masculinity and femininity. Whereas biological sex identity is determined by reference to genetic and anatomical characteristics, socially learned gender is an acquired identity gained through performing prescribed gender roles. Moreover, because societies place different values on masculine and feminine behaviors, gender is also the basis for relations of inequality between men and women. Finally, gender is a particularly powerful lens through which all of us see and organize reality. (Gender as a lens is explored more thoroughly in Chapter 2.)

6

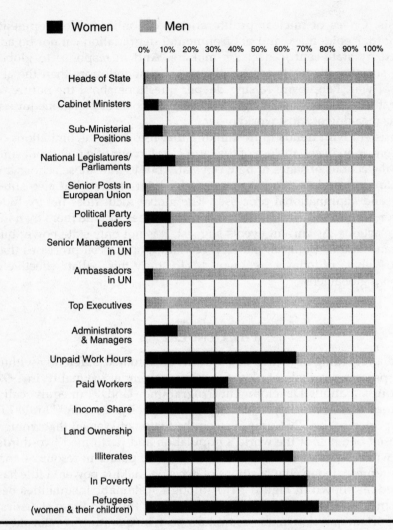

FIGURE 1.1 Global Gender Inequalities: Percentages of Women and Men in Various Important Categories. *Sources:* Data from United Nations, *The World's Women 1995: Trends and Statistics* (New York: United Nations, 1995); United Nations Development Program, *Human Development Report 1995* (New York: Oxford University Press, 1995); United Nations Development Program, *Human Development Report 1997* (New York: Oxford University Press, 1997); Inter-Parliamentary Union, *Towards Partnership Between Men and Women in Politics, Reports and Documents No. 29* (Geneva: Interparliamentary Union, 1997); Ruth Leger Sivard, *Women . . . A World Survey,* 2nd ed. (Washington, D.C.: World Priorities, 1995); Noleen Heyzer, ed., *A Commitment to the World's Women* (New York: UNIFEM, 1995); Joni Seager, *The State of Women in the World Atlas,* 2nd ed. (London: Penguin Press, 1997).

We *learn*, through culturally specific socialization, what characteristics are associated with masculinity and femininity and how to assume the identities of men and women. In this sense, "gender refers to characteristics linked to a particular sex by one's culture."[5] The specific meanings of and values given to masculinity and femininity vary dramatically over time and across cultures. For example, Western ideals of "manliness" have undergone historical shifts: From the early Greeks through the feudal period, the emphasis was on military heroism and political prowess through male bonding and risk-taking, whereas more modern meanings of masculinity stress "competitive individualism, reason, self-control or self-denial, combining respectability as breadwinner and head of household with calculative rationality in public life."[6] Moreover, not all cultures have associated either of these conceptions of masculinity with leadership qualities: "Queen mothers" in Ghana and "clan mothers" in many Native American societies have been accorded power and leadership roles in these matrilineal contexts on the basis of the feminine quality of regeneration of the people and the land.[7] It is also the case that there is some play in gender roles even within patrilineal or patriarchal cultures given that men are not exclusively leaders and warriors, and women are not exclusively in charge of maintaining the home and caring for children in these contexts. Due to the variation in meanings attached to femininity and masculinity, we know that expressions of gender are not "fixed" or predetermined: The particulars of gender are always shaped by context. However, these variations still rest on concepts of gender differences and do not necessarily disrupt gender as a relation of inequality.

We focus on gender in this text not because other axes of difference and bases of inequality (race/ethnicity, class, religion, age, etc.) are less important than—or even extricable from—gender. Rather, gender is our primary lens because the worldwide institutionalization of gender *differences* is a major underpinning of structural inequalities of significance to world politics. Through a complex interaction of identification processes, symbol systems, and social institutions (which we explore in subsequent chapters), gender differences are produced—typically in the form of a **dichotomy** that not only opposes masculinity to femininity but also translates these oppositional differences into **gender hierarchy,** the privileging of traits and activities defined as masculine over those defined as feminine. Thus, although it is important to recognize the cultural variation in how gender differences are formed and expressed, it is also important to stress the political nature of gender as a system of difference construction and hierarchical dichotomy production that is constitutive of almost all contemporary societies. Gender is about power, and power is gendered. We begin to make this power visible by examining the relationship between masculinity and femininity.

Here we make two points in regard to this relationship in order to elucidate what we mean by gender dichotomy and hierarchy. First, masculinity and femininity are not "independent" categories, such as fruit, children, or labor, but are defined in oppositional *relation* to each other: More of one is understood to mean less of the other—as with ripe versus unripe fruit, active versus passive children, mental versus manual labor. Specifically, the dominant masculinity in Western culture is associated with qualities of rationality, "hardheadedness," ambition, and strength. To the extent that a man displays emotionality, "softheadedness," passivity, and weakness, he is likely to be identified as nonmasculine, which is to say, feminine. Similarly, women who appear hardheaded and ambitious are often described as masculine.

Second, the relationship between masculinity and femininity shows considerable constancy in assigning greater value to that which is associated with masculinity and lesser value to that which is associated with femininity. Again, the terms are not independent but form a hierarchical (unequal) relation that we refer to as a dichotomy (explored further in Chapter 2). Thus, in most—but not all—situations, rationality, hardheadedness, ambition, and strength are perceived as positive and admired traits that are in contrast to less desirable feminine qualities. This hierarchy is readily observed. Consider (in the United States) how different our response is to women wearing pants and even business suits compared to our response to men wearing dresses, ruffles, or flowery prints. Similarly, girls can be tomboys and adopt boyish names, but boys avoid behaving in ways that might result in their being called "sissies" or girlish names. And we applaud women who achieve success in previously male-dominated activities (climbing mountains, becoming astronauts, presiding over colleges), but men who enter traditionally female arenas (water ballet, child care, nursing) are rarely applauded and often treated with suspicion. Females dressing or acting like males appear to be copying or aiming for something valued—they are attempting to improve their status by "moving up." But because feminine characteristics are less valued, boys and men who adopt feminine dress or undertake female roles are more likely to be perceived as "failing" in their manhood or "moving down."

Because of the interdependent nature of this relationship, we learn about both men *and* women when we study gender. When we look at activities associated with masculinity (e.g., team sports, politics, the military), it appears simply that men are present and women are absent. Moreover, it appears that we can explain what is happening simply by attending to the men engaging in these activities. Gender analysis offers a more comprehensive explanation; it enables us to "see" how women are in fact important *to* the picture (enabling men's activities, providing "reasons" for men to fight), even though women and the roles they are expected to play are obscured when we focus only on men (see Figure 1.2). Through a gender-sensitive lens, we see how constructions of masculinity (agency, control, aggression) are not independent of, but rely upon, contrasting constructions of femininity (dependence, vulnerability, passivity). In a sense, the dominant presence of men depends on the denial and absence of women. Because of this interdependence, a gender analysis of women's lives and experiences does not simply "add something" about women but *transforms* what we know about *men* and the activities they undertake. Hence, we study gender to enhance our understanding of the conventional foci of IR: men, masculinity, and masculine activities (power politics, war, economic control).

Gender shapes not only how we identify ourselves and view the world but also how others identify and relate to us and how we are positioned within social structures. For now, we will look at gender divisions of labor as exemplifying the either-or construction that constitutes the dichotomy of masculine and feminine. Consider that women are traditionally associated with childbearing, child rearing, emotional caretaking, and responsibility for the physical maintenance of the household. In contrast, men are associated with the activities of wage labor, physical prowess, intellectual achievements, and political agency. This gender labeling is so strong that even when women work for wages (and women have been wage workers as long as men have), they typically do so in areas regarded as "women's work": taking care of others and providing emotional and maintenance services (counseling, welfare services, clerical support, cleaning).

Labor markets are thus segregated horizontally by gender, with women and men clustered in different occupational roles. They are also segregated vertically, with women concentrated in the lowest-paid, least-protected, and least-powerful positions. And when individual women move up corporate ladders, they run into a "glass ceiling" that obstructs their access to the most powerful positions. This horizontal and vertical

FIGURE 1.2   Gender and War. Gendered explanations for war are lampooned in this cartoon. Copyright © 1982 by Nicole Hollander. From *Mercy, It's the Revolution and I'm in My Bathrobe* by Nicole Hollander. Reprinted by permission of St. Martin's Press, Incorporated.

gender segregation accounts in part for the fact that women—about 40 percent of the paid workforce worldwide—earn approximately 74 cents for every dollar earned by men.[8]

The point is that stereotypes of gender (masculinity and femininity) have consequences for the difference between men's and women's experience in, for example, earning money and exercising public power. Around the world, women are relatively absent from the top decision-making positions of political, economic, and ideological power: Consider the leadership of nations, militaries, corporations, religions, and media. And women are absent in part because gender stereotypes establish leadership as a masculine activity and in part because gender labeling and structures discriminate against women seeking positions of power (as illustrated in Chapter 3). It is in this sense that where women are absent, principles of gender are at work. That is, the disproportional presence or absence of women (or men) does not suggest gender neutrality but in fact demonstrates the personal, political, systemic, and structural effects of gender differentiation. The latter involves defining different qualities, roles, and activities for men and women and ensuring the reproduction of these discriminatory structures.

Gender is not a traditional category of analysis in IR, in terms of either "what" we study or "how" we study it. Nor has gender been raised very often as an issue in IR policy-making. But this picture is changing. In the past several decades, we have accumulated increasing evidence that gender equity is strongly related to the quality of life for everyone in every country.[9] The fundamental message is that "empowering women and improving their status are essential to realizing the full potential of economic, political and social development."[10] Hence, all those who seek a "better world" are advised to take seriously the bettering of women's conditions. This text provides tools for understanding these relationships and how we might more effectively move toward gender equity.

As the text illustrates, gender is salient both as a substantive (empirical, concrete) topic and as a dimension of how we study (analyze, think about) world politics. The former we characterize as the effects of IR on gender, or the *position of women:* where and how women are situated differently than men as a consequence of the practices, processes, and institutions we identify as world politics. We deal with gender as a dimension of the way world politics is studied by referring to the effects of gender on IR, or the *power of gender:* how gender is a category of our mental ordering (a filter or lens) that has consequences for practices, processes, and institutions that we think of as world politics. The position of women (which also reveals the position of men) and the power of gender are two *interacting* themes—two sides of the same coin—that frame the material presented in this text.

The Position of Women in World Politics

We can observe historical changes in men's and women's lives that are elements of world politics and (like developments in state interactions) require that we modify our analytical frameworks if we are to accurately and effectively make sense of our world.

Although the influence of gender is not new (any more than transnational processes are), our awareness of and ability to analyze gender has grown dramatically in the past three decades. The roles of women and the gender issues they raise are particularly obvious in the following developments: the impact of feminist movements; the roles of women in struggles for human rights, nationalist and indigenous self-determination, economic justice, and environmental protection; new understandings of security in the face of systemic gendered violence (war, rape, domestic violence); shifting international divisions of labor in the context of global capitalism; the significance of gender in designing and implementing economic development and structural adjustment policies; the backlash against feminist gains; the role of patriarchy in fundamentalist religions and practices; gender-differentiated effects of state reduction of welfare services; the urgency of reproductive issues and population-planning policies; and, in general, small but significant improvements in the percentages of women engaged in formal politics. The UN Decade for Women (1976–1985) marked the convergence of many of these issues and movements; it also generated—for the first time—worldwide data on the actual conditions of women. Global women's conferences (Mexico City, Copenhagen, Nairobi, Beijing) have nourished international connections among women and illuminated both commonalities and differences (see Figure 1.3). In addition, activities of the United Nations itself—especially the declarations of women's equal rights and the convention to eliminate sex discrimination—have focused attention on the specific conditions of women and on global commitments to gender equality.

The confluence of these and other developments has enabled us to assess the *position of women:* We now have extensive data documenting how women and men are affected differently by global processes.[11] More specifically, we can identify gendered divisions of power, violence, labor, and resources (examined in depth in subsequent chapters) and describe how they have concrete consequences that differ for men and women—how they, in fact, constitute systemic conditions of gender inequality. To make sense of these *concrete* effects, we must also consider how gender functions as a filter or lens that shapes our ways of thinking about and understanding world politics.

FIGURE 1.3   Global gender issues, as articulated by women around the world. Courtesy of International Women's Tribune Center, Inc. Illustrator: Anne S. Walker.

The Power of Gender in World Politics

Today we know a great deal about gender, due to the growth of women's studies programs and gender-sensitive research by scholars in all disciplines. Perhaps the most profound insight emerging from this scholarship is recognition of the pervasiveness of gender as a filtering category. (We elaborate on gender as a lens in the next chapter.) That is, gender-sensitive research does more than document the pattern of excluding or trivializing women and their experiences. It documents how gender—characterizations of masculinity and femininity—influence the very categories and frameworks within which scholars work.

In short, how we understand and value masculine and feminine characteristics profoundly shapes how we care about, perceive, understand, analyze, and critique the world in which we live. Gender thus influences not only who we are, how we live, and what we have, but also "how" we think, order reality, and claim to know what is true, and, hence, how we understand and explain the social world. As subsequent chapters illustrate, gender shapes our identification of global actors, characterization of state and nonstate actions, framing of global problems, and consideration of possible alternatives.

These interacting phenomena—the position of women in world politics and the power of gender as a lens on the world—indicate that gender is important for contemporary understanding of world politics. It is no longer acceptable—and was never accurate—to treat gender as irrelevant to our knowledge of world politics. For these reasons, we offer in this text a *gender-*sensitive lens on global processes. Through this lens, not only the "what" of world politics but also "how" we view—and therefore understand—world politics is different. We see the extent and structure of gender inequality, the role of gender in structuring the experience of women *and* men worldwide, the significance of gender in shaping how we think about world politics, and the process by which gendered thought shapes world politics itself. A text on global gender issues affords more adequate and comprehensive understanding of world politics than do approaches that ignore the effect of world politics on gender relations and the effect of gender on world politics.

WHY ISSUES?

In this book, we examine the "dilemma" of global gender inequalities as a central, not peripheral, dimension of world politics. The text introduces gender as a lens through which to examine traditional IR categories and makes gender *visible* in additional ways that inform our understanding. It is organized around central themes of IR inquiry: politics, security, economics, equity, and ecology. We present and analyze these topics by examining the gendered divisions of power (politics), of violence (security), of labor (economics), and of resources (equity and ecology).

These gendered divisions become the issues in this text. Questions we raise in regard to these issues include: How do we understand power and politics? Where is power located, and who is invested with it? Who has access to political power, and who is accountable for what? How do we understand security, and who is it for? How do we understand work, and who gets paid for what? How are resources distributed and controlled? How do we understand our relationship to nature, and what are the consequences of that understanding?

We cannot address all the concerns raised by a critique of global gender inequalities. Nor can we explore how IR theories might be transformed by an awareness of gender bias. Other books and an extensive body of multidisciplinary journal literature that address themes we cannot treat in depth here are now available.[12] Our presentation of global gender issues is suggestive, not definitive: We attempt to suggest to what extent and in what ways gender is at work in—and a consequence of—world politics. This includes exploring how gender shapes traditional categories and frameworks, thus making gender visible, and asking how gender sensitivity enables new insights to emerge, thus making transformation possible. By restating old questions and/or raising new questions, we reveal how current approaches are selective and omit important dimensions of world politics. We also open up new ways of seeing, and therefore understanding, issues that confront all students of world politics.

THE IMMEDIACY AND IMPORT OF GLOBAL GENDER ISSUES

As ways of being and knowing become institutionalized, we begin to see them as "natural" rather than as socially constructed. Hilary Lips argues that "this apparent naturalness is a source of power for those who would maintain things as they are . . . because they help to make the system [of power relations] invisible, like water to a fish."[13]

Real world developments force us to revise our categories and frameworks to make better sense of those developments. In IR, notions of security have been revised in light of post–Cold War geo- and ethno-politics, technological developments, and spiraling costs of militarization. The meaning of economic development and social well-being has been reexamined in light of global restructuring, the decline of state welfare provisioning, and increasing disparities between "haves" and "have-nots" within and between developed and developing countries. Similarly, recognition of global gender inequalities and the power of gender to order our thinking and shape our reality forces us to acknowledge and make sense of the role of gender in world politics.

Gender issues surface *now* because new questions have been raised that cannot be addressed within traditional frameworks. The amassing of global data reveals the extent and pattern of gender inequality: Women everywhere have less access to political power and economic resources and less control over processes that reproduce this systemic inequality. Moreover, our knowledge of the world of men and the politics they create is biased and incomplete in the absence of knowledge about how men's activities, including their politics, are related to, even dependent upon, what women are doing—and why.

Additionally, recognizing the power of gender as a lens forces us to reevaluate traditional explanations, to ask how they are biased and hence render inadequate accounts. As in other disciplines, the study of world politics is enriched by acknowledging and systematically examining how gender shapes categories and frameworks that we take for granted. This is necessary for answering the new questions raised and for generating fresh insights—about the world as we currently "know" it and how it might be otherwise.

Finally, gender-sensitive studies improve our understanding of global crises, their interactions, and the possibilities of moving beyond them.

These include crises of political legitimacy and security as states are increasingly unable to protect their citizens against economic, epidemic, nuclear, or ecological threats; crises of maldevelopment as the dynamics of our global economic system enrich a few and impoverish most; and crises of environmental degradation as the exploitation of natural resources continues in unsustainable fashion.

These global crises cannot be understood or addressed without acknowledging the structural inequalities of the current world system, inequalities that extend well beyond gender issues: They are embodied in interacting hierarchies of race, class, ethnicity, nationality, sexual orientation, physical ability, age, and religious identification. In this text, we focus on how the structural inequalities of *gender* work in the world: how the hierarchical dichotomy of masculinity-femininity is institutionalized, legitimated, and reproduced, and how these processes differentially affect men's and women's lives. We also begin to see how gender hierarchy interacts with other structural inequalities. The dichotomy of masculinity and femininity is not separate from racism, classism, ageism, nationalism, and so on. Rather, gender both structures and is structured by these hierarchies to render complex social identities, locations, responsibilities, and social practices.

Gender shapes, and is shaped by, all of us. We daily reproduce its dynamics—and suffer its costs—in multiple ways. By learning how gender works, we learn a great deal about intersecting structures of inequality and how they are intentionally and *unintentionally* reproduced. We can then use this knowledge in our struggles to transform global gender inequality by also transforming other oppressive hierarchies at work in the world.

In short, *Global Gender Issues* not only addresses traditional IR concerns but also expands our understanding of global processes. By examining how men and women are differently affected by these global processes and how gender as a lens shapes the way we think about—and in part "create"—the world we live in, this text reframes and expands our knowledge of world politics. By including women's experience—of politics, security, economics, ecology, and equity—the book generates understanding that is more comprehensive and adequate because it is more inclusive and less distorted than conventional accounts.

NOTES ABOUT THIS TEXT

Some final clarifications are in order. First, there is considerable diversity even within mainstream approaches to world politics. It is therefore inappropriate to characterize IR as one school of thought with a set of basic and unchanging principles. However, because of space constraints and the orientation of this text, we tend to present traditional approaches as having a variety of features in common that generally differ from the gender-sensitive approach we undertake here.

Second, we assume that readers are relatively unfamiliar with gender analyses. In a text of this size, we cannot address all the relevant issues or do more than introduce the scholarship on gender that underpins our arguments: The text makes no pretense of surveying the issues completely. We focus, instead, on providing data and analyses that introduce students to the significance of gender generally and to its role in shaping world politics specifically. To facilitate comprehension, we have included a glossary that enables the reader to look up all words printed in boldface in the text, a bibliography of "Suggested Readings," discussion questions, and a selected list of internet/web resources related to feminist IR theory and practice. And we encourage students to read the chapter endnotes, which often contain clarifying material. We hope that readers will gain a broader and deeper understanding of these new subjects of study and debate and perhaps pursue them further.

As we argue throughout this text, *gender* refers to *both* men/masculinity and women/femininity. Yet the text focuses on the position of *women*. It does so not because men are unimportant or even less important through a gender-sensitive lens, but because men and masculinity have been and remain the focus of virtually all mainstream IR texts.[14] Despite the fact that men/masculinity dominate these texts, their authors fail to acknowledge how gender informs their representations of IR theory and practice. In contrast, we bring women into focus and render them visible in order to reveal the power of gender in world politics. Our focus on women illuminates how men/masculinity and women/femininity are *differently* affected by, and have differing effects upon, international relations.

Because we recognize that a gender-sensitive approach is unfamiliar, we have presented what is now a rich and sophisticated literature in extremely simplified form. This simplification imposes its own distortions. Because it is an important political issue, we wish especially to point out that our attention to gender, which distinguishes primarily between masculine and feminine as identities associated with men and women, tends to underplay the considerable differences *among* men and *among* women.[15] We remind readers that men, women, masculine, feminine, masculinist, and feminist are not homogeneous or unchanging categories. Like references to racism, liberalism, developed countries, or the Third World, our references to these general and familiar categories always risk obscuring differences *within* the categories. We try throughout the text to note and analyze how women and men are in reality divided along multiple dimensions: class, race, physical abilities, age, ethnicity, sexual orientation, nationality, and so on. Nevertheless, the demands of introducing unfamiliar material have prompted our use of many generalizations. In reality, as well as in our own thinking, things are always more complex.

Third, we acknowledge our normative commitments. Every lens is shaped by historical context and has normative and political implications. Diverse approaches, though they offer alternative perspectives, cannot simply be "added up" to gain a greater understanding of a static world. Rather, how we think about the world affects the world we think about: Different approaches have different concrete effects.

Just as realism makes conflict more visible and idealism makes cooperation more visible, this text makes gender more visible. In the process, it exposes distortions and limitations of conventional accounts. Existing frameworks do not adequately explain the nature, sources, and levels of conflict and cooperation in world politics. In fact, one begins to see that traditional IR accounts can misread situations of conflict and cooperation by failing to analyze the difference that gender makes.

We acknowledge that our gender-sensitive lens affords often critical accounts of both the "what" and "how" of contemporary world politics. Our perspective challenges a variety of institutions and practices in world politics because we are concerned with changing the negative conditions experienced by a majority of women, men, girls, and boys in our world. Many perspectives, in addition to gender-sensitive ones, are legitimate and necessary for understanding world politics and its current inequalities. We attempt to build upon and engage with these. In sum, we examine world politics through a gender-sensitive lens to enable a broader and deeper understanding of how the world works—or does not work—for all of us.

MAPPING THE BOOK

The focus of Chapter 2 is on the *power of gender*, elaborating on the meaning of a gender-sensitive lens as seen through various feminist perspectives, how such a lens works in shaping our lives, and how it filters our understanding. Here, after examining how the interaction of stereotypes, dichotomies, and ideology obscures the power of gender in shaping our world, we introduce the issue areas to be discussed throughout: gendered divisions of power, violence, labor, and resources.

In Chapter 3 we begin to examine the *position of women*—how and where women and men are differently situated—in relation to the gendered division of power. We present data and analyses of women as political actors in state structures. Then we examine how and why the presence of these powerful women is rendered invisible by asking: Why so few? How do the few succeed? What effect do they have? What makes actors powerful?

Chapter 4 contains our examination of how women and men are differently situated in relation to gendered divisions of violence (security is-

FIGURE 1.4   "It's a Man's World." This cartoon suggests that when men rule the world, they leave destruction in their wake. Reprinted with permission of King Features Syndicate.

sues), labor (economic issues), and resources (equity and ecology issues). Within each issue area, we ask what dichotomies are at work, how they differently affect men and women, and what their consequences are, especially in relation to global processes and crises.

In Chapter 5 we explore the politics of resistance by surveying and analyzing gender as a dimension of nonstate, antistate, and transstate movements. After reviewing varying feminist orientations to political practice and discussing the relationship between practical and strategic gender interests, we examine gender at work in activities promoting peace, antimilitarization, and antiviolence, in nationalist and antinationalist movements, and in movements for economic justice and sustainable ecology.

In our conclusion, Chapter 6, we review the main points of the foregoing chapters and their implications for studying world politics. We then take a final, integrative look at the gender divisions of power, violence, labor, and resources. We ask how a gender-sensitive lens informs the objectives of participatory politics, security based on the minimization of indirect as well as direct violence, equitable economic systems, and sustainable ecology. We close with policy recommendations, suggesting how individuals, social movements, and institutional actors can promote a world less burdened by the dilemma of gender—and other—inequalities (see Figure 1.4).

NOTES

1. Paul R. Viotti and Mark V. Kauppi, *International Relations Theory* (New York: Macmillan, 1987), pp. 2–3.

2. Patrick M. Morgan, *Theories and Approaches to International Politics*, 4th ed. (New Brunswick, N.J.: Transaction Books, 1987), p. 2.

3. United Nations Development Programme (UNDP), *Human Development Report 1997* (New York: Oxford University Press, 1997), p. 39.

4. J. Ann Tickner, *Gender in International Relations* (New York: Columbia University Press, 1993), p. 75.

5. Francine D'Amico and Peter R. Beckman, "Introduction," in Peter R. Beckman and Francine D'Amico, eds., *Women, Gender, and World Politics: An Introduction* (Westport, Conn.: Bergin & Garvey, 1994), p. 3.

6. Charlotte Hooper, "Masculinist Practices and Gender Politics: The Operation of Multiple Masculinities in International Relations," in Marysia Zalewski and Jane Parpart, eds., *The "Man" Question in International Relations* (Boulder: Westview Press, 1998), p. 33.

7. See, for example, Kamene Okojo, "Women and the Evolution of a Ghanaian Political Synthesis," in Barbara J. Nelson and Najma Chowdhury, eds., *Women and Politics Worldwide* (New Haven: Yale University Press, 1994), p. 286; and M. A. Jaimes * Guerrero, "Exemplars of Indigenism: Native North American Women for DeColonization and Liberation," in Cathy J. Cohen, Kathleen B. Jones, and Joan C. Tronto, eds., *Women Transforming Politics* (New York: New York University Press, 1997), p. 215.

8. As Ruth Leger Sivard points out, "The ILO for 1995 put women at 42 percent of the total force (women and men) in developed countries and at 34 percent in developing. . . . Comparisons available for manufacturing industries (26 countries reporting to the ILO) indicate that in 1992 women's hourly earnings averaged 74 percent of men's." See Sivard, *Women . . . A World Survey* (Washington, D.C.: World Priorities, 1995), pp. 11, 14. For more statistical information on women's labor force participation, see also United Nations (UN), *The World's Women 1995: Trends and Statistics* (New York: United Nations, 1995); and Naomi Neft and Ann D. Levine, *Where Women Stand: An International Report on the Status of Women in 140 Countries, 1997–1998* (New York: Random House, 1997). All of these sources point to the notorious undercounting of women's labor force participation; indeed, Neft and Levine estimate that at least 70 percent of the world's women work outside the home, even though many do not show up in formal labor force figures.

9. For the comprehensive statistical study most definitively making this claim, see Riane Eisler, David Loye, and Kari Norgaard, "Women, Men, and the Global Quality of Life" (Pacific Grove, Calif.: Center for Partnership Studies, 1995). This point is also made in most contemporary studies of gender and development.

10. UN, *The World's Women 1995*, p. xvii.

11. We caution our readers: Although data are increasingly available, difficulties remain in collecting timely (current), accurate, and appropriately comparable data worldwide.

12. Major books on feminist IR theory include Cynthia Enloe, *Bananas, Beaches & Bases: Making Feminist Sense of International Politics* (Berkeley: University of California Press, 1989); Rebecca Grant and Kathleen Newland, eds., *Gender and International Relations* (Bloomington: Indiana University Press, 1991); V. Spike Peterson, ed., *Gendered States: Feminist (Re)Visions of International Relations Theory* (Boulder: Lynne Rienner Publishers, 1992); Tickner, *Gender in International Relations*; Cynthia Enloe, *The Morning After: Sexual Politics at the End of the Cold War*

(Berkeley: University of California Press, 1993); Christine Sylvester, *Feminist Theory and International Relations in a Postmodern Era* (Cambridge, Eng.: Cambridge University Press, 1994); Peter R. Beckman and Francine D'Amico, eds., *Women, Gender, and World Politics: Perspectives, Policies, and Prospects* (Westport, Conn.: Bergin & Garvey, 1994); Jan Jindy Pettman, *Worlding Women: A Feminist International Politics* (London: Routledge, 1996); Zalewski and Parpart, eds., *The "Man" Question in International Relations;* and Jill Steans, *Gender and International Relations* (Cambridge, Eng.: Polity, 1998).

13. Hilary Lips, *Women, Men, and Power* (Mountain View, Calif.: Mayfield, 1991), p. 11.

14. See Marilyn Myerson and Susan Stoudinger Northcutt, "The Question of Gender," *International Studies Notes* 19, no. 1 (1994): 19–25. From their analysis of six popular IR textbooks, Myerson and Northcutt conclude that women are virtually absent (p. 22) and that gender as an analytic question is ignored in all of them (p. 24). A few recent (single-author) IR textbooks do include feminist perspectives, most notably Ralph Pettman's *International Politics: Balance of Power, Balance of Productivity, Balance of Ideologies* (Boulder: Lynne Rienner Publishers, 1991) and *Understanding International Political Economy* (Boulder: Lynne Rienner Publishers, 1996) as well as Joshua Goldstein's *International Relations*, 2nd ed. (New York: HarperCollins, 1996). Other scholarly treatments of IR are also increasingly acknowledging the existence of feminist perspectives on and/or women's movements in world politics, such as Mark A. Neufeld's *The Restructuring of International Relations Theory* (Cambridge, Eng.: Cambridge University Press, 1995), Jim George's *Discourses of Global Politics* (Boulder: Lynne Rienner Publishers, 1994), Richard Falk's *Explorations at the Edge of Time: The Prospects for World Order* (Philadelphia: Temple University Press, 1992), and R.B.J. Walker's *One World, Many Worlds: Struggles for a Just World Peace* (Boulder: Lynne Rienner Publishers, 1988). However, with the exception of Pettman and Neufeld, feminist insights and activisms are not necessarily integrated into these authors' accounts and rethinkings of IR. Acknowledgment without integration is also typical of recent edited volumes that include a single chapter from a feminist perspective. Although adding feminist viewpoints is a welcome development, it is inadequate insofar as "most work that appears throughout the rest of these anthologies seems unfamiliar with, and unaffected by, feminist scholarship" (Sandra Whitworth, *Feminism and International Relations* [London: Macmillan, 1994], p. x). Nevertheless, we note that male scholars in the field are increasingly engaged in and with feminist IR scholarship as evidenced by contributions to, for example, James N. Rosenau, ed., *Global Voices: Dialogues in International Relations* (Boulder: Westview Press, 1993); and Zalewski and Parpart, eds., *The "Man" Question in International Relations.*

15. For many contemporary feminists, the significance of differences and, especially, hierarchies among women is one of the most challenging and politically crucial issues we confront. It is a key dilemma in current feminist theory and practice. In brief, at issue is how to bring an awareness of and respect for differences among women into productive relation with commitments to and action in support of "women's" political agency and efficacy, insofar as the latter presupposes commonalities of experience, interest, and strategic objective.

TWO

□ □ □

Gender as a
Lens on World Politics

There are many lenses (or theoretical perspectives) through which world politics has been viewed historically and in the contemporary context. These lenses have been variously labeled over time as idealism (or liberalism), Marxism, realism, behavioralism, neorealism, neoliberalism (or neoliberal institutionalism), neo-Marxism (or critical perspectives), postcolonialism, postmodernism (or poststructuralism), and feminism (which has drawn upon and yet significantly alters liberal, critical, postcolonial, and postmodern perspectives). Lenses act to foreground some things, while backgrounding others. (Neo)realist lenses bring the conflictive behavior of states to the fore, whereas (neo)liberal lenses focus attention on interstate cooperation and organization. (Neo-)Marxist lenses direct our gaze to class inequalities and conflicts within and across states, whereas postcolonial lenses call attention to racial inequalities, nationalist identities and conflicts, and imperialist practices within and across states. As these examples suggest, lenses often vary by what aspects of reality they find problematic—a process that involves normative as well as substantive commitments—and, relatedly, by what conceptual schema they find useful in explaining particular problematics. At the same time, topics and commitments may be variously mixed and comprise elements of several lenses. For example, because Marxists focus on economic inequalities, their conceptual frameworks privilege economic variables and practices, although these are inextricable from political dimensions and some Marxists pay particular attention to culture. Both neorealists and neoliberals assume a model of human nature that presents emotion or irrationality, rather than rationality, as problematic, although their different foci lead them to different expectations about behavior. Institutionalists share a focus on institutions but may be liberal or conservative and interested in foreign policy or labor markets.

21

When we are considering different theoretical lenses, a further distinction is useful: between *what* objects (variables, topics, issues, levels of analysis) are focused on and *how* knowledge/truth about those objects is produced (empirically, analytically, comparatively, intuitively). Stated simplistically, the former refers to ontology (the nature of "being": *What* is reality?) and the latter to epistemology (the study of truth claims: *How* do we know?), and they are always intertwined because claims about "what *x* is" are necessarily also claims about how we know what *x* is. We cannot engage these issues in depth, but they are important for comprehending the complexity and range of theories (or lenses) in both IR and feminism. And they are key to current theoretical debates, which center on how we understand the relationship between knowledge and power (see Figure 2.1).

In brief, epistemological preferences cut across normative/political commitments and substantive foci (objects of inquiry), though this is not often visible or readily acknowledged. As one consequence, conventional labeling boxes are inadequate. They especially mislead us into thinking that individuals do—and should—fit in one box, rather than spanning several, as the above examples suggest. In reality, of course, not only do individuals employ multiple (sometimes complementary, sometimes conflicting) lenses, but the "mix" itself changes, depending on a variety of personal and contextual factors.

These points are most salient here in regard to the distinction typically drawn between positivist (sometimes called modernist, Enlightenment, rationalist, empiricist) and postpositivist orientations (including constructivist, critical, interpretive, reflexive, and postmodernist perspectives). Briefly stated, positivists make two fundamental assumptions: first, that through the application of the scientific method, facts can be separated from values, and, second, that subjects (knowers, observers) and objects (that which is known, observed) can also be categorically separated. Combining the two assumptions, positivists argue that social reality exists independent of the observer and that the observer can see this reality objectively (separating fact from value) by employing the scientific method to control for bias or emotional investments. Hence, the knower can stand "outside of" the reality observed, as categorically separate from the object of her or his observations. Similarly, positivists assume that social reality is "given" (separate from the knower) and is the product of unchangeable laws of (human and physical) nature and rational action.

In contrast, postpositivists argue that reality is a *social construction*, in the sense that humans/subjects "create" meaning and intelligibility through the mutual constitution of symbols, language, identities, practices, and social structures. The point here is not that the physical world does not exist independent of subjects but, rather, that it has no social *meaning* independent of that which is "imposed" by human thought and

FIGURE 2.1 Changing Lenses. Shown here is a graphic depiction of how lenses affect fields of vision and how women at the bottom of the world politics hierarchy are struggling to make elite men see the world more clearly. Courtesy of the United Nations, "The State of the World's Women 1985." Illustrator: Wendy Hoile.

action. Hence, knowers cannot stand "outside of" the reality they observe because their participation in that reality is a necessary condition for the object observed to have any meaning; both subject and object gain their meaning and intelligibility by reference to their location in a system of meaning (language and thought) that encompasses both. On this view, subjects and objects are *not* categorically separate but exist in a relationship that shapes what is known. As a consequence, objectivity must be rethought, the relationship between knowledge and power becomes central, and language becomes political insofar as it constitutes the meaning system of intelligibility and order.

By denying the categorical separations (fact from value and subject from object) that are fundamental to positivism, postpositivists thus challenge conventional claims about scientific objectivity and castigate "either-or" thinking (dichotomies) as a distortion of social reality. Later in this chapter we examine how this critique of dichotomies relates to gender and lenses; throughout the text we apply this critique to global gender issues. But first, in the next section, we consider postpositivism in relation to objectivity and the ways in which we label theoretical lenses.

Because observers are always implicated in the context of their observations, postpositivists argue that neither social identities nor structures are products of laws of nature (independent of social life). Because they are not given or fixed for all time, they can be changed, and, thus, what is taken to be reality can be altered. Postpositivists further claim that what is taken for reality is too often what those in positions of power say reality is. By arguing that "[t]heory is always *for* someone and *for* some purpose,"[1] postpositivists advance the position that no inquiry is value-free, nor could it be. What questions we ask, problems we focus on, methods we use, resources we commit, and emotional investments we make in our pursuit of "knowledge" are *all* shaped by the social context, therefore power relations, in which they occur. There is no escaping this. When we recognize that knowledge is inseparable from power, we are more apt to take responsibility for how our *particular* identities and locations inevitably affect our worldviews and, thus, our inquiries about and actions in the world.

Accepting that knowledge is socially situated and thus productive, at best, of only partial accounts of reality makes us more open to other perspectives, other (partial) accounts of reality, especially those advanced by people(s) not in formal positions of power. Such accounts do not just give us additional pictures of reality; they also cause us to question and rethink dominant portrayals of reality. When we see that dominant portrayals are just as value-laden as alternative (often contending or oppositional) accounts of reality, we can begin to debate which values are productive of the least partial—or "objective"—accounts of social reality.

The latter are often more complex and less exclusivist accounts. Sandra Harding refers to this approach to knowledge production as practicing "strong objectivity," which "permit[s] one to abandon notions of perfect, mirror-like representations of the world, the self as a defended fortress, and 'the truly scientific' as disinterested with regard to morals and politics, yet still apply rational standards to sorting less from more partial and distorted belief."[2] In other words, we must recognize that all perspectives, problems, methods, and so on, are value-laden (shaped by power and commitments), but this is not to argue that they are equally valid, or that we cannot comparatively assess them. It is to argue that all claims must be situated: interpreted in their historical context and in terms of how subjects (observers) and objects (that which is observed) are *related* (mutually constituted, interdependent) within that context. It is to argue that absolute, transcendent, universal claims, because they *deny* context, must be abandoned in favor of *comparative* claims.

In our simplified presentation, postmodernism is one among many postpositivist lenses. Although there is little agreement on the meaning of postmodernism, we simply note that postmodernists are especially attentive to the power, therefore politics, of symbols, conceptual frameworks, and language. Relatedly, they insist not just on the constructed nature of reality but also on the constructed nature of lenses themselves. In particular, postmodernists[3] question whether we can refer unproblematically to collective social identities—such as "*the* working-class perspective" or "*the* Third World perspective"—as sources of alternative accounts of reality that counter dominant representations by elites. If all social identities are constructed through complex and intersecting histories, experiences, and structures, then there is no such thing as a purely "working-class" identity. Rather, people have socially constructed identities other than and in addition to class, such as gender, race, and national and familial identities that can conflict with or mediate their class identities. Thus, there is no way to speak of a singular working-class perspective that can speak for all working-class people. This does not mean that class oppression does not exist or that it should not be resisted. But it does mean that we must be careful not to reduce complex social formations into simplistic, homogeneous characterizations (or labels).

Feminist perspectives (which we introduce here and elaborate upon in Chapter 5) foreground the position of women and the power of gender, whether in the study of literature, history, philosophy, science, or world politics. But there is no universal meaning of feminism, and neither feminists nor women constitute a homogeneous category. As with the theoretical lenses or perspectives in IR, there are many variations of feminism. And as with IR, the variations are patterned by normative/political commitments (liberal, socialist), substantive focus (peace, trade, culture), and conceptual frameworks (positivist, interpretive, postmodernist). Most important, endless "mixing" is the rule, not the exception. Hence, as argued earlier, conventional "boxes" misrepresent the diversity and range of perspectives and, especially, the extensive overlap among many perspectives. Although, as in IR, we can provide labels for various lenses, it is crucial to remember that the labels rarely refer to discrete (either-or, mutually exclusive) positions or belief systems. Indeed, individuals make assumptions that may be common to various lenses, they may make different assumptions when focusing on different substantive topics or normative issues, and our "mix" of assumptions changes as an effect of experiences and learning. And finally, as we noted above, epistemological preferences cut across other differences (in topical focus or normative commitment), so that a simplistic picture of discrete lenses or boxes is wholly inadequate. In sum, although we will draw familiar distinctions among feminist lenses, we warn readers against the positivist habit of assuming homogeneity within a lens or categorical separation between lenses.

In Chapter 1, we distinguished between substantive and conceptual aspects of gender, as two interactive sides of the gender coin. The former we identified as the effects of IR on gender, or the *position of women*, and the latter we identified as the effects of gender on IR, or the *power of gender*. The former is familiar as a reference to substantive (empirical, concrete) issues, whereas the latter marks a more recent interest in the power of concepts and language. Now we can relate substantive and conceptual gender aspects to epistemological positions. In brief, for those wedded to positivist commitments, gender is comprehensible *only* as an empirical category. That is, sex can be added as a variable (we can distinguish male and female prime ministers, workers, citizens), but gender is ostensibly an irrelevant factor in how we think. Because positivists separate subject and object and take meaning systems as given, they are unable to "see" gender as a theoretical (conceptual, analytical) category; they deny the role of gender in the construction of meaning and lenses. In contrast, postpositivists acknowledge the power of language and the centrality of meaning systems; they are therefore much more likely to comprehend gender as *both* empirically and conceptually significant. Throughout this book, and as the focus of this chapter, we attempt to make the less familiar *power of gender*—gender as an analytical category—visible.

Feminist inquiries that focus on empirical women (our *position of women*) often employ positivism to show that there is no rational basis for women's exclusion from or marginalization within such male-dominated fields as science, economics, and international relations. If, as positivists argue, reality can be apprehended by an observer whose personal attributes and values can be kept from affecting his or her view of reality through the scientific method, then it should not matter if the observer is male or female, white or black, American or Asian, rich or poor. The fact, however, that women (and especially those who are non-white, non-Western, and/or non-middle class) have been traditionally denied significant roles in these fields, and that women's experiences and concerns are not addressed in these fields, suggests that inquiry is not bias-free.

For the most part, however, feminists employ postpositivism to show how the marginalized and subordinated position of women is inextricably tied to the power of gender as a value and valuing system that permeates our concepts and meaning systems, and hence our actions. Claims to being value-free merely mask the power of gender (along with other entrenched systems of oppression) to shape the production of knowledge. Because inquiry is a social practice and so is always value-laden, it is incumbent on inquirers to critically examine their social locations and values that arise from them. In this way, normative commitments that underlie inquiry are made visible and can become the subject of political debate about what values inquiry should advance.

In sum, positivists may recognize the empirical role of gender and accept the need to examine sex as a variable, but their dichotomizing assumptions obscure and even deny the relevance of gender to concepts and thought. In contrast, postpositivists are critical of rigid dichotomies and recognize the centrality of meaning systems; they variously explore how agents and structures, subjects and objects, are mutually constituted. At the same time, postpositivists vary tremendously in how and to what extent they prioritize meaning systems, with postmodernists paying the most attention to the power of concepts and language.

All feminist lenses foreground some dimensions of world politics in relation to some aspects of gender inequality and oppression, while backgrounding others.[4] Most early typologies of feminist theory differentiated perspectives by how they framed the question of women's oppression: Was it due to women's exclusion from political power (liberal feminisms), to class inequalities (Marxist feminisms), or to sociocultural practices that denigrate the feminine and control women's sexuality (radical feminisms)? The simplicity and separability of these categories soon gave way to more complicated typologies. Socialist feminisms acknowledged both political and economic sources of oppression, psychoanalytic feminisms emphasized the unconscious and psychic codification of sex difference, lesbian feminisms problematized heterosexism, and "women of color" feminisms highlighted interactive oppressions and decried the exclusionary practices of mainstream feminisms. More recently, postcolonial feminisms and postmodern feminisms have become key lenses as well. As with all typologizing efforts, the possible permutations are endless and the value of any particular schema depends on its purpose and use.

In our discussion of gendered social movements (see Chapter 5), we explore five feminist lenses that are especially relevant to global gender issues. These are briefly introduced here to convey the diversity among feminisms and to suggest how they illuminate varying aspects of social life and global dynamics. Liberal feminisms gained formal expression in the eighteenth-century bourgeois revolutions that advocated equality but limited its application to (propertied) males. Shaped by its historical context, liberal feminism has for the most part assumed positivist epistemological commitments. At the same time, liberal feminisms do engage postpositivist insights when they link women's exclusion from political power to the undervaluing of women's responsibilities in the home and recognize that simply "adding women" to formal power structures is insufficient for transforming male-defined structures.

Radical feminisms problematize the cultural denigration of femininity and the sexual manifestations of male dominance. They expose how experiences and activities associated with women and the female body are devalued, how sexual violence is a form of social control of women, and how **heterosexism** (clarified below) prevents women from identifying primarily with other women and reproduces the objectification of and violence against women's bodies. Hence, they highlight the security issue of the relationship between sexual and international violence. Whereas liberal feminisms tend to emphasize equal opportunities for women to secure male-defined privileges, radical feminisms foreground the need for women's autonomy and freedom from male-defined norms, heterosexist norms, and male sexual violence.

Socialist feminisms draw upon various neo-Marxist or critical traditions as well as upon radical feminist insights. They foreground economic forces, revealing how capitalism and patriarchal gender relations interact to disadvantage women in the workplace *and* the home. By contesting the categorical separation between public and private spheres (and men's and women's work), socialist feminisms are more likely to exhibit postpositivist commitments against dichotomized thinking. They are thus more likely to interrogate, rather than take for granted, the conventional use of gendered dichotomies (explained below).

Postcolonial feminisms emerge from the experiences of women of color; they are also known as anti-racist or anti-imperialist feminisms. They typically draw upon economic critiques but are especially distinguished by their emphasis on the *interaction* of oppressive dynamics and on race/ethnicity as a primary axis of oppression. They put into sharp relief how gender, race, class, nationalist, and imperialist hierarchies are interwoven in ways that particularly undermine the lives of Third World women—physically, politically, economically, and culturally. This systematic undermining is implicated in a variety of global crises, as we subsequently illustrate in this book by analyzing gendered divisions of power, violence, labor, and resources. One may engage this perspective from a range of epistemological commitments, as evidenced by postcolonial feminist work that exhibits various positivist and postpositivist orientations.

Postmodernist feminisms constitute our fifth lens. This lens is distinguished less by substantive focus than by explicitly problematizing positivist and modernist commitments and the power relations that they sustain. As intimated above, postmodernist feminisms take the power of gender, women's oppression, and women's struggles seriously, but are concerned that we avoid reducing both gender and women into simplistic, homogeneous categories. As Sandra Harding puts it, "[I]n a certain sense there are no 'women' or 'men' in the world—there is no 'gender'—but only women, men, and gender constructed through particular historical struggles over just which races, classes, sexualities, cultures, religious groups, and so forth, will have access to resources and power."[5] We are mindful of this admonition as we present the following explication of gender and the power it has in world politics, which draws upon this variety of feminist perspectives.

DENATURALIZING GENDER

Too typically, and quite erroneously, the term *gender* is understood as interchangeable with the term *sex*, which conventionally refers to biological distinctions between male and female. Instead, gender should be understood as a social, not physiological, construction: "*Femininity* and *masculinity*, the terms that denote one's gender, refer to a complex set of characteristics and behaviors prescribed for a particular sex by society and learned through the socialization experience."[6] (In this book, the term *gender* also refers to masculinity and femininity as they shape our thinking.)

The particular characteristics associated with femininity and masculinity vary across cultures, races, classes, and even age groups. "Acting like a man" (or a woman) means different things to different groups of people (e.g., heterosexual Catholics, Native Americans, British colonials, agriculturists versus corporate managers, athletes versus orchestra conductors, combat soldiers versus military strategists) and to the same group of people at different points in time (e.g., nineteenth- versus twentieth-century Europeans, colonized versus postcolonial Africans, prepuberty versus elderly age sets, women during versus after wars). It is especially important to recognize that gender is typically racialized (models of masculinity and femininity vary among Africans, Indians, Asians, Europeans) and race is gendered (gender stereotypes shape racial stereotypes of "Africans," "Indians," "Asians," "Whites"). Moreover, different types of masculinity may be more or less valued in particular contexts (aggressive masculinity may be good for fighting but less desirable as a management style and inappropriate in conflict resolution processes).

Because models of appropriate gender behavior vary, we know that femininity and masculinity are not timeless or separable from the contexts in which they are observed. Thus, gender rests not on biological sex differences but on *interpretations* or constructions of behavior that are culturally specific and may or may not have anything to do with biological differences.

In other words—and this is a key point—although biology is ostensibly the basis for establishing gender models, it plays an ambiguous and often purely symbolic role in our actual use of gendered concepts. Consider that a man (e.g., Mahatma Gandhi) may be characterized as "feminine" and a woman (e.g., Margaret Thatcher) as "masculine." Even activities and institutions are characterized in gender terms, regardless of whether they are associated mainly with men or women. For example, computer programming and government bureaucracies are often described as "masculine." Finally, because masculinities and femininities vary (by class, race/ethnicity, age), some expressions of gender (Hispanic in the United States, Muslim in India, Turkana in Kenya) are subordinated to *dominant* constructions of gender (Anglo, Hindu, Kikuyu). Although we do speak at various points to the complexity and diversity of gender constructions in this text, our use of the terms *masculinity* and *femininity* typically refer to their dominant Western/Anglo forms.

Recognizing the complexity of gender is important for clarifying distinctions between the *biological* categories of male and female, the *socially constructed* models of masculine and feminine, and the *political* perspectives of **masculinism** and **feminism.** The distinctions among, but also interrelations of, these concepts are reviewed in the following pages.

Although the specific traits that mark gender-appropriate behavior vary cross-culturally, they constitute systems of politically significant structural power because males are expected to conform to models of masculinity (that are privileged) and females to models of femininity (that are subordinated). And within particular cultures, these expectations are taken very seriously because they are considered fundamental to who we are, how we act, and how we think. That is, the construction of gender identities is closely related to how cultures organize work, power, and pleasure along gender-differentiated lines. In short, the way we think about who people are (images and identities) is inextricable from what we expect people to do (roles and activities).

Because (dominant) masculine activities are more highly valued or privileged than feminine activities in most of the world, the identities and activities associated with men and women are typically unequal. Thus, the social construction of gender is actually a system of power that not only divides men and women as masculine and feminine but typically also places men and masculinity above women and femininity. We observe this power at work when we notice how systematically those institutions and practices that are male dominated and/or representative of masculine traits and style are valued more highly and considered more important than institutions and practices associated with femininity.

Because the dichotomy of masculine and feminine constructs them as mutually exclusive, when we favor or privilege that which is associated with masculinity we tend to do so at the expense of that which is associated with femininity. Politics in a broad sense is about differential access to power—about who gets what and how. Therefore, the privileging of masculinity is political insofar as relations of inequality, manifested in this case as gender inequality, represent men's and women's differential access to power, authority, and resources. In this text, the term *masculinist* refers to individuals, perspectives, practices, and institutions that are masculine in orientation (embodying and privileging the traits of masculinity) and, thus, engaged in producing and sustaining relations of gender inequality.

Like other social hierarchies, gender inequality is maintained by various means ranging from direct violence (rape, domestic battering) and structural discrimination (job segregation, inadequate health care) to psychological mechanisms (**sexist** humor, blaming the victim, internalization of oppressive stereotypes). And like many social hierarchies, gender inequality is "justified" by focusing on physical differences and exaggerating their significance as determinants of what are in fact social, *learned*, behaviors. Thus, Arthur Brittan argues that by denying the social construction of gender, *masculinism* serves to justify and "naturalize" (depoliticize) male domination because "it takes for granted that there is a fundamental difference between men and women, it assumes that heterosexuality is normal, it accepts without question the sexual division of labour, and it sanctions the political and dominant role of men in the public and private spheres."[7]

These points are fundamental to the focus and arguments of this text. To repeat: Like the abstract concepts of family, race, and nation, gender "in the real" is always inflected by dimensions of race/ethnicity, class, and so on, that vary depending on context. What renders gender so fundamental a dichotomy in all contexts (hence the focus of this text) is that gender structurally organizes not just sexual practices but virtually all aspects of social life in all cultures. The assumptions that follow from the dichotomy or polarization of gender are (1) that males and females are unambiguously distinguishable; (2) that there are different scripts (ways of identifying, being, and knowing) for males and females; (3) that sex difference is important enough to shape all social relations; and (4) that the dichotomy of gender is so important that persons deviating from sex-appropriate scripts are problematic (suspect as "unnatural" or "immoral").[8] Hence, heterosexism (belief in heterosexuality as the only "normal" mode of sexual orientation, family life, and social relations) is inextricable from the dichotomy of gender that privileges unambiguous distinctions between males/masculinity and females/femininity and that promotes gender-differentiated lives and social structuring. Because heterosexism is currently the dominant model worldwide and is key to social reproduction, *all* groups/societies manifest *gendered* dichotomies, myths, practices, and institutions, however much these may vary in particular contexts. This gendering is structurally maintained, for example, through reproduction of masculinist myths and stereotypes, but also through customs, policies, and legislation that impose heterosexist family forms, **androcentric** (male-as-norm) citizenship, and sex-differentiated labor markets.

It is the oppressive structural effects of gender/heterosexism, premised on unequivocal distinctions between femaleness and maleness, on which we focus in this text. Masculinism is one way of referring to these effects and the ideology that justifies them (as "natural" or god-given). In short, we argue that the realization of global equity and justice among all people *requires* that the dichotomy of gender, which is naturalized and reproduced through androcentrism and heterosexism, be subverted.

Feminism, in contrast, is a more complicated and contested term. There are, in fact, many forms of feminism, as we have indicated in the introduction to this chapter and will further discuss in Chapter 5. Here we suggest that the common thread among feminisms is an orientation valuing women's diverse experiences and taking seriously women's interests in and capacities for bringing about social and political change. It is our position that feminism is not about promoting a simplistic role reversal in which women gain power over men or femininity becomes more valued than masculinity. Rather, *feminist* individuals, organizations, perspectives, practices, and institutions seek an end to social constructions of gender inequality (see Figure 2.2). For us, this entails transforming the stereotypes and polarization of gender identities and contesting how masculinity is privileged in concepts, practices, and institutions. For us, this *also* entails transforming related hierarchies (racism, homophobia, colonialism, etc.) that are legitimized by denigration of the feminine.

We further note that masculinist perspectives can be held by women and that feminist perspectives can be held by men, because these perspectives are politically, not biologically, grounded. As we illustrate in this text, many of the most serious global issues facing humankind and the planet today are caused, in part, by the practices, processes, and structures of gender hierarchy (the power system that privileges maleness/masculinity over femaleness/femininity). Thus, it is neither appropriate nor defensible to ignore this feature of the international system.

THE INCREDIBLE SHRINKING WOMAN

FIGURE 2.2 "The Incredible Shrinking Woman" is one who fails to advocate feminism at the behest of masculinist power structures, according to this cartoon. Reprinted by special permission of Kirk Anderson.

Through a gender-sensitive lens, not only the "what" of world politics but also "how" we think about it looks different. In the chapters that follow, we demonstrate how IR affects gender: As a consequence of gendered divisions of power, violence, labor, and resources, women and men are positioned differently—a fact that represents the *position of women* side of the gender coin. In the remainder of this chapter, we consider how gender affects IR, or the *power of gender*—the lens side of the gender coin. Specifically, we consider how gendered lenses shape our thinking, our ordering of reality, our claims of knowing what is true, and, therefore, our understanding and explanation of the social world. Because a gender-sensitive lens is unfamiliar to most students of IR, the rest of the chapter focuses on such a lens and its implications for the study of world politics.

THE SOCIAL CONSTRUCTION
OF GENDER AND GENDER HIERARCHY

To understand how gender works, we examine two interacting dimensions of social systems: the formation of gendered identities and the reproduction of gendered social structures. The first is about **socialization:**

how individuals are taught, and how they internalize, culturally appropriate attitudes and behaviors. Families, schools, religious institutions, and media are important sources of this socialization. The second dimension is about systemic, or structural, control: how practices and institutions keep gender hierarchy in place by generating conformity and compliance. Moral and intellectual control is effected through the privileging of certain belief systems (e.g., myth, religion, and even science). More direct social control is effected through job markets, laws, governance, and physical coercion.

From birth on, the way we are treated depends on our gender assignment, and we learn in multiple ways how to adopt gender-appropriate behaviors. There are few occasions or interactions where our gender is truly irrelevant: Our names, clothes, games, rewards, threats and punishments, the attention we get, the subjects we study, the knowledge claims we make, the jobs we work at, and the power we have are all profoundly shaped by gendered (and racialized) expectations. As individuals, we differ considerably in the extent to which we conform to cultural expectations. But none of us escapes gender socialization or the systemic effects of gender inequality: Not only females but males, too, suffer from rigid gender roles.[9]

> Everyone is born into a *culture*—a *set of shared ideas* about the nature of reality, the nature of right and wrong, *evaluation of what is good and desirable,* and the nature of the good and desirable versus the bad and nondesirable. . . . As totally dependent infants we are *socialized*—taught the rules, roles and relationships of the social world. . . . [I]n the process we learn to think, act, and feel as we are "supposed to."[10]

More than two thousand years ago, Plato recognized that the most effective way to maintain systems of rule was not through direct violence but by persuading those who are subordinated that social hierarchy is natural, therefore inevitable, and even desirable. When people believe that differences in status and wealth are part of the "natural order of things," they are less likely to challenge how society is organized to benefit some more than others. Such people do not require constant external policing because they have internalized their own policing in terms of selective perceptions and lowered expectations. As a consequence, they internalize an acceptance of their own, and others', inequality.

In the next two sections we examine how gender inequality is produced, reinforced, and reproduced through gender stereotypes, dichotomies, and masculinist ideology. (In subsequent chapters we focus on the gender-differentiated consequences of social control: how divisions of power, violence, labor, and resources affect women and men differently, and how women and men resist gender hierarchies.)

Gender Stereotypes and Dichotomies

Stereotypes are pictures in our heads that filter how we "see." They are composite images that attribute—often incorrectly and always too generally—certain characteristics to whole groups of people. Thus, groups are seen as others want or expect to see them, not necessarily as they are. The oversimplification in stereotypes encourages us to ignore complexity and contradictions that might prompt us to challenge the status quo. Moreover, the use of stereotypes suggests that particular behaviors are timeless and inevitable.

By providing unquestioned categories and connections, stereotypes can mask actual relationships and in effect "excuse" discrimination. For example, the underrepresentation of women in political office is often "explained" by the stereotype of their being uninterested in power and politics. Similarly, high unemployment among African-Americans is often "explained" by the stereotype of their being lazy and irresponsible. In such pictures, stereotypes render *structural* or societal (in contrast to individual) causes invisible.

Stereotypes, because they oversimplify, overgeneralize, are resistant to change, and promote inaccurate images, significantly affect how we see ourselves, others, and social organization generally. Stereotypes are political because they both reproduce and naturalize (depoliticize) unequal power relations. They reproduce inequalities by being self-fulfilling: If we *expect* certain behaviors, we may act in ways that in fact create and reinforce such behaviors. (Expecting girls to hate mechanics and math affects how much encouragement we give them; without expectations of success or encouragement, girls may avoid or do poorly in these activities.) And stereotypes naturalize inequalities (making them appear "natural" rather than political) by presenting subordinated groups negatively, as inferior, undesirable, or threatening. When members of such groups internalize oppressive stereotypes, they may hold themselves—rather than social structures—responsible for undesirable outcomes. (Females are more likely to blame themselves for ineptness or poor grades than to ask how social structures discourage girls from exploring mechanics and discriminate educationally in favor of boys.) Those who believe they are acting out the inevitable are, in effect, reconciled to discriminatory treatment.

In the United States, dominant gender stereotypes depict men/masculinity as "strong, independent, worldly, aggressive, ambitious, logical, and rough" and women/femininity as the opposite: "weak, dependent, passive, naive, not ambitious, illogical, and gentle."[11] Such depictions exemplify the binary nature of models of gender, constructing man/masculinity and woman/femininity as two poles of a *dichotomy*—as mutually exclusive or oppositional—that define each other. Through this either-or lens, women are not simply different from men: "Woman" is defined by what is "not man," and characteristics of femininity are those that are inappropriate for or contradict masculinity.

In every aspect of our lives, we are bombarded with gender stereotypes. Consider the depiction of men and women on television and in musical lyrics: How often is there a politically powerful or physically "rough" woman, especially one who is likable? Or a man who is nurturing and sensual as a way of being all the time, not just in certain circumstances? And most telling, why are there so few images of gender-neutral individuals—people whose gender status is not immediately and unequivocally apparent? Why are we so uncomfortable with gender ambiguities, virtually insisting that individuals be patently *either* men/masculine *or* women/feminine?

Our discomfort reflects two important points. First, gender ambiguity is uncomfortable because we simply do not know how to respond. That is, our expectations and behavior regarding gender are so taken for granted that when we are confronted with ambiguous gender signals, we become confused; we literally do not know how to act. This reveals how unconsciously "programmed" by gendered expectations we are: When those expectations are disrupted—forcing us to think consciously about how to act or respond—we realize how much they (unconsciously) shape our habitual behavior. Second, and relatedly, we typically resent the discomfort and confusion. This reveals how significant our unacknowledged commitments to gender are. That is, when people confront us with gender ambiguity, we resent both not knowing how to act *and* the questions that our confusion raises. For if gender identities are not reliable and stable, what does this mean for one's own identity? Because gender identification is so important for "knowing who we are" and how to act, and for securing self-esteem when we "do gender well," confusion about gender identification can feel very threatening.

Insecurity about one's gender identity is especially acute for males in the context of masculinist/heterosexist culture. Because femininity is devalued and expressions of femininity render men's masculinity suspect, men face tremendous pressures to be "real men"; and being a "real man" requires that gender distinctions are unambiguous. Given the high stakes, it is not surprising that men consistently demonstrate greater discomfort with gender ambiguities than women do. For example, men are much more likely to express homophobia (the abhorrence of homosexuality), in part because homosexuality disrupts conventional gender distinctions and raises questions about what it means to be a "real man."[12] Moreover, and significantly, in masculinist/heterosexist cultures, men are motivated to *enhance* their masculinity and to exaggerate their difference from women and homosexual men.[13]

In other words—and this illustrates how gender is constructed rather than "natural," obvious, or unchanging—men are not sufficiently masculine simply because they have the appropriate genitalia. Rather, they must continuously *demonstrate* their claims to being "real men" by distancing themselves from that which is defined as feminine. This distancing may involve avoidance of body decorations, bright colors, ballet, quiche, flowers, child care, gentleness, and asking directions. It may involve fear of acknowledging emotion, needs, vulnerabilities, and desire for affection/intimacy. It may involve exaggerating one's rationality, competitiveness, and power, or encouraging tough and even violent behaviors. It may involve a preference for scotch, meat-and-potatoes, heavy-metal music, computer games, and exploring unknown territory.

The point here is that gender is not established biologically but comes to pervade all aspects of social life. Consider that, in the context of masculinist/heterosexist culture, demonstrating that we are "real men" and "real women" *matters* emotionally and materially; there are a variety of "costs"—from mild to deadly—for not conforming to gender stereotypes. Because biological criteria alone do not *establish* our status as real men and real women, we must continuously "perform" (demonstrate, act out) gender attitudes and behaviors to "prove" that we are conforming appropriately. Doing so makes all of social life a test of our performance: Gender comes to matter in what we wear, eat, and drink; what entertainment and activities we prefer; how we approach risk-taking and dependence; and how we measure intelligence, courage, and leadership.

In short, the acting out of gender—and the importance we put on doing so appropriately—demonstrates both how gender is not biologically determined (it is not "given" by a difference in sex organs) and how polarized gender-differentiation produces and sustains male-female inequalities. Putting so much weight on the *differences* between men/masculinity and women/femininity ensures that what we share is obscured and that any blurring of gender boundaries—and concomitant erosion of masculinism/heterosexism—feels threatening and is resisted.

This discussion leads us into considering how gender stereotypes interact with Western patterns of thinking to institutionalize acritical and typically conservative patterns in how we think about, act upon, and therefore shape reality. In Cynthia Epstein's words, "No aspect of social life—whether the gathering of crops, the ritual of religion, the formal dinner party, or the organization of government—is free from the dichotomous thinking that casts the world in categories of 'male' and 'female.'"[14] Our argument here expands on the work of contemporary nonfeminist scholars who are critical of dichotomies for their role in sustaining status quo inequalities (elaborated below). But we go beyond their general critique to argue that dichotomized (either-or) thought cannot be adequately understood and therefore cannot be effectively transformed without attention to gender.

In brief, the gender dichotomy gains its "givenness" by (mistaken) association with biological ("natural") sex difference. And dichotomies acquire the status and authority of givens in part because they so readily "map onto" the dichotomy of gender that we reproduce, consciously and unconsciously, as we "act out" gender in all areas of social life. Because of this interaction, gender stereotypes have political significance far beyond their role in male-female relations: They not only reproduce *gender* hierarchy but also sustain other relations of domination by promoting and naturalizing the practice of thinking in terms of hierarchical dichotomies that legitimate domination of that which is associated with femininity. We clarify these claims by examining how the structure, status, and androcentrism (use of male as norm) of dichotomies interact to (re)produce and legitimate social inequalities.

The structure of dichotomies severely constrains our thought and therefore action. The image of only two mutually exclusive choices keeps us locked into those—and only those—choices. Polarities (right versus wrong, rational versus emotional, strong versus weak) forestall our consideration of nonoppositional constructions (right in relation to plausible, persuasive, reasonable, coherent; rational in relation to consistent, instrumental, logical; strong in relation to effective, principled, respected).

The meanings of the polar terms also appear fixed, as if they are givens of logic and language rather than social conventions.[15] In this sense, polarities resist critical reflection by presenting what appear to be inevitable ways of categorizing. Social reality, however, is complex and conditioned by multiple variables. Categorical oppositions misrepresent (distort) *social* relations by eliminating this complexity and interdependence of terms. For example, in IR, we posit state sovereignty as independence and autonomy, the opposite of dependence and constraints. Until recently, this dichotomy prevented our seeing *interdependence* as a third option and, for many, a more accurate picture of actual relationships between states. Similarly, when we define the field's theoretical debates as "idealism versus realism," we make it impossible to address how virtually all theorists in fact adopt a mixture of idealist and realist positions.

In addition, the oppositional form of dichotomies denies any overlap or commonalities between terms: It puts difference in focus at the expense of viewing terms *relationally*. As humans, men and women exhibit more commonalities than differences. But the gender dichotomy (and heterosexism's insistence on clear distinctions) highlights differences, not shared characteristics, as primary. In reality, not all females bear children and no female bears them throughout her lifetime. But the dichotomy pitting men as performing **productive labor** (working for wages, creating ideas and products) against women as performing **reproductive labor** (maintaining the household, bearing and caring for children) masks the variation among females and the commonality between males and many females (see Figure 2.3).

The dichotomies of sovereignty-anarchy, politics-economics, realism-idealism, and center-periphery similarly structure how we think about and therefore act in the world. They emphasize polarized and hierarchical difference rather than how states, transnational processes, and people are embedded in complex and ever changing relationships that are not adequately characterized or analyzed in either-or terms. In sum, the structure of dichotomies promotes patterns of thought and action that are static (unable to acknowledge or address change), stunted (unable to envision alternatives), and dangerously oversimplified (unable to accommodate the complexities of social reality).

Whereas the *structure* of dichotomies makes gender stereotypes harder to "see," critique, and alter, the *status* of dichotomies in Western thought poses additional problems. Although all cultures employ categories of comparison, Western thought is singular in the extent to which binarism

FIGURE 2.3 The Productive-Reproductive Labor Split. This cartoon shows how it undermines shared parenting. Reprinted by special permission of Kirk Anderson.

(thinking in either-or oppositions) is privileged. This is due in large part to the prominence of science in Western culture. Science takes two dichotomies as givens: the categorical separation of fact from value, and of knower (subject) from that which is known (object). Deeply embedded in Western thought, these dualisms are accorded particular status because of their association with science and with claims to "objective knowledge" and "Truth." But they are not gender-neutral categories. On the contrary, the knowing subject, rationality, and objectivity are gendered in meaning and practice.[16] Take a moment to consider how the dichotomies in Table 2.1 are linked both to gender stereotypes and the stereotype of scientific knowledge claims.

To repeat: Dichotomies are so pervasive and privileged in Western culture that they lend authority to the particular dichotomy of gender. And the dichotomy of gender is so taken as given that it lends authority to the "natural" separation of other categories into dualistic form. To the extent that other dichotomies have gendered connotations (culture-nature, reason-emotion, autonomy-dependency, realism-idealism), they buttress the stereotypes of masculine and feminine when they are reproduced. Such reciprocal interaction will be elaborated throughout this text, inasmuch as gender dichotomies (the *power of gender*) create social effects (the *position of women*) and these effects in turn reproduce gendered thought and practice.

Finally, these dichotomies are not only hierarchical (privileging the first term over the second) but also androcentric: The first term is associated with masculinity or assumes a male-as-norm point of view.[17] This androcentrism has three interacting effects. First, because the primary term is androcentric and privileged, it effectively elevates the values of the primary term over those of the "other" term. Thus, reason, order, culture, and action are associated with maleness and are privileged over emotion, uncertainty, nature, and passivity. Second, and closely related, characteristics and activities associated with femaleness are deemed not only less important but also unworthy or undesirable because they appear to

TABLE 2.1   Gender and Science Dichotomies

Masculine/Subject	Feminine/Object
Knower/self/autonomy/agency	Known/other/dependence/passivity
Objective/rational/fact/logical/hard	Subjective/emotional/value/illogical/ soft
Order/certainty/predictability/ control over	Anarchy/uncertainty/unpredictability/ subject to control
Mind/abstract/transcendence/ freedom/intellectual	Body/concrete/contingency/ necessity/manual
Culture/civilized/exploiter/ production/public	Nature/primitive/exploited/ reproduction/private

threaten the values represented by the primary term. Thus, attitudes and activities associated with women (emotion, dependence, reproduction, caretaking) are given less attention and are often disparaged.[18]

Androcentrism has a third effect: It assumes that men are the most important actors and the substance of their lives the most important topic to know about. As long as the realities of women, nonelite men, and children are treated as secondary to the "main story"—as the "background" that is never important enough to warrant being spotlighted—we in fact are unaware of what the background actually is and what relationship it actually has to the main story. What we are unaware of we cannot understand or analyze. Nor can we understand to what extent and in what ways the main story *depends on* background that is "hidden"—forced into darkness or silence by focusing illumination and attention elsewhere. Rendering "invisible" the experience or realities of "others"—of those not privileged—tends to present that which we do "know about" as real and authoritative, as if it were "natural" and knowing about it were all we needed to understand the story.

In sum, an interaction of gender stereotypes, dichotomies, hierarchies, and masculinism/androcentrism powerfully filters our understanding of social reality. Because we rarely question the dualism of male-female, we fail to see how the male-dominated hierarchy of masculine-feminine is socially constructed rather than natural. Recognizing the power of these filtering devices is an important first step toward analyzing their effects accurately and improving our knowledge of the world we both produce and are produced by.

Gender Ideology

As used in this text, the term **ideology** refers to systems of belief—including notions of human nature and social life—that distort reality while they maintain it by justifying status quo social, economic, and political arrangements. In Margaret Andersen's words: "Ideologies serve the powerful by presenting us with a definition of reality that is false and yet orders our comprehension of the surrounding world. When ideas emerge from ideology, they operate as a form of social control by defining the status quo to be the proper state of affairs."[19]

Ideologies are thus political: They order how we "see" and in turn "create" differential access to power. Whereas stereotypes are expectations about certain groups of people, ideologies are beliefs about the nature of social systems and the relationships among groups of people within them. They buttress the effects of stereotyping by further filtering our perceptions and actions in ways that reproduce discrimination by "naturalizing" social hierarchies.

For example, social Darwinism refers to the belief that only the fittest survive and rise to the top. It emerged in the context of European capitalist and colonial expansion. As an ideology, social Darwinism justified the accumulation of wealth by powerful men while fostering a racist belief that inferiority—rather than European imperialism—explained the subordinated status of people of color.[20]

As noted earlier, the dominant gender ideology in the United States fuses gender stereotypes with masculinist/heterosexist beliefs about families, sexuality, divisions of labor, and constructions of power and authority. The belief that men are by nature aggressive and sexually demanding and that women are naturally passive and sexually submissive encourages other beliefs ("men can't help it," "women actually want it") that legitimate systemic sexual abuse. It "excuses" the pattern of male rape behavior and controls the behavior of girls and women, who attempt to avoid or diminish the effects of this violence. Although some males are targets of assault because of their cultural choices, sexuality, class, or race/ethnicity, *all* females are potentially threatened and therefore socially controlled by virtue of simply being female in a masculinist world. At the same time, beliefs that "women are mothers by nature" and that "a woman's place is in the home" legitimate the social practice that holds women disproportionately responsible for child care, maintenance of family relations, and household tasks while denying that this is socially necessary *work*.

Ideologies, although they appear timeless, are context dependent and alterable to suit the interests of those with power. Depending on what the situation calls for, gender ideology may promote women as physically strong and capable of backbreaking work (e.g., slave women, frontier women), as competent to do men's work (e.g., Rosie the Riveter in World War II), as dexterous and immune to boredom (e.g., electronics assembly industries), or as full-time housewives and devoted mothers (e.g., postwar demands that women vacate jobs in favor of returning soldiers and repopulate the nation). The point is that ideologies are reconfigured to suit the changing interests of those in power, not those whose lives are most controlled by them (see Figure 2.4).

Ideologies are often couched in terms of biological determinism, positing narrow genetic or biological causes for complex social behaviors. In the real world, human behavior is always mediated by culture—by systems of meaning and the values they incorporate. The role that biology actually plays varies dramatically and can *never* be determined without reference to cultural context. Ideological beliefs may exaggerate the role of biological factors (the argument that men's testosterone explains male homicide rates) or posit biological factors where none need be involved (the argument that because some women during part of their life bear children, all women should *care* for children and are unfit for political

FIGURE 2.4 Changing Gender Ideologies. Such shifts suit those in power, as this cartoon indicates. Reprinted by special permission of Kirk Anderson.

power). Reliance on biological determinism means that ideologies tend to flourish in periods of disruption or transition, when political conservatism serves to buttress traditional power-wielders.[21] And when traditional power-wielders are threatened by change, it is easy and often effective for them to repeat ideological claims that emphasize how natural and therefore unchanging inequality is.

In the late twentieth century, individuals and societies worldwide are experiencing a variety of profound and rapid transformations associated with the end of the Cold War and the rise of global capitalism. Partially responding to (and taking advantage of) the turbulence and uncertainty these changes bring, right-wing activists and religious fundamentalists in the United States (and elsewhere) crusade for a return to "traditional values." Implicitly, and sometimes explicitly, the policies they promote (such as anti-homosexual legislation, reduced welfare for single mothers, and restricted abortion in the United States) rely on and reproduce gender hierarchy and its inequalities. They also reflect hierarchies of race and class.[22] In this example, an understandable desire for security and stability in the face of disturbing changes is translated into a resurgence of masculinist and racist practices that sustain traditional (affluent, white, heterosexual, and male) power-holders.

Finally, ideologies are most effective when most taken for granted. They resist correction and critique by making the status quo appear natural, as "the way things are" rather than as the result of human intervention and practice. Like stereotypes, ideologies depoliticize what are in fact differences in power that serve some more than others. Religion, myths, educational systems, advertising, and the media are variously involved in reproducing stereotypes and ideologies that make the world we live in seem inevitable and, for some, even desirable. The point is not that the world is as bad as it could be but that ideologies present only a partial and particular view of the world. Most important, ideologies prevent us from seeing inequalities, comprehending how they impoverish the majority and threaten all of us, and determining how we can act to change them.

Our final point is that much of our behavior *unintentionally* reproduces status quo inequalities. We cannot simply locate an "enemy" to blame for institutional discrimination and its many consequences. Although there are, of course, individuals who actively pursue discriminatory policies and the perpetuation of injustice, few people positively identify with such a characterization. Rather, most of us wish to be and think of ourselves as good family members, friends, neighbors, and citizens.

But stereotypes and ideologies play a particular role in shaping our expectations and behaviors. We begin to be socialized into these belief systems early in life, well before we have the capacity to reflect critically on their implications for our own or others' lives. Hence, for the most part, we internalize these beliefs and do not think to question them. Moreover, because ideologies are supported and sustained by those with power in our societies, there are powerful incentives for subscribing to these belief systems—and negative consequences of not doing so. (Consider the risks a man takes by wearing a dress, or a woman takes by hiking alone.) Unless something or someone prompts us to "see things differently," these belief systems become unconscious assumptions that shape decision-making throughout our lives. They serve to reinforce the status quo and to blunt criticism of it. As such, they involve all of us in the often *un*-intentional reproduction of various social hierarchies, including those that hurt us.

At the same time, we know that the real world of inequality and oppression is a function of actions taken—and not taken—by actual people, not abstract "structures." It is real people who engage in physical violence, pass discriminatory legislation, deny citizenship claims, pollute our environment, sell dangerous products, promote hatreds, and denigrate those who pursue social change. Yet individuals may—in fact, frequently do—engage in these activities while insisting that their intentions are good (being a good soldier often means having to engage in physical violence; getting to the emergency room may require driving a vehicle that pollutes; participating in a consumer culture to meet our needs and wants promotes waste and dangerous risks). Obviously, *intending to be harmful* is not likely to produce good outcomes, and presumably warrants blame and perhaps punishment. But in a context of structural oppressions, *intending to be helpful* does not *inevitably* contribute to good outcomes, because actions taken may unintentionally reproduce structurally oppressive consequences. In short, although the absence of bad intentions or the presence of good intentions is presumably a necessary condition for ensuring good outcomes, it—unfortunately!—is not a sufficient one.

Ensuring good outcomes requires more; it requires both good intentions and consciousness of how structural dynamics may frustrate or facilitate good outcomes. Even with these in place, the social world is determined by so many factors and their interactions that we can never guarantee or absolutely predict outcomes. Rather, we can, to the best of our current abilities, promote normative commitments—to equity and justice—as we constantly and critically improve our understanding of patterns and structures.

Complicating the picture is our frequent ignorance of structural hierarchies and our varying positions within them. In particular, when we occupy positions of privilege or advantage (in relation to hierarchies of class, ethnicity, physical ability, age, religion, nationality, sexual orientation, etc.), we rarely recognize how that structural positioning grants us power and/or resources that the disadvantaged are denied. For example, although not all whites endorse racism, all men masculinism, or all heterosexuals homophobia, *all* whites, men, and heterosexuals *benefit* from their positions of relative privilege within the structures of racism, sexism, and heterosexism. It is in this sense that the hierarchies are *structural* and not simply individual or idiosyncratic. In an eye-opening essay, Peggy McIntosh provides telling examples of how much those who are privileged can take for granted, how much they do not have to think about (or be angered, hurt, or impoverished by) the effects of structural hierarchy (see Box 2.1).[23]

Blame and punishment may be appropriate in regard to intended harms. But they tend to be counterproductive and "backward looking"[24] in relation to structural hierarchies, which are by definition not reducible to individual acts. The point we wish to emphasize is that structural privilege or advantage confers power. Hence, although individuals alone are, appropriately, not held accountable for institutional hierarchies, the privileged in every hierarchy have greater power *and therefore greater responsibility* for transforming those hierarchies. Rather than be caught up in blaming, and in its defensive responses, we encourage readers to become aware of structural oppressions and how all who are privileged necessarily play a part in the reproduction of oppressions. In particular, we hope

BOX 2.1 ILLUMINATING INVISIBLE PRIVILEGE

The following selections have been adapted from Peggy McIntosh, "White Privilege and Male Privilege," reprinted in Margaret L. Andersen and Patricia Hill Collins, eds., *Race, Class, and Gender* (Belmont, Calif.: Wadsworth Publishing), pp. 70–81. We have expanded and revised McIntosh's examples to reflect our global focus in particular.

* * *

Privilege constitutes an "invisible package of unearned assets" that can be counted on and about which the privileged are encouraged to remain oblivious (p. 71). It is hard not to desire and to enjoy privilege! We are not trained to see ourselves as oppressors, as unfairly advantaged, or as participants in damaged cultures (p. 72). Hence, we often unintentionally participate in reproducing oppression simply by taking our privilege—and the culture and structures that sustain it—as "normal." The following suggest everyday ways in which the privileged can take for granted advantages that are denied to others. This is the nature of structural oppression: advantages to some are premised upon their denial to others.

WHITE/ANGLO PRIVILEGE

[Many of the following examples apply to elite privilege more generally.]

1. I can turn on the television or read the paper and see people of my race/ethnicity widely and positively represented. I can be sure that my children will be given educational materials that testify to the existence and value of their race, and I do not have to teach them about systemic racism for their own daily protection.
2. I am never asked to speak for all the people of my racial/ethnic group. I can behave in an unconventional or unattractive manner without having people attribute these "faults" to my race. I am not made acutely aware that my shape, mode of dress, abilities, or body odor will be taken as a reflection on my race. When I perform well, I am not called a credit to my race.
3. I can remain oblivious to the language, customs, desires, and injuries of persons of color (who constitute the majority of the world). And within my culture, I suffer no penalty for this ignorance and insensitivity. If I do protest racism, my efforts are not disparaged as self-interested or self-seeking.
4. I can be confident that if I seek accommodation, a job, social services, legal help, or medical care, my race will not work against me.
5. I can count on the presence of English-speakers even in foreign countries, and that most professional meetings I attend will be conducted in English.

MALE PRIVILEGE

1. I can watch, listen to, and read multiple media and count on most of the actors, directors, athletes, speakers, authors, teachers, politicians, scientists, religious leaders, and corporate decision-makers to represent my gender and interests. At school, I (and my children) can count on learning about what men find interesting, what they have said and done (mostly about and with other men) throughout history and across cultures, and how men's ideas, theories, discoveries, experiments, and conquests have determined "human" history and progress.
2. I can go walking, drinking, working, and playing wherever I want to without fear of violence on the basis of my sex. I can dress as I like without being held responsible if I am harassed or attacked. If I behave assertively, aggressively, dogmatically, and/or unsympathetically, I will usually be applauded for "taking control."
3. I can attend religious services and count on celebrating the experiences, authority, power, and spiritual teachings of men. I can readily access visual and written materials that objectify women and cultivate male dominance.
4. Aside from personal relationships (and often even then), I can remain oblivious to the fantasies, life experiences, health concerns, distresses, and injuries of women (who constitute more than half the world's population). And I rarely suffer any penalty for this ignorance and insensitivity. If I protest sexism, I am not dismissed as being self-interested.
5. I can choose not to participate in parenting without being branded unnatural or immoral.
6. If I am successful and single, it is assumed to be my choice rather than my inability to attract women.

HETEROSEXUAL PRIVILEGE

1. I can enjoy virtually all popular cultural media as a celebration of desires, humor, stories, relationships, intimacy, romance, and family life that I participate in and identify with. My children are exposed to cultural and educational materials that support our kind of family unit and do not turn them against my choice of domestic partnership. I can enjoy the taxation, legal, health insurance, adoption, and immigration benefits of being able to marry.
2. I have no difficulty finding neighborhoods, schools, jobs, recreational activities, or travel arrangements where people approve of our family unit. I can express feelings of affection for my partner in public, without fear of censure or physical attack.
3. If in my work or play I spend time with children of my sex, my motives and actions are not treated with suspicion. If I am critical of heterosexism, I am not dismissed as self-interested.
4. I, and my children, can talk about our home life or the social events of the weekend without fearing most listeners' reactions. I am not asked to deny or "hide" who I am, in the important sense of my sexual identity, desires, loving relationships, and family life.
5. If the person I love does not share my citizenship, we have the option of marriage, which permits us to live together and have a family.

that readers, by becoming aware of their own positioning and privileges, will more effectively take responsibility for transforming oppressive power dynamics.

Oppressive hierarchies are not in fact inevitable. If we are to change the world, we have to change ourselves as well as the social structures that both produce and are produced by those selves. We cannot change either without changing how we think. And in that regard, understanding the role of stereotypes and ideologies is crucial.

THE GENDERED WHO, WHAT, AND HOW OF WORLD POLITICS

The increasing salience of women's issues and the resurgence of women's movements have raised popular consciousness about the politics of gender relations. And three decades of feminist scholarship have placed gender on the agenda of most academic disciplines. In the humanities, history, anthropology, and even in sociology and political science, feminist critiques have altered disciplinary givens, challenged conventional explanations, and expanded the reach of intellectual inquiry. In this section we look at *who* does IR, *what* it is about, and *how* it is studied and practiced in order to see how international relations scholars and practitioners do—and do not—address gender issues.

International relations has been and continues to be male-dominated. The preponderance of male scholars and practitioners partly explains the silence on gender: Men checked with each other about what men were doing that was considered relevant to other men and was written by men for primarily male audiences! Though important, the absence of women from these activities is insufficient to explain why these men failed, until very recently, even to comment on this gender imbalance. Other reasons include IR's relative insulation as a discipline, which has distanced it from developments in those disciplines where feminist theories and research have been most influential.

But it is also the particular nature of IR inquiry—what it is about—that produces resistance to taking gender seriously. International relations distinguishes itself from political science generally by valuing matters of foreign policy over matters of domestic policy: Relations between but not within states define its focus. Whereas domestic political observers and policymakers have had to grapple with voting behavior, welfare state issues, domestic public interest groups, and social movements—areas in which gender issues figure prominently—IR practitioners have focused on national security (defined most often in terms of military might), economic power (defined typically by gross national product indicators), and international organizations and regimes (made up of government and financial elites). Not only are women infrequent actors in these matters of state, but also IR orthodoxy sees no place for women in these high-stakes games.

Yet the "what" of IR is changing. The end of the Cold War and its East versus West tensions, the expansion of global capitalism, the revival of nationalisms and development of regionalism, and the growth of new social movements have altered the practical and theoretical terrain of IR. More specifically, peace studies and development studies have challenged conventional definitions of security and economic growth. Proponents of these studies argue that militarized national security, particularly in this nuclear age, and economic development strategies, which put profits before the needs of people and a sustainable ecology, compromise both individual and global security. By focusing on the security needs of people and the planet, these approaches open the field to gender issues. They permit the articulation of demands for peace, economic justice, and global equality, and they permit work in defense of the environment, upon which women and all other living things ultimately depend.

In addition to rethinking the meaning of security, IR analysts are rethinking the meaning of states and sovereignty. The growth of transnational power has not eliminated but has certainly altered the power of states. In the context of unregulated global financial markets (therefore not under state control) and expansion of transnational institutions, organizations, and social movements, states confront a transformed political, economic, and sociocultural environment. All of these are variously gendered and have varying implications for the positions of women and men.

For instance, although barely present at the top, women are active members of local, national, and transnational organizations. In numerous ways, issues that transcend national borders are becoming increasingly important today, making nongovernmental organizations (NGOs), composed of private individuals and groups, increasingly important actors in world politics. Women have historically been very active in NGOs and through these activities "have taken issues previously ignored—such as violence against women and rights to reproductive health—and brought them into the mainstream policy debate."[25] This observation relates to a further and extremely significant change. IR theorists increasingly recognize that the conventional separation between domestic and international politics is untenable. Issues that have traditionally received little attention from students of IR (race/ethnic divisions, democratization, unionization, welfare provision, citizenship rights, health care) are inescapable dimensions of today's world politics.

Finally, recent developments point to the growing impact of "people power." Although direct violence grabs most of the headlines, nonviolent transformation are also prominent. Throughout history, women have participated in all types of struggle; however, they play a particularly central role in nonviolent resistance, which requires mass mobilization to induce the populace to cease cooperation with, and, thereby, delegitimize regimes. Both women's activism in nongovernmental organizations and their traditional roles in sustaining families and communities uniquely position them to mobilize people at the grass-roots level and to devise alternative networks for food, clothing, shelter, and health services. In addition, women have taken great risks to protest governmental crimes and bear witness to human rights violations. These actions have not in themselves toppled governments, but they have been significant factors in bringing about political change. Indeed, they are key features of today's much touted "global democratization" or "global civil society"; yet the gender dynamics of these changes remain largely unexamined.

Politics itself has to be redefined in view of the wide range of political activities in which women and men are involved. Neither can politics be defined narrowly as an activity of governmental officials and elite influence-peddlers, nor can popular participation be reduced to voting and membership in political parties. Instead, **politics** is about differential access to resources—both material and symbolic—and how such power relations and structures are created, sustained, and reconfigured. According to this broader definition, politics operates at all levels, ranging from the individual and her identifications, to family and community, and to the state, transnational agencies, and global dynamics. All people act politically in their everyday lives. When feminists claim that the "personal is political," they mean that all of us are embedded in various kinds of power relationships and structures that affect our choices and aspirations on a daily basis (see Box 2.2). Most important, changes among individuals and communities both affect, and are affected by, inter- and transnational processes. In Cynthia Enloe's words, "the personal is international" *and* "the international is personal."[26]

Recognition of gender inequality as a global phenomenon with global—and local—implications challenges traditional definitions of IR. Sarah Brown argues that "the proper object and purpose of the study of international relations is the identification and explanation of social stratification and of inequality as structured at the level of global relations."[27] Compared to a standard definition, Brown's draws greater attention to political, economic, and social forces below and above the level of the state, thereby revealing the greater complexity of global politics, which cannot be reduced to the actions of state leaders and their international organizations. It also highlights inequality as a significant source of conflict in international relations in addition to, but also in tension with, notions about the inevitable clash of states with differing ideologies and interests. Finally, it speaks to global patterns of inequality operating across states, creating divisions among people along not just national lines but also gender, race, class, and culture lines. The corollary of this is that people are finding common cause with each other across national boundaries and, thus, creating a different kind of international relations, or world politics, from that of elite policy-makers.

Whereas world leaders and those who study them concentrate on sustaining the balance of power among the most powerful—in the interests of stability—nonelites around the world and those who study them focus on the imbalances of power that are created in the name of stability and that compromise the security of the majority of the world's people. People around the world struggling against the tyrannies of sexism, racism, classism, militarism, and/or imperialism seek justice, which requires upsetting the status quo. An IR lens focused exclusively on elite interstate actors and narrow definitions of security keeps us from seeing many other important realities.

In recent years, IR scholars and practitioners have become more sensitive to a variety of forces that divide and bind in the international system, as a result of both changing world conditions and the emergence of postpositivist perspectives within IR. They pay more attention to power struggles happening within and across states over land, religion, language, race, class, and general access to resources. They also study the historical processes that created the inequalities that have erupted into conflict. And even though much IR literature continues to speak of states and their leaders as unitary actors in world affairs, IR observers are becoming less likely to assume that the interests of a political leader are necessarily shared by the people whom he or she rules, even in so-called democratic countries. What most IR scholars and practitioners, even many of those who have adopted postpositivist perspectives, continue to avoid dealing with in any depth is gender inequality, despite evidence that it is integrally tied into all other inequalities and many global problems.

GENDERED DIVISIONS OF WORLD POLITICS

In this section we introduce the issue areas examined in the following chapters and begin to expose the "hidden" gender at work in conventional accounts of IR.

Politics and Power

Masculinism pervades politics. Wendy Brown writes: "More than any other kind of human activity, politics has historically borne an explicitly masculine identity. It has been more exclusively limited to men than any

BOX 2.2 SELECTED QUOTATIONS

ON SEXISM

Sexism is a many-headed, ubiquitous monster that has manifested itself in different ways in different historical periods and in different cultures. It is a belief system based on the assumption that the physical differences between males and females are so significant that they should determine virtually all social and economic roles of men and women. It holds that not just their reproductive functions are determined by sex, but that sex is the factor that rules their entire lives, all their functions in society and the economy, and their relation to the state and all public institutions and especially to each other. Sexism is manifest in all forms of behavior from subtle gestures and language to exploitation and oppression, and in all human institutions from the family to the multinational corporation.

—Betty A. Reardon, *Sexism and the War System*
(New York: Teachers College Press, 1985), p. 16.

ON OPPRESSION

Consider a birdcage. If you look very closely at just one wire in the cage, you cannot see the other wires. If your conception of what is before you is determined by this myopic focus, you could look at that one wire, up and down the length of it, and be unable to see why a bird would not just fly around the wire. . . . Furthermore, even if, one day at a time, you myopically inspected each wire, you still could not see why a bird would have trouble going past the wires to get anywhere. . . . It is only when you step back, stop looking at the wires one by one, microscopically, and take a macroscopic view of the whole cage, that you can see why the bird does not go anywhere; and then you will see it in a moment. . . . It is perfectly *obvious* that the bird is surrounded by a network of systematically related barriers, no one of which would be the least hindrance to its flight, but which, by their relations to each other, are as confining as the solid walls of a dungeon.

—Marilyn Frye, *The Politics of Reality*
(New York: Crossing Press, 1992), pp. 4–5.

ON MASCULINISM AS OBJECTIFICATION

Objectification involves more than the subjection of the female body. Fundamentally, it is rooted in the human assertion of power over nature. It is men who, for a variety of reasons, come to see themselves as being the tamers of nature, as the vanguard fighting scarcity. In their subjection of nature they simultaneously begin to subjugate other human beings. The masculine ideology is the ideology of objectification. As such, it naturalizes the distinction between subject and object. In so doing, it distinguishes between the agency of man the maker, and the passivity of nature. The pacification of nature involves the pacification of women, as well as the subordination of other men perceived as potential rivals. Hence . . . masculinity as an ideology elevates the primacy of technique, rationality, and power. In objectifying nature, men lay the foundation for the objectification of all social and personal relationships.

—Arthur Brittan and Mary Maynard, *Sexism, Racism, and Oppression* (Oxford: Basil Blackwell, 1984), pp. 201–202.

ON POWER AND RESPONSIBILITY

The penalties for inequality between women and men are very severe. And they are not borne by women alone. They are borne by the whole world.

Power, tempered by the wisdom and restraint of responsibility, is the foundation of a just society. But with too little responsibility, power turns to tyranny. And with too little power, responsibility becomes exploitation. Yet in every country in the world power and responsibility have become unbalanced and unhitched, distributed unequally between men and women. . . . The penalties of women's too-great burden of responsibility and their too-small slice of power . . . are hardship, sickness, hunger, even famine. But the penalties of man's disproportionate share of the world's power (without the intimate day-to-day knowledge of the effects of that power, or the responsibility for ensuring that the basic needs of the household are met) are just as great.

Of course, not all men are tyrants or despots and not all women are martyrs to duty and hard work. But *masculine* and *feminine* social roles have tilted the majority of men and women in those directions.

—Debbie Taylor, *Women: A World Report* (New York: Oxford University Press, 1985), p. 87.

other realm of endeavor and has been more intensely, self-consciously masculine than most other social practices."[28]

In IR, as in political science, power is usually defined as "power-over"—specifically, the ability to get someone to do what you want. It is usually measured by control of resources, especially those supporting physical coercion. This definition emphasizes separation and competition: Those who have power use it (or its threat) to keep others from securing enough to threaten them. The emphasis on material resources and coercive ability obscures the fact that power reckoning is embedded in sociocultural dynamics and value systems. Also obscured is the way that power presupposes relationships—among actors, resources, meaning, situation—and its inability to be accurately understood when separated from these relationships.

In IR, the concept of "political actor"—the legitimate wielder of society's power—is derived from classical political theory. Common to constructions of "political man"—from Plato and Aristotle to Hobbes, Locke, and Rousseau—is the privileging of man's capacity for reason. This unique ability distinguishes man from other animals and explains his pursuit of freedom—from nature as well as from tyranny. Feminists argue that the models of human nature underpinning constructions of "political man" are not in fact gender neutral but are models of "male nature," generated by exclusively male experience. They are not universal claims about humankind but masculinist claims about gendered divisions of labor and identity that effectively and sometimes explicitly exclude women from definitions of "human," "moral agent," "rational actor," and "political man."

Conceptually, "woman" is excluded primarily by denying her the rationality that marks "man" as the highest animal. Concretely, women have historically been excluded from political power by states' limiting of citizenship to those who perform military duty and/or are property owners. Under these conditions, most women are structurally excluded from formal politics, even though individual women, in exceptional circumstances, have wielded considerable political power. In this century, women have largely won the battle for the vote, though definitions of citizenship continue to limit women's access to public power, and their political power is circumscribed by a variety of indirect means (discussed elsewhere in this text). Most obvious are the continued effects of the dichotomy of **public-private** that separates men's productive and "political" activities from women's reproductive and "personal" activities.

These constructions—of power, "political man," citizenship, public-private, and so on—reproduce, often unconsciously, masculinist and androcentric assumptions. For example, sovereign man and sovereign states are defined not by connection or relationships but by autonomy in decision-making and freedom from the power of others. And security is understood not in terms of celebrating and sustaining life but as the capacity to be indifferent to "others" and, if necessary, to harm them. Hobbes's androcentrism is revealed simply when we ask how helpless infants ever become adults if human nature is universally competitive and hostile. From the perspective of child-rearing practices—necessary for life everywhere—it makes more sense to argue that humans are naturally cooperative: Without the cooperation that is required to nurture children, there would be no men or women. And although Aristotle acknowledged that the public sphere depends upon the production of life's necessities in the private sphere, he denied the power relations or politics that this implies.

Gender is most apparent in these constructions when we examine the dichotomies they (re)produce: political-apolitical, reason-emotion, public-private, leaders-followers, active-passive, freedom-necessity. As with other dichotomies, difference and opposition are privileged and context and ambiguity are ignored. The web of meaning and human interaction within which political man acts and politics takes place remains hidden, as if irrelevant. The point is not that power-over, aggressive behavior, and life-threatening conflicts are not "real" but that they are only a part of a more complicated story. Focusing on them misrepresents our reality even as it (to some extent unnecessarily) reproduces power-over, aggressive behavior, and life-threatening conflicts.

Security and Violence

Claims about men's superior strength are favored justifications for gender hierarchy. But such claims are misleading. On the one hand, men's strength varies cross-culturally and within cultures, and a considerable number of women are in fact stronger than men. On the other hand, what do we mean by strength? Anyone who has observed women of Africa on lengthy treks carrying heavy loads of firewood and water cannot help seeing how arbitrary our indicators of strength are. Why do we consider men's upper-body muscular strength more significant than women's burden-carrying strength and greater endurance? On what basis do we assume that bigger is better? (Consider the plight of dinosaurs!) Ashley Montague undertook a comprehensive review of scientific literature and concluded that only androcentric lenses prevent our acknowledging the "natural superiority of women." Specifically, "the female is *constitutionally* stronger than the male": She has greater stamina, lives longer, fights disease better, and endures "all sorts of devitalizing conditions better than men: starvation, exposure, fatigue, shock, illness and the like."[29] Superiority is often defined in terms of the most effective survival traits— but apparently not when women's abilities are assessed.

Historically, the greater muscular strength of (some) males has been a crucial factor when the outcome of conflicts depended on this particular strength. Today's technology dramatically alters the relationship of muscular strength to success in battle or in the workplace. But there continues to be a preoccupation with power and strength defined in masculine terms—upper-body strength as well as access to and use of weapons. And there is no denying that men, worldwide, engage in violent behaviors more frequently and with greater negative effect than do women. Males are encouraged to act aggressively in more situations than females and are systematically placed in situations where proving their manhood requires aggressive behavior. In fact, most models of masculinity include elements of courage, competition, assertiveness, and ambition that are difficult to disassociate from physical aggression and even violence. Ancient, classical, and modern depictions of warriors and political actors typically identify risking life—one's own and that of others—as the surest mark of a free man: "A real man lays his life on the line. For what is death risked? For honor, for glory, for a value greater than life, for freedom from enslavement by life, for immortality, or for the 'ultimate value' of the state."[30]

A willingness to engage in violence is built into our constructions of masculinity and is exacerbated by **militarization**—the extension of military practices into civilian life. And to the extent that we define national security as the defense and protection of sovereignty, militarization becomes hard to avoid. Believing that peace requires preparation for war, we become locked into arms races and other self-perpetuating cycles. These involve sacrificing social welfare objectives in favor of defense spending and training young people—men *and* women—to risk lives and practice violence in the name of putatively higher objectives.

There are no simple formulas for determining appropriate trade-offs between "butter" and "guns," and we are not suggesting that security concerns are illusory or easily resolved. But in a climate of militarization, we must be careful to assess the ostensible gains from encouraging violence because the actual costs are very great.

Moreover, the construction of security in military terms—understood as direct violence—often masks the systemic insecurity of indirect or **structural violence**.[31] The latter arises from social, economic, and political structures that increase the vulnerability of particular groups to forms of harm (e.g., greater infant mortality among poor women who have reduced access to health-care services). Structural violence especially affects the lives of women and other subordinated groups. When we ignore this fact, we ignore the security of the majority of the planet's occupants. Finally, because violence is gendered, militarization has a reciprocal relationship to masculinist ideologies: The macho effects of military activities, the objectifying effects of military technologies, and the violent effects of military spending *interact*, escalating not only arms races but also direct and indirect sexual violence.

What the gendered division of violence constructs is a world shaped by hostile forces and the naturalization of war against "the feminine." In a self-repeating cycle, threats (real or fictive) increase preparations for defense and/or retaliation that are inextricable from conditions of structural violence. An oppositional lens magnifies and legitimates self-other, us-them, friend-enemy, aggressive-passive, soldier-victim, and protector-protected dichotomies. The latter dichotomy is institutionalized in protection rackets: creating a threat and then charging for protection against it. Some theorists argue that nation-states engage in such rackets by creating a system of mutually threatening centralized governments and charging citizens taxes and military service to support effective defense of state boundaries.[32] Feminists have similarly identified marriage as a protection racket. Under conditions of systemic male violence, women are forced to seek protection by entering into disadvantageous marriages to individual men. People often fail to see the repetition of the same pattern in different situations, to recognize the self-perpetuating and costly nature of this violence, and to seek a way to break these self-destructive cycles.[33]

Economics and Labor

The division of gender and identities is nowhere clearer than in the ways we define "work" and in which kinds of work are most valued, who does what, and how much they are paid. The stereotypes of women and femininity here interact powerfully with the ideology of public-private to generate quite rigid patterns in what men and women do. Just as the public is seen as more important than the private, women's jobs and the status and pay they are accorded tend to be seen as "secondary," as providing the support system for "more important"—the "primary"—work that men, especially elite men, do. Thus we find that women's work is largely of a servicing nature: taking care of the emotional (e.g., counseling, nursing), "entertainment" (e.g., performing arts, sex industries), production (e.g., word processing, assembly-line jobs), and maintenance (e.g., cleaning, clerical, child care, teaching) needs of men as individuals and the masculinist social system generally.

Treated as secondary, these jobs are not assigned high status and are not well paid. And women who earn a paycheck rarely do less unpaid work at home. Instead, women worldwide have a "double workday": earning money for the family while also being held responsible for child care and household maintenance. It seems that women are expected, consistent with the stereotype of femininity, to labor both at home and in the workplace, not for status or income as we expect men to do, but for the joy of serving others. Whereas men may be asked to volunteer their time and energy for a special cause or specific occasion, women are expected to volunteer their entire lives in the service of male needs and masculinist social orders. Of course, women are not entirely without benefits in these societies. Nor do *all* men benefit equally from the exploitation of women's labor. But as a generalization, all men do benefit in various ways from the systemic masculinism that treats women's energies, lives, intellects, demands, and needs as secondary (see Figure 2.5).

Economic relations are addressed in IR almost exclusively through the lens of neoclassical economics. The ostensible "free market" of capitalist global relations is assumed to be the most efficient and therefore most desirable approach to national and international economic relations. Through this lens, an expanding world economy provides an ever larger pie, and, through a process of "trickle down," ever bigger pies translate into larger slices—theoretically, even for those with few initial resources. Economic-development policies promote growth as the way to provide more goods and services to the world's increasing population. And capitalism is identified as the most effective system for securing growth.

In addition, formal modeling of exchange relations and market systems are popular in IR. These models appear to provide analytically powerful tools for understanding human decision-making and its cumulative consequences. On the basis of a rational actor's ("his") utilitarian assessment of market trade-offs, projections of other decision-making activities and their consequences are mapped. Thus game theory models are said to illuminate a wide range of human behaviors, such as responding to deprivation, making threats, risk-taking, and developing nuclear strategies. All such models leave out the complexity of human behaviors in real life be-

FIGURE 2.5   The World on Women's Backs. Shown here is a cartoon emphasizing women's enormous responsibilities but minimal power in the world. Copyright © 1979 by Nicole Hollander. From *I'm Training to Be Tall and Blond* by Nicole Hollander. Reprinted by permission of St. Martin's Press, Incorporated.

cause to make models workable, the variables they include must be reduced to a very few. The complex, ambiguous, and nuanced *context* of decision-making must be sacrificed to generate clear patterns that accommodate quantifiable analysis.

Left out are the hard-to-quantify dimensions of social reality, such as culture, emotional investments, and normative commitments. And once preference formation, prior conditions, and the context are considered irrelevant, it becomes hard to say what the relevance of the actual findings is. What does the study of behavior in poorly modeled situations tell us about behavior in the real world, in real-life decision-making? We do not argue that rational-actor modeling is useless. Rather, we ask and attempt to evaluate whether, in a context of scarce research resources, alternative approaches to IR would not contribute more to our ability to resolve global crises and reduce global inequality.

On the face of it, advocates of traditional approaches tend to reproduce rather than challenge the status quo because the questions they frame result in answers that confirm the assumptions upon which the questions are based. Gender dichotomies are built into the dualities favored by economic analysis: paid-unpaid work, providers-dependents, production-reproduction, and independence in the marketplace versus dependence. Just as women are deemed feminine by their dependence within the family, the Third World is "unmanned" by its position of dependence in the global economy. Finally, "trickle down" theories tend to benefit those who control the most resources by promoting the continued growth that delivers the biggest pieces of pie to those in power. Many argue that not only do the poorest never see the benefits of "trickle down" but that, even if they get marginally larger pieces, today's ecological crises (which hurt the poorest most) challenge the entire premise of ever expanding growth.

Equity, Ecology, and Resources

Traditional texts in world politics often contrast "high" and "low" politics. High politics are state-centric security and military affairs; low politics, economic relations. Even more removed from the traditional core of IR concerns are matters of ecology, which are often called "soft politics." Once again, a hierarchy is at work, pitting high over low and hard over soft politics. In recent years, the seriousness of environmental degradation and the dependence of *all* of us on sustainable ecology have prompted much greater attention to environmental issues. When we begin to take the environment seriously, we are forced to examine how resources are distributed and who controls them. It is not simply an increasing population but also the disproportionate and, to a large extent, irresponsible consumption of resources on the part of industrialized nations that exacerbate resource depletion.

What are the causes of ecological irresponsibility? We observe first that numerous variables interact in sometimes unpredictable ways to shape environmental use. Industrialization promotes resource consumption because it accelerates the consumption of fuels and other raw materials and fosters a growth mentality that condones environmental destruction and the waste of material and human resources. Tragically, the "success" of industrialization and expansion leads to many failures. For example, in the United States the apparent wealth of resources contributes to wasteful attitudes such as "bigger is better" and "growth is the answer," which dull environmental sensibilities, discourage recycling, and ignore the need to reduce consumption. We put short-term profit and convenience ahead of long-term security.

Nonindustrialized peoples rarely have the luxury of a throw-away mentality. Without the illusion of constant growth, many live in a symbiotic relationship with their environment. There is neither need for nor advantage in wasteful or unnecessary consumption. However, the presence of growing populations in resource-poor environments also creates environmental degradation. People are forced to secure their everyday subsistence by depleting the very resources they depend upon. Water, food, and fuel for domestic use are essential for life, but the acquisition and consumption of these goods in much of the Third World conflict with long-term ecological planning and resources. At the macrosocietal level, development policies—whether securing foreign currency through the sale of timber or building an industrial base with fossil-fuel-driven factories—often have costly ecological consequences. The choices are not easy.

Gender divisions are played out in terms of who has access to what resources, who controls resources and to what ends, who suffers most from environmental degradation, and how gender stereotypes relate to irresponsible resource use. At core, the characteristically Western ideology of limitless growth presupposes a belief in "man's" dominion over nature (promoted, for example, in Christian and capitalist belief systems) and the desirability of "man's" exploiting nature to further his own ends. Conquering nature, digging out her treasures and secrets, proving man's superiority through manipulation of nature—these are familiar and currently deadly refrains. The identification of nature as female is not an accident but a historical development that is visible in justifications by elites for territorial and intellectual expansion. Exploitation is most readily legitimated by "objectifying"—treating something or someone to be exploited as an "object" devoid of intelligence or feelings. Thus, "natural resources" are deemed exploitable by right, no questions asked, "there for the taking." Historically, women, colonies, and the earth's bounty have all been treated as such natural resources. The gendered dichotomies of culture-nature, subject-object, exploiter-exploited, agency-passivity, and leader-follower are reproduced in the process and justification of exploiting human mothers and "mother nature."

Gender dynamics undermine sustainable ecology and the equity required to achieve it. Worldwide, females are more dramatically affected by environmental degradation than males. As food providers, women bear a workload that increases when water, food, and fuel resources deteriorate; as caretakers, they have to work harder when family and community members are victims of environmental disasters; as last and least fed, they suffer most from starvation and malnutrition; as poorest, they are least able to quit jobs, acquire adequate health care, purchase safer products, or move away from immediate environmental threats. As we illustrate in this text, women have long been active in ecological movements. But it is no longer "just women" who are systemically threatened by environmental crises.

CONCLUSION

We conclude this chapter by looking at gender in world politics along three dimensions: normatively (how we evaluate), conceptually (how we categorize and think), and organizationally (how we act). In contrast to our approach in this text, writers of conventional accounts tend to deny the importance of gender, its relation to social inequalities, and, therefore, the moral costs imposed by gender hierarchy. In regard to the *normative dimension*, blindness to gender inequality is a consequence of reigning ideologies—religious and secular—that naturalize status quo masculinism. A paradox operates here inasmuch as the exaggeration of gender differences both confirms the existence of gender inequality and depoliticizes that inequality by characterizing and trivializing it as "natural" gender difference.

Some writers "ignore" the politics (and costs) of gender hierarchy by claiming that gender is irrelevant to topics such as governmental politics or national security. Therefore, they "avoid" acknowledging gender inequality and the moral issues it raises. In this case, the moral costs of masculinism remain invisible on the false assumption that unless women are explicitly part of the picture or sexuality is central to the topic, gender is irrelevant. The assumption is false because the position of men and masculinity as dominant features of IR reveal this position as pervasively gendered. In contrast, stereotypical differences between men and women and the lives they lead are not only acknowledged by some writers—they are celebrated. In such accounts, the moral costs of masculinism remain invisible on the false assumption that gender differences are not *political*—and bear no moral costs—but are natural, the inevitable consequence of biological difference. This assumption is false because gender hierarchy fuels systemic inequalities and, hence, injustice. Moreover, gender hierarchy is not separate from but intersects with and sustains multiple other hierarchies, each of which exacerbates injustice and shapes world politics. In both cases, denying the pervasive effects of gender has the consequence of obscuring gender inequality and the moral issues it raises.

Not only gender difference, but also the privileging of men and masculinity over women and femininity, is "justified" by the assumption that male being and knowing are the norm and are more valuable than female being and knowing. Androcentric moralities thus do not take into account how men's and women's lives differ and that such differences limit the applicability of evaluations based on male experience only. The problem is twofold: Androcentric moralities exclude or silence women's experience and moral orientations and also fail—normatively—to be critical of gender inequality and injustice.[34] In sum, gender remains normatively invisible as long as we do not see how extensively it operates and as long as we take for granted the differences and inequalities we do see—as givens rather than as political and moral problems.

In world politics, the inequalities of power, the effects of direct and indirect violence, the disparities between rich and poor, and the unequally distributed costs of environmental degradation are most often deemed the regrettable but unavoidable price of "progress." Through a gender-sensitive lens we begin to ask how the highly acclaimed benefits of progress are distributed and who pays the greatest costs for them. We also ask what kind of morality operates to keep current inequities and their individual and systemic costs from becoming daily matters of public outrage.

We observe that progress looks most acceptable, even desirable, to those most advantaged by the status quo. If system transformations had only win-lose ramifications, these people would have the most to lose. As noted in our earlier discussion, those who benefit the most are seldom aware of the extent of their privilege or its relation to the poverty of others (just as most residents of the First World remain ignorant of Third World poverty and its relation to First World abundance and consumption). Of course, some of those who benefit endorse improvements for "others" who are "less fortunate" (trickle down). The point is that no conspiracy of greed or malintent need be posited. And although we can identify particular groups as generally benefiting more than others from systemic inequities, it is neither adequate nor accurate to hold particular individuals or groups solely responsible for structural effects. What we want to emphasize is that, however they originated in historical time, systemic or structural inequities are reproduced through the interaction of multiple variables, including the internalization of oppression by subordinated individuals, the abuse of power by those who wield it, the unaccountability of the marketplace, and the institutional structures of racism, classism, ageism, and heterosexism. These are what we must become aware of and transform.

It is in this sense that masculinism is key to understanding how we normatively accept rather than struggle against systemic inequities. As we argue in this text, masculinism and its twin, androcentrism, are ideologies that pervade our thinking, doing, and evaluating. They are ubiquitous and largely unquestioned. They not only institutionalize the particular hierarchy of masculine over feminine but also perpetuate belief in the inevitability of hierarchies in general. They emphasize abstract reason, objectification, and instrumentalism too often at the expense of attention to context and normative consequences. Their codification of oppositional, mutually exclusive categories promotes a silence on responsibility: By denying the *relationship of (inter)dependence* between fact and value, subject and object, exploiter and victim, direct and indirect violence, culture and nature, they obscure who has the greatest power—and therefore responsibility. Finally, these ideologies, to the considerable extent that they inform other normative orientations, blind us to how gender both creates and reproduces a world of multiple inequities that today threatens all of us.

The *conceptual dimension* refers to the ways in which patterns of thought make gender hierarchy invisible—including not only the forms our thought takes (e.g., categories, dichotomies, stereotypes) but also more encompassing or more structured systems of thinking (e.g., ideologies, theoretical frameworks, religion, science). Language is extremely important for patterning our thought; a vast literature now documents how gender—and the hierarchy it constructs—is built into the English language. As Laurel Richardson and Verta Taylor note:

> Embedded in the language are such ideas as women are adjuncts to men (e.g., the use of the generic "man" or "he"); women's aspirations are and should be different than men's (e.g., "The secretary . . . *she*," "the pilot . . . *he*"); women remain immature and incompetent throughout adult life (e.g., "The girls—office staff—have gone to lunch"); women are defined in terms of their sexual desirability (to men) whereas men are defined in terms of their sexual prowess. (Contrast the meanings of the supposedly equivalent words *spinster* and *bachelor, mistress* and *master, courtesan* and *courier,* etc.) As long as we speak the language we have acquired, we are not only speaking but also thinking in sex-stereotyping ways.[35]

English and other languages structure our thinking in dichotomies that emphasize difference, suggest timeless polarities, and thus obscure the interdependence, mutability, and complexity of the social world. The ideology of scientific objectivity structures subject-object and fact-value in dichotomies and thus directs our attention away from the actual and relevant sociopolitical relations of context. Finally, the privileged status of claims to "objectivity"—like claims to "reality"—marginalizes potential critiques.

The systematic effect of thinking in nonrelational categories is to exaggerate difference, separation, and inevitability. Rather than intimate a longer story and a larger picture, nonrelational categories render events and beliefs as "givens"; by being presented as ahistorical and decontextual, they are made to seem inevitable. If we are looking through the lens of "naturally given," we cannot even ask a variety of questions and cannot take seriously other challenges. Normative questions appear irrelevant or pointless, and alternative visions appear necessarily utopian. If we think only in dichotomies—of objective-subjective and realist-idealist—then our attempts to criticize objectivity and realism are rendered immediately suspect, as irrational, illogical, idealistic, unreal. And it looks as though any critique of objectivity or realism *must* entail its opposite: a complete denial rather than a partial critique.[36]

Gender is at work here because dichotomies, masculinism, and androcentrism are present. In academe as elsewhere, we rely on what men have thought, written, and concluded to establish the "givens" of our discourses. That which pertains to the lives and experience of elite males is taken as the norm and privileged. Thus, autonomy and freedom, independence from and power over others, separation from and control over nature, military and technological mastery, exploring and taming frontiers—these are given privileged status and held to be good for everybody. However, not only do such values fail to benefit everybody, but they no longer (if ever) unproblematically benefit elite men. And they have never afforded accurate understandings of the world. These orientations are not all bad, but their pursuit at the expense of other values has always been costly. Without exposing and examining the trade-offs, we continue to live irresponsibly and limit ourselves intellectually.

In terms of the *organizational dimension,* gender is rendered invisible primarily by the androcentric focus on what men do. By taking male experience as the norm and privileging it as the most important to know about, we find ourselves focusing on some activities at the expense of others. This is most obvious in terms of public-private domains and the elevation of men's issues, experiences, and activities over women's. But it is also present in academe, where "hard sciences" (chemistry, biology) and fields noted for logic (physics, philosophy) and instrumentalism (engineering, business administration) are male dominated and accorded the greatest prestige and authority. Outside of the academy, we pay more attention to areas of masculine interest (heart disease, rocketry, corporations) over feminine concerns (breast cancer, contraception, child care). In world politics we focus on national and international leaders, wars and militarization, and the high stakes of global economics.

What these patterns obscure are the relationships between activities, how they are mutually structured, and how alternatives can be pursued. They also obscure the social costs of separating production from reproduction, science from social values, politics from economics, and public from private life. Losing sight of history—forgetting that we *make* our world—locks us into patterns that have never served global justice and may now threaten even the most advantaged. For example, the expansion of global capitalism is associated with the increasing power of transnational corporations and their decision-making elites as well as with a greater reliance on high technologies and the professional class they foster. These developments threaten the majority of the planet's inhabitants in at least two profound ways.

First, the concentration of resources and power in the hands of a few is always suspect; when those few are not accountable to any public constituency, the threat is even greater that they will abuse their power. Second, the consumption of resources in relation to global ecology is dramatically shaped by the operations of giant corporations. The abuse of power through its concentration and the misuse of resources through their control by a small elite in the pursuit of profit combine in today's world, restricting the opportunities available to the vast majority in every country and throughout the world. In various ways, we *all* participate in reproducing the inequity and imbalance that maintain the status quo. And in quite different but also costly ways, we *all* are impoverished by the status quo and the structural violence it entails.

NOTES

1. Robert W. Cox, "Social Forces, States and World Orders: Beyond International Relations Theory," in Robert O. Keohone, ed., *Neorealism and Its Critics* (New York: Columbia University Press, 1986), p. 207.

2. Sandra Harding, *Whose Science? Whose Knowledge?* (Ithaca: Cornell University Press, 1991), p. 159.

3. This brief account draws mostly from Sandra Harding, *The Science Question in Feminism* (Ithaca: Cornell University Press, 1986.)

4. Accounts of the history and analysis of feminist theory use varying categorizations to describe particular forms of feminism. Two contemporary sources are Rosemarie Putnam Tong, *Feminist Thought: A More Comprehensive Introduction* (Boulder: Westview Press, 1998); and Judith Lorber, *Gender Inequality: Feminist Theories and Politics* (Los Angeles: Roxbury Publishing Company, 1998). For a survey of postcolonial feminisms, readers are directed to M. Jacqui Alexander and

Chandra Talpade Mohanty, *Feminist Genealogies, Colonial Legacies, Democratic Futures* (New York: Routledge, 1997).

5. Harding, *Whose Science? Whose Knowledge?* p. 151.

6. Sheila Ruth, *Issues in Feminism* (Dallas: Houghton Mifflin, 1980), p. 17. In this chapter, our discussion focuses primarily on U.S. culture because it is familiar to most of our readers.

7. Arthur Brittan, *Masculinity and Power* (New York: Blackwell, 1989), p. 4. We also recommend the extraordinarily accessible yet penetrating analysis of masculinism provided by Allan G. Johnson in *The Gender Knot: Unraveling Our Patriarchal Legacy* (Philadelphia: Temple University Press, 1997). We became aware of Johnson's important book too late to deploy his clear argumentation and effective examples more systematically in this second edition of our own text.

8. These points draw on the extended discussion in Sandra Lipsitz Bem, *The Lenses of Gender* (New Haven: Yale University Press, 1993).

9. See, for example, R. W. Connell's *Gender and Power* (Cambridge, Eng.: Polity Press, 1987) and *Masculinities* (Berkeley: University of California Press, 1995).

10. Laurel W. Richardson and Verta A. Taylor, eds., *Feminist Frontiers: Rethinking Sex, Gender, and Society* (Reading, Mass.: Addison-Wesley, 1983), p. 1; emphasis in original.

11. Hilary Lips, *Women, Men, and Power* (Mountain View, Calif.: Mayfield, 1991), p. 19.

12. For example, among a study of freshmen entering U.S. colleges in the fall of 1997, 45.2 percent of males and 24.1 percent of females "agreed strongly or somewhat that . . . [i]t is important to have laws prohibiting homosexual relationships." See *Chronicle of Higher Education* 44, no. 1 (August 1997): 20. See also the discussions and studies cited in Bem, *The Lenses of Gender;* and Virginia Sapiro, *Women in American Society* (Mountain View, Calif.: Mayfield Publishing, 1994).

13. Bem, *The Lenses of Gender*, pp. 163–166.

14. Cynthia Fuchs Epstein, *Deceptive Distinctions* (New Haven: Yale University Press, 1988), p. 232.

15. English-language training exacerbates this tendency by teaching word meanings as opposites. Learning antonyms forces us to think in apparently unchanging oppositions: right-wrong, hot-cold, friend-foe, boy-girl, night-day, us-them. Dichotomized or dualistic thinking is criticized from diverse perspectives but especially those identified as postpositivism, postmodernism, or poststructuralism.

16. A vast feminist literature supports these claims but cannot be elaborated here. See, for example, Sandra Harding and Merrill Hintikka, eds., *Discovering Reality* (Dordrecht, Netherlands: Reidel Publishing, 1983); Evelyn Keller, *Reflections on Gender and Science* (New Haven: Yale University Press, 1985); and Susan Hekman, *Gender and Knowledge* (Cambridge, Eng.: Polity Press, 1990).

17. For a particularly accessible and comprehensive treatment of androcentrism, see Bem, *Lenses of Gender*. This excellent book identifies three interacting gender lenses: androcentrism; gender polarization (similar to the discussion of gendered dichotomies here), as "the more subtle and insidious use of that perceived [gender] difference as an organizing principle for the social life of the culture"; and biological essentialism, "which rationalizes and legitimizes both other lenses by treating them as the natural and inevitable consequences of the intrinsic

biological natures of women and men" (p. 2). Bem makes especially good use of innumerable examples and studies to clarify and substantiate her claims. She also integrates a critique of heterosexism throughout the book, in part by analyzing "how the individual who has internalized the culture's gender lenses *self*-constructs a gendered personality, a gendered body, an androcentric heterosexuality, and an abhorrence of homosexuality" (p. 4); emphasis in original.

18. Consider how cultural media and academic studies highlight issues and activities that are masculinist or male dominated: making money, competitive sports, crime, spying, fighting, killing, war, death, sexual pursuits and conquests, male bonding, public figures and events, diplomacy, national and international politics. In comparison, media and academic studies rarely focus on issues and activities associated with women's lives: poverty and physical victimization (assault, rape, homicide), caretaking (of children and other dependents), building cooperative interpersonal and community relations, reproducing everyday life and activities—in the home, family, workplace, public forums—and, especially, reproductive issues involving women's mental and physical health and when, whether, and under what circumstances to bear children.

19. Margaret L. Andersen, *Thinking About Women: Sociological and Feminist Perspectives* (New York: Macmillan, 1983), p. 213.

20. Ibid., p. 39.

21. Ibid.

22. Welfare provisioning is inherently classist, especially in the United States, where, as Mark Zepezauer and Arthur Naiman argue, government welfare for the rich (social security, military waste and fraud, tax breaks) costs "about 3–1/2 times as much as the $130 billion we spend each year on welfare for the poor." (See Zepezauer and Naiman, *Take the Rich Off Welfare* [Tucson, Ariz.: Odonian Press, 1996], p. 6). Welfare is also a racial issue, because women of color are disproportionately poorer than ethnic white women in the United States. Finally, class and race (and age, physical ability, religion, etc.) structure women's access to safe and affordable contraception and abortion.

23. Peggy McIntosh, "White Privilege and Male Privilege," in Margaret L. Andersen and Patricia Hill Collins, eds., *Race, Class, and Gender* (Belmont, Calif.: Wadsworth Publishing, 1992), pp. 70–81.

24. Iris Marion Young, *Justice and the Politics of Difference* (Princeton: Princeton University Press, 1990), p. 151. Our discussion of structural oppression and the dilemmas of evaluating intentional versus unintentional actions is indebted to Young's thoughtful and comprehensive treatment of these topics. For a classroom exercise that illuminates patterned commonalities as well as differences among structural oppressions, see V. Spike Peterson, "Social Hierarchies as Systems of Power," *PS: Political Science and Politics* (December 1994): 719–720. This exercise also draws out the relationships among less direct (humor, myths, educational discrimination, labor market segregation) and more direct (harassment, political exclusions, physical violence) expressions of various hierarchies, thus effectively demonstrating how jokes, for example, must be taken seriously in critiques of oppression.

25. United Nations (UN), *The World's Women 1995: Trends and Statistics* (New York: United Nations, 1995), p. xx.

26. Cynthia Enloe, *Bananas, Beaches & Bases: Making Feminist Sense of International Politics* (Berkeley: University of California Press, 1989), p. 196.

27. Sarah Brown, "Feminism, International Theory, and International Relations of Gender Inequality," *Millennium* 17 (Winter 1988): 461.

28. Wendy Brown, *Manhood and Politics* (Totowa, N.J.: Rowman and Littlefield, 1988), p. 4.

29. Ashley Montague, *The Natural Superiority of Women* (New York: Collier Books, 1974), pp. 61–62.

30. Brown, *Manhood and Politics*, p. 182.

31. See Simon Dalby, "Security, Modernity, Ecology: The Dilemmas of Post–Cold War Security Discourse," *Alternatives* 17 (1992): 95–133; and V. Spike Peterson, "Security and Sovereign States: What Is at Stake in Taking Feminism Seriously?" in V. Spike Peterson, ed., *Gendered States* (Boulder: Lynne Rienner Publishers, 1992), pp. 31–64.

32. For example, see Charles Tilly, "War Making and State Making as Organized Crime," in Peter Evans, Dietrich Rueschemeyer, and Theda Skocpol, eds., *Bringing the State Back In* (New York: Cambridge University Press, 1985).

33. On the politics of protection rackets generally, see Peterson, "Security and Sovereign States," pp. 49–54.

34. Historically, moralities generated from women's lives and experiences have been silenced or subordinated. In regard to facing difficult moral choices, Carol Gilligan argued that women are more likely to emphasize responsibility and care, whereas men are more likely to emphasize a weighing of rights. See Gilligan, *In a Different Voice* (Cambridge, Mass.: Harvard University Press, 1982). Important feminist treatments of justice include Susan Moller Okin, *Justice, Gender and the Family* (New York: Basic Books, 1989); Iris Marion Young, *Justice and the Politics of Difference* (Princeton: Princeton University Press, 1990); and Iris Marion Young, *Intersecting Voices: Dilemmas of Gender Political Philosophy and Policy* (Princeton: Princeton University Press, 1998).

35. Richardson and Taylor, eds., *Feminist Frontiers*, p. 2.

36. For a critique of dichotomized thinking as it relates to gender and IR, see V. Spike Peterson, "Transgressing Boundaries: Theories of Knowledge, Gender and International Relations," *Millennium* 21 (Summer 1992): 183–206.

THREE

□ □ □

Gendered Divisions of Power

What is power? Which gender "has" it? And how does it affect "who rules the world"? In this chapter we look at how gender shapes the meaning of power and how inequalities of power have gendered effects. We focus on the gendered division of power in terms of where women are positioned (and how they get there)—in comparison to men—as state actors in world politics.

The definition of power conventionally favored in IR, as in political science generally, is one of **power-over.** Power-over is captured in Robert Dahl's classic definition: the ability of A to get B to do something that B would not otherwise do. Defining power in this way emphasizes control of material—especially military—resources and a willingness to use them in order to enforce one's preferences. It is power-over in the sense of being top-down (those on top, where the most resources are concentrated, are determined to have the most power) and coercive (the ability to "force" compliance is determined to be the surest sign of power). When we use only this narrow definition of power to study world politics, however, we neglect investigating how other dimensions of social reality—moral commitments, religious beliefs, ethnic allegiances, sociopolitical ideologies—shape how power works and who rules the world. Finally, and singularly relevant to our thesis, this definition of power is masculinist to the extent that it presupposes androcentric notions of strength, competition, aggression, and coercion, and because it focuses on power understood only in terms of public-sphere activities that are dominated by men.

As noted earlier, IR texts often draw a distinction between "high" and "low" politics. The former concerns the strategic interests of states, understood in political and military terms, and involves the activities of those who wield power in the international "public sphere." Through a high-politics lens, the focal points of inquiry are national security and military might, and the actors of greatest significance are heads of state and military leaders. National security and military might are preeminently masculine activities and have long been dominated by male actors (see Figure 3.1). Nevertheless, throughout history, women have been crucial to the success of states and militaries, and individual women have effectively exercised state power.

Because states are viewed as the primary units in traditional IR, our aim in this chapter is to look at where women are positioned as political actors within the formal power structures of states: as heads of states or governments, diplomats, foreign service and military officers, as UN and other intergovernmental organization (IGO) officials, and as members of national legislatures and elite administrative bodies. We address the following questions: Where are the women who wield power in public-sphere activities? What proportion of formal political power is held by women? Why are women so underrepresented in public office, and how do the few manage to get there?

This chapter demonstrates how gender is systematically at work in the "high politics" of IR by engaging an apparent paradox. We begin the chapter with data on the position of women as powerful state actors. Our listing of women who in the past held or were holding (at this writing) positions of state power *challenges* the gender stereotype that portrays women as uninterested in or unfit for political leadership. In the rest of the chapter, by contrast, we take gender stereotypes seriously. We do so in order to analyze the gendered division of political power—that is, to determine how a gendered concept of power and the gendered consequences of international relations interact to position men and women very differently in relation to global power. We also address how and why the gender imbalance of political power remains so invisible in conventional accounts.

WOMEN AS STATE ACTORS

Women Acting as Heads of States and Governments

Individual elite women have, throughout history, wielded considerable political power and influence. (We consider woman warriors and military power in the next chapter.) An adept international politician, Cleopatra, ruler of Egypt in the first century B.C., exemplified a tradition of politically powerful women in ancient Egypt. It was under the strong and skillful rule of Queen Elizabeth I that England first rose to power in the sixteenth century; in the nineteenth century, Queen Victoria's alliance strategies in Europe and colonizing policies abroad secured Great Britain's position as the

FIGURE 3.1 Male-Dominated IR. (*top*) On November 29, 1980, the all-male Security Council voted on resolutions to use force against Iraq if it did not withdraw from Kuwait by the January 15, 1991, deadline. Courtesy Andrew Lichtenstein, Impact Visuals. (*bottom*) Male ministers met during the Uruguay Round of the GATT (General Agreement on Tariffs and Trade) on December 4, 1990. Courtesy Wim Van Cappellen, Impact Visuals.

world hegemon. Similarly, in the eighteenth century, Catherine the Great's imperialistic foreign policy achieved world-power status for Russia.

Heads of government are among the world's most powerful political actors, and a number of women have held these powerful positions in the twentieth century (see Table 3.1). On the one hand, heads of state are key executive decision-makers and policy-implementors within the nations they lead. On the other hand, their power "within" the state has international consequences to the extent that the military, political, economic, and cultural priorities they establish extend beyond territorial borders. Additionally, heads of government "represent" their states culturally as well as politically: In varying ways they come to symbolize the values of the country they represent. Female heads of state and government are no exception.

As prime minister (1960–1965, 1970–1977), Siramovo Bandaranaike was largely responsible for the constitution of 1972 that transformed Ceylon into the Republic of Sri Lanka; in international affairs, she also served as chair of the Nonaligned Movement. Golda Meir, having served as minister of labor, and then for ten years as minister of foreign affairs, in 1969 became prime minister of Israel and led Israel through five tumultuous years. In the Philippines, Corazón Aquino was elected president in 1986 and governed during a period of severe economic problems—exacerbated by natural disasters—and difficult foreign policy decisions. Until her assassination in 1984, Indira Gandhi ruled as a formidable prime minister of India, overseeing the defeat of Pakistan and Indian dominance of the subcontinent. In 1988 Benazir Bhutto was elected head of state in Pakistan, remaining in power until ousted in a constitutional coup two years later. She returned to power in 1993, serving again as head of state until she was dismissed in 1996.

In power until recently, Vigdis Finnbogadottir promoted both pacifist and feminist causes as a member of the Women's Alliance Party and as president of Iceland from 1980 until 1996. In a dramatic rise to power, Violeta Barrios de Chamorro became president of Nicaragua in 1990 and remained in power until 1996. Assuming leadership in the midst of military and economic crises, Chamorro was credited by *Time* magazine with "end[ing] the *contra* war in less than a month and quell[ing] riots without bloodshed."[1] Tansu Ciller served as prime minister of Turkey from 1993 to 1996, Agathe Uwilingiyimana as prime minister of Rwanda from 1993 to 1994, and Claudette Werleigh as prime minister of Haiti from 1995 to 1996.

In 1997 Rosalia Arteaga, vice president of Ecuador, was named interim president during a constitutional crisis. Also in 1997, Social Democratic Party member Charity Kaluki Ngilu and environmentalist Wangari Maathai became the first women candidates for the Kenyan presidency;

TABLE 3.1   Women Presidents and Prime Ministers in the Twentieth Century
as of 1997

Presidents		
Argentina	Isabel Martinez de Peron	1974–1976
Bolivia	Lidia Gueiler	1979–1980*
Ecuador	Rosalia Arteaga	1997*
Haiti	Ertha Pascal-Trouillot	1991*
Iceland	Vigdis Finnbogadottir	1980–1996
Ireland	Mary Robinson	1990–1997
	Mary McAleese	1997–
Liberia	Ruth Perry	1996–
Malta	Agatha Barbara	1982–1987
Nicaragua	Violeta Chamorro	1990–1996
Philippines	Corazón Aquino	1986–1992
Sri Lanka	Chandrika Bandaranaike Kumaratunga	1994–
Yugoslavia	Milka Planinc	1982–1986
Prime Ministers		
Bangladesh	Khaleda Zia Rahman	1991–1996
	Hasina Wazed	1996–
Burundi	Sylvie Kinigi	1993
Canada	Kim Campbell	1975–1976
Central Africa Republic	Elisabeth Domitien	1980–1995
Dominica	Mary Eugenia Charles	1991–1992
France	Edith Cresson	1991–1992
Haiti	Claudette Werleigh	1995–1996
India	Indira Gandhi	1966–1977, 1980–1984
Israel	Golda Meir	1969–1974
Lithuania	Kazimiera Prumkini	1990–1991
Netherlands Antilles	Maria Liberia-Peters	1984–1986, 1988–1994
Norway	Gro Harlem Brundtland	1981, 1986–1989, 1990–1996
Pakistan	Benazir Bhutto	1988–1990, 1993–1996
Poland	Hanna Suchocka	1992–1993
Portugal	Maria de Lourdes Pintasilgo	1981–1985*
Rwanda	Agathe Uwilingiyimana	1993–1994
Sri Lanka	Siramovo Bandaranaike	1970–1977, 1994
	Chandrika Bandaranaike Kumaratunga	1994–
Turkey	Tansu Ciller	1993–1996
United Kingdom of Great Britain and Northern Ireland	Margaret Thatcher	1979–1990

*Interim post

Sources: United Nations, *The World's Women 1995: Trends and Statistics* (New York: United Nations, 1995), p. 152; Naomi Neft and Ann D. Levine, *Where Women Stand: An International Report on the Status of Women in 140 Countries, 1997–1998* (New York: Random House, 1997), p. 20.

losing their bids to the incumbent but are planning to try again. Still in office as of 1998 are Hasina Wazed, prime minister of Bangladesh, and Ruth Perry, president of Liberia, both of whom were elected in 1996, as well as Chandrika Bandaranaike Kumaratunga, who was appointed prime minister and then elected president of Sri Lanka in 1994.

In Europe, Gro Harlem Brundtland headed social-democratic governments as prime minister of Norway three times; Brundtland also chaired the UN World Commission on Environment and Development, which in 1987 produced a global report on the environment.[2] She was recently appointed as the first woman head of the World Health Organization (WHO). In France, Edith Cresson served as prime minister from 1991 to 1992 after holding important positions in the ministries of agriculture, industry, trade, and European affairs. Mary Robinson served as the president of Ireland from 1990 to 1997. In spite of the power of the Roman Catholic Church, Robinson advocated the liberalization of laws relating to contraception, abortion, and divorce. Her high international profile recently won her the post of the United Nations high commissioner for refugees, and her support for women in politics led the four main political parties in Ireland to nominate women candidates to succeed her as president.[3] Mary McAleese, a law professor representing the nationalist Fianna Fail party in Northern Ireland, won the race. And perhaps most familiar is the first woman prime minister of Great Britain, Margaret Thatcher. After twenty years as a member of parliament, Thatcher served as prime minister from 1979 until 1990. Her forceful response to the Malvinas/Falkland Islands dispute and her resolute conservative commitments won her the attribution of "Iron Lady."

UN and Other IGO Officials

It is not only national leaders who are powerful actors on the stage of world politics: Observers of IR cannot help but acknowledge the increasing significance of international organizations—especially the United Nations—in shaping world events. To the extent that IGOs play key roles, their elite officials are powerful actors. Women have a long history of support for and participation in international organizations; some have served in leadership positions, and many more are moving "up through the ranks" in order to do so. Other women wield political power by representing their states as ambassadors to the United Nations.

In 1972 Helvi Sipila, appointed assistant secretary-general for social development and humanitarian affairs, was the first woman to serve at the highest level of the United Nations below the secretary-general. Two women have been elected to preside over the General Assembly: Vijaya Lakshmi Pandit of India in 1953 and Angie Brooks of Liberia in 1969.[4] As of 1996, women holding top-level positions in the United Nations included Nafis Sadik, executive director of the UN Fund for Population Activities (UNFPA); Carol Bellamy, executive director of the UN Children's Fund (UNICEF); Elizabeth Dowdeswell, director of the UN Environment Programme (UNED); Catherine Ann Bertini, executive director of the World Food Programme (WFP); and Noleen Heyzer, director of the UN Development Fund for Women (UNIFEM).[5] In 1997 Mary Robinson became the UN high commissioner for refugees, and in 1998 Louise Frechette, Canada's former deputy minister of national defense, became deputy secretary-general of the United Nations, the highest-ranking political office ever to be held by a woman.[6]

Whereas in 1949 only 4 percent of the delegates to the UN were women, by 1994 this figure had increased to 20 percent. Women constitute the highest percentages of delegates from the Caribbean (29 percent) and Latin America (22–24 percent), but the lowest percentages of delegates from Eastern Europe (5 percent) and southern and western Asia and Oceania (8–9 percent).[7] In addition to delegates, each nation identifies a single "permanent representative" or ambassador—who constitutes the national spokesperson—to the UN. Most familiar in the United States are Jeane Kirkpatrick, an independent thinker and outspoken public official who served as U.S. representative in the early 1980s, and Madeleine Albright, who served as representative before being appointed secretary of state by President Clinton. As of 1997, six women were serving as ambassadors to the UN, representing Guinea, Jamaica, Kazakhstan, Liechtenstein, Trinidad and Tobago, and Turkmenistan.[8]

Many more women have served as ambassadors to other countries, practicing the art of diplomacy that is well recognized as a dimension of effective international relations. In providing the personal link between governments, diplomats play significant roles in promoting successful communication and negotiating mutually desirable outcomes. They are frequently key actors in preparing for and carrying out major political, economic, and military projects. However, because women's numbers still remain comparatively small in diplomatic circles, women have organized lobbying and policy groups that both expose and influence gender dynamics in ministries, departments, and committees dealing with foreign affairs. Such organizations include the Diplomatic Service Wives Association, Great Britain (DSWA); the Association of American Foreign Service Women, United States (AAFSW); and the Women's Action Organization, United States (WAO).

What remains most problematic is that as of 1995 no women had been appointed heads of any of the eighty-nine autonomous or specialized United Nations agencies, such as the very powerful bodies of the World Bank, the International Monetary Fund (IMF), or the World Trade Organization

(WTO), where crucial decisions are made with respect to the world economy. In addition, no woman has ever served as a judge on the International Court of Justice (ICJ).[9]

Bureaucratic Elites and Members of National Legislatures

Women elected to national legislatures shape international (and domestic) relations through their votes on foreign policy issues and their participation on legislative committees. At the cabinet or ministerial level, women holding foreign policy and/or military/defense portfolios participate directly in shaping national policy and practice; those holding other portfolios effect a less direct, but still powerful, influence on national policies having international consequences.

Around the world, the percentage of women in legislative bodies had steadily increased from 1975 into the early 1990s but has been declining in recent years (a trend we discuss in the next section).[10] The political power of these women is manifested in numerous ways: through committee reports, legislative objectives, and policy implementation. Women who have had ministerial and cabinet posts, particularly posts with a nondomestic focus, can more directly affect international politics and even emerge as particularly significant international political actors by becoming heads of state. Examples include Golda Meir and Edith Cresson, both of whom headed important ministries before assuming the position of prime minister.

The first woman to serve as a cabinet member in the United States was Frances Perkins, secretary of labor from 1933 to 1945. The percentage of women appointed to cabinet-level positions has risen steadily under the last four presidents: from 14 percent under Carter and 17.9 percent under Reagan to 35.3 under Bush and 40.9 percent in the Clinton administration.[11] As of 1997, four of the executive departments were headed by women: Janet Reno as attorney general and Donna Shalala, Madeleine Albright, and Alexis Herman as secretaries of the health and human services, state, and labor departments, respectively. Four more women held cabinet-level positions: Environmental Protection Agency Administrator Carol Browner, Small Business Administration Administrator Aida Alvarez, U.S. Trade Representative Charlene Barshefsky, and Council of Economic Advisors Chair Janet Yellen.[12] President Clinton's appointments were exemplary in that they marked inroads into departments traditionally reserved for male leadership. Even more significant, Secretary of State Albright, just after taking office, sent a directive to all U.S. embassies to "consider the advancement of women's human rights as an integral objective of U.S. foreign policy."[13]

As of 1994, women held 15 percent of the ministerial positions in only eight countries and 15 percent of subministerial positions in only twenty-three countries.[14] Among the twenty-five countries with no women in ministerial or subministerial posts at that time was Iran, which appointed Massoumeh Ebtekar to the office of vice president for the environment in 1998. Ebtekar thereby became the first woman cabinet member in Iran's Islamic Republic.[15]

The highest percentage of women in ministerial positions is found in the Nordic countries, where male-only cabinets have not been the norm since the early 1970s. Particularly striking is the fact that in Denmark, Finland, the Netherlands, Norway, and Sweden, women constituted between 30 and 52 percent of cabinet ministers by 1996.[16] Also notable is the European Parliament, where women have a higher percentage of representation (approximately 28 percent of its 626 members[17]) than in national assemblies, and where women's increased presence appears to have made a difference in the amount of legislation benefiting women.[18]

Military and Peacekeeping Officers

As we discuss in the next chapter, women have played significant roles in military activities throughout history: as leaders, warriors, and camp supporters (nursing and "housekeeping"), and in keeping the home fires burning. In the twentieth century, women's participation in state militaries has expanded, especially in the West. For example, in the United States women accounted for only 2 percent of the military in 1973, which marked the beginning of the All Volunteer Force. As of 1996, however, women constituted approximately 12 percent,[19] serving in all branches and holding most jobs—including "many in nontraditional 'combat type' jobs, such as pilots, security police, truck drivers, and missile gunners,"[20] even though many combat exclusions remain in effect.

Thirty-five thousand U.S. women served in the Persian Gulf war; of these, two were held as prisoners of war and thirteen lost their lives.[21] Their distinguished performance generated congressional and public support for expanding women's roles in the military, as exemplified by the Senate's overturning of a forty-three-year ban on women flying combat missions. Because high-command positions require cumulative experience, the number of female senior officers is slowly increasing as women achieve seniority in the military.

Only one country conscripts women (Israel) and only a few countries have either no combat restrictions for women (Australia, Belgium, Canada, Denmark, Eritrea, Ethiopia, the Netherlands, Norway, Spain, Venezuela, and Zambia) or only some combat restrictions (Finland, France, Ghana, Israel, Japan, the United Kingdom, and the United States).[22] This situation may account, ironically, for the very low military participation of women in peacekeeping operations: Women constituted only 2 percent of the military contingents engaged in seventeen peace-keeping missions in 1993. In contrast, women made up one-third of the international civilian staff for peacekeeping activities that same year, although 70 percent of those served in clerical-grade positions.[23]

HOW AND WHY ARE THESE WOMEN RENDERED INVISIBLE?

The preceding identification of national leaders, governmental officials, and civil service officers suggests that there are a number of women joining the ranks of elite men as powerful national and international actors. It is hard to deny the power wielded by women who have governed First World states that hold seats on the UN Security Council (Thatcher) or Third World states that are or were geopolitically strategic (Aquino, Gandhi, Chamorro). Yet our lack of familiarity with the many other women named above suggests how invisible they—and the power they wield—remain. Moreover, even the presence of numerous women has not prompted gender-sensitive analyses in international relations. In other words, not only are there very few women "at the top," but even those who succeed in achieving positions of power remain largely gender-invisible in conventional accounts of how power works in the world. How can we explain this failure to acknowledge gender in the face of women as global actors?

We turn first to the most obvious explanation: Although women constitute approximately 50 percent of the population worldwide, the percentage of women in positions of national and international power is indeed very small—and their ascension to these positions very recent. Fewer than thirty women have been elected to the highest national office (president or prime minister), and half of these have been elected *since 1990*. In 1995 Ruth Leger Sivard noted that "of the 190 independent states in the world, less than 1 percent of the presidents or prime ministers are women."[24] And Joni Seager points out that fifty-nine governments had *no* women in cabinet positions, and that by the beginning of 1997 only three women were heads of government.[25] In 1997 only 13 percent of parliamentary seats and 7 percent of national cabinet posts were held by women.[26] Men continue to constitute more than 90 percent of the top decision-makers in the United Nations, embassies, militaries, and business. Thus gender continues to be "invisible," in part because so few women appear in the world's most powerful decision-making positions.

Although most women in the world finally have the right to vote, women remain dramatically underrepresented in political institutions of "numerical representation" (on the basis of "one person, one vote").[27] Women's participation in national legislatures has historically been highest in the Nordic countries (reaching 35 percent or more) and in Eastern

Europe and the former Soviet Union (reaching 25 percent or more). Elsewhere, until very recently, women's parliamentary representation rarely exceeded 10 percent and was surprisingly low (5–8 percent) in the United Kingdom and the United States, where women's movements for political representation have been organized for more than a century.

In 1993 we reported that women's participation in national legislatures was steadily increasing (between 1975 and 1987) in all regions of the world, but it was still low compared to men's. Today, the increase is no longer steady. The percentages among regions and countries vary dramatically (see Figure 3.2); but worldwide, the proportion of women in national parliaments has actually stagnated. The record world average (14.8 percent women) was reached in 1988.[28] In 1994 the proportion dropped to 11 percent, which was no higher than the figure in 1975.[29] Political restructuring in Eastern Europe and the former Soviet Union has been particularly costly to women's political power: Data from recent elections show women rapidly losing "representational ground." From an average of 29 percent in the mid-1980s, women's representation dropped to 7 percent in 1994.[30] The loss of women's political representation that we are witnessing in former communist countries is a grim reminder of the fragility of women's political power: Gains secured at great cost in one period are all too frequently abandoned, renounced, or traded away in other periods. Indeed, throughout history, women have found themselves fighting similar battles, in different periods or contexts, for their rights and status as political actors.

The pattern of male dominance in political institutions of "numerical representation" is replicated in IGOs, governmental bureaucracies, and, especially, the increasingly powerful institutions of economic decision-making. In the United Nations, women have always constituted the majority of clerical (general services) workers but the minority of professional staff. Although the UN Charter established the principle of gender equality, the UN performed little better than other corporate bodies in realizing this objective.[31] After decades of activism both within and outside of the UN, institutional commitments to affirmative action were initiated in 1985 and have recently borne fruit.

The goal of 30 percent women in professional posts by 1990 was met in 1991. But in senior management positions, women had reached only 13 percent in 1995. From 1972 to 1982, between one and three women served at the undersecretaries-general level; from 1986 to 1991, between three and five women; and in 1993–1994, twelve women. Yet there were approximately sixty comparable positions at this level.[32] The aforementioned paucity of senior management women in autonomous and specialized agencies of the UN as well as the lack of female judges on the ICJ are particularly telling of the failure of affirmative action efforts thus far.

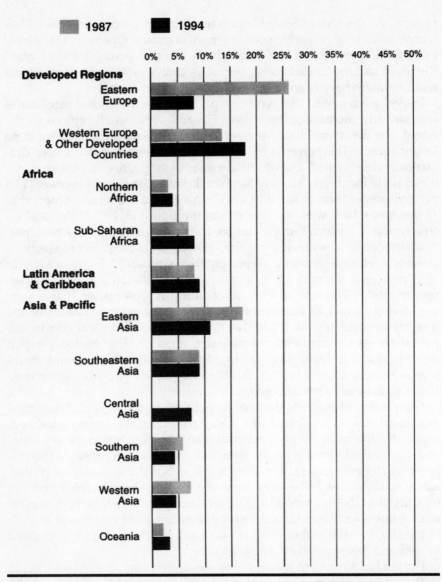

FIGURE 3.2   Gendered Parliamentary Representation by Region, 1987 and 1994. Shown here are the average percentages of women in parliamentary assemblies (unicameral assembly or lower chamber of bicameral assembly). *Source:* United Nations, *The World's Women 1995: Trends and Statistics* (New York: United Nations, 1995), p. 154.

Whereas women are fairly equally represented in entry-level grades, where competitive examinations determine hiring, their low representation at higher levels is due in part to recruitment practices that favor men. For example, outside recruitment depends on the submission of candidates by member states, which frequently choose from among their delegates to the United Nations, where women are underrepresented (20 percent in 1995). And as Sivard notes, "Of the 185 national missions which act as embassies to the United Nations, 3 percent are headed by women."[33]

In unions, political parties, special interest organizations, and bureaucracies, women may constitute a significant proportion of membership/ employees, but typically they form only a small minority (usually fewer than 5 percent) of officeholders or top decision-markers. Historically, trade unions have been key institutions of civil society because they enable workers to collectively resist and negotiate with the concentrated power of governments and corporate elites. It is of considerable political significance, then, that (with the exception of Scandinavia) trade union activities have been declining in most industrialized countries[34] and are variously repressed by governments around the world. In 1994 a record-high total of ninety-eight countries were cited for violating basic labor rights, 528 workers were murdered, 1,983 injured, and 4,353 arrested, "all for asserting their rights."[35] Women's union membership and leadership varies by region, political system, and type of union. Since World War II, the highest percentages of women in unions have been in Nordic and Eastern European countries and the lowest in developing countries.[36] Even these generalizations are no longer adequate, however. Transformations in formerly communist countries have altered women's employment patterns and therefore their union participation. Unemployment rates are especially high for women, and women confront a variety of pressures to take home- and family-making as their primary identity and profession. In other industrialized countries, both women and men confront declining living standards, shifting labor markets, and the necessity for two wage-earners to support families. Even in Nordic countries, women's share of national legislative leadership far outpaces their share of union leadership. As of 1990, women held only 17 to 20 percent of trade union leadership posts in Denmark and Sweden.[37] In the same year in the United States, 83 percent of the members of the International Ladies Garment Workers Union (ILGWU) were women, yet women constituted only 22 percent of its leadership.[38]

Some unions have made women a target of membership drives, though with varying commitments to sharing elite decision-making power. Most notable have been the efforts of the International Confederation of Free Trade Unions (ICFTU) and, more recently, the Congress of South African Trade Unions (COSATU) to build women's leadership in their ranks.[39]

In developing countries, unionization has historically been and remains less institutionalized because fewer workers—including men but especially women—are in the formal sector where labor organizing is more likely. This picture is complicated by **globalization,** the internationalization of the capitalist economy in which states, markets, and civil society are restructured to facilitate the spread of global capital. On the one hand, in pursuit of apparent economic gains, governments often accommodate the interests of transnational corporations at the expense of workers' rights, especially by constraining—or even outlawing—unions. At the same time, transnational production has moved many workers—including women but especially men—*out* of formal waged labor and into less secure and rarely organized "informal-sector" activities. The latter includes any work done to earn money that occurs outside of formal agreements between employers and employees and is unregulated by the state. Under these conditions, union organizing is unlikely to develop and civil society is weakened. On the other hand, transnational production has shifted global divisions of labor. In many countries, women's proportion of formal-sector employment has significantly increased—with women sometimes displacing men—as employers seek the cheapest, most reliable, yet most vulnerable workers.[40] In this case, women are gaining employment, but typically under conditions that exacerbate worker vulnerabilities and exploitation. Because unions have historically afforded the only organized power against worker exploitation, their role remains important politically, though they confront formidable obstacles.

In regard to political parties, women in developed countries are active but tend to remain outsiders at elite levels. Underrepresented in leadership positions, they are less likely to be put forward for office, which keeps the proportion of officeholding women low. To the extent that executive and ministerial elites are drawn from the pool of prior officeholders, women again face disadvantages, resulting in continued underrepresentation in top decision-making positions. This "route to the top" is confirmed by studies that find a strong correlation between percentages of women in legislative bodies and in ministerial positions.[41]

Women tend to be even more marginalized in business and economic-interest organizations than in "representational" channels of political power. Their absence is particularly significant in the face of increasing corporate power in world politics in this age of globalization. In 1993 women constituted only 1 percent of the chief executive officers in the largest United States corporations, and only 2 percent of the senior managers.[42] A 1996 study of women at the top of Fortune 500 companies in the United States found that more than a hundred of these had no women serving as corporate officers. Among the hundred biggest companies with no women officers were oil giants such as Exxon and Mobil, major financial institutions such as Merrill Lynch and Lehman Brothers, and

At the current rate of progress, it would take **475 YEARS** for women to reach equality with men as senior managers.

| YEAR: 1990 | 2150 | 2310 | 2470 |

Source: 1994 World Survey on the Role of Women in Development, United Nations, 1995

FIGURE 3.3   Gendered Corporate Power. Women clearly have a long way to go to reach parity with men in economic decision-making. Courtesy of the United Nations Department of Public Information.

huge conglomerates such as Rockwell International and Archer Daniels Midland, not to mention a number of telecommunications and computing TNCs. The study also found that women constituted only 2 percent of the 2,500 top earners in Fortune 500 companies.[43] And the situation is even worse outside of the United States, where there are no women at the top level and only 1 percent at the second tier.[44]

It is worth noting that these proportions are far *lower* than the figures reflecting women's already low representation among national leaders. As such, they confirm the "minuscule influence of women in the world of big business,"[45] which in reality is the world of big power (see Figure 3.3).

Power exercised by business both directly and indirectly shapes political power. Women's exclusion from leadership in economic decision-making bodies thus has considerable political significance, in two ways. First, business and interest organizations produce and effectively promote candidates for political office. Second, these organizations often "come together with governments and bureaucracy to form a corporate policy-making channel."[46] As long as women are excluded from business power, their political power is diminished. This is especially the case as political power is increasingly shaped by corporate interests outside of the traditional channels of representative government.

This discussion confirms that few women are situated at what is considered the apex of international political power. But it also raises the following questions: *Why* are so few women in power? *How* did women in power get there? And *what* are the gendered consequences of their being in power?

WHY SO FEW?

Explaining *why* people do or do not engage in political activities (traditionally defined "political behavior") has long been a focus of political science. Researchers have extensively studied gender differences in political participation—in particular, the low percentage of women in high political office. Two conclusions emerge repeatedly from this research. First, women do not lack interest in or motivation for political action: Studies of women's participation in grass-roots organizing, community politics, election campaigns, and political organizations suggest that "women are as likely (if not more likely) to work for political causes or candidates as are men."[47] Second, a point related to the first, women's underrepresentation in political office and leadership positions is linked to gender-differentiated patterns pervasive in today's world. Gender socialization, situational constraints, and structural obstacles interact in favoring men and discriminating against women as candidates for and effective holders of political office.[48]

Gender Socialization

Early studies tended to focus on the effects of sex-role stereotyping—that is, on the enduring consequences of childhood socialization of girls and boys into mutually exclusive gender roles. Presumably, socialization into appropriate "feminine" behavior makes women less likely than men to pursue traditionally defined political activities. For example, feminine identity formation is inextricable from cultural expectations that motherhood is the primary role of women, that women's domestic role is antithetical to public-sphere activities, and that traits associated with political efficacy (ambition, aggression, competitiveness, authority) are distinctly *un*feminine. To the extent that women internalize these stereotypical norms, then, they are less likely to perceive themselves as political actors or aspire to public office.

As a corollary, socialization into appropriate "masculine" behavior makes men more likely than women to identify with political activities. Just as important, gender stereotypes, because they are held by men *and* women, create a "climate" that encourages male participation while discouraging female participation in politics. Thus, individual women who seek leadership positions must struggle not only with their own internalized stereotypes but also with the fact that gender stereotyping in general fuels *resistance* to women as political actors. Finally, for women who do achieve positions of power, expectations of appropriately "feminine" behavior are often in conflict with qualities required for successful leadership. In short, gender stereotypes suggest that appropriately feminine women (passive, dependent, domestic; engaged in meeting private, familial needs) are by definition inappropriate political agents (active, autonomous, public oriented; engaged in meeting collective, not personal needs).

This picture is further complicated by men's and women's positions in relation to race/ethnicity, religion, sexual orientation, ability, age, and so on. Masculinities and femininities vary along these dimensions, and not

DRESS FOR SUCCESS

FIGURE 3.4 "Dress for Success." This cartoon shows the lengths to which a woman of color must go to have the privileges of a white, upper-class male. She must first become male to enter power structures and then become white to reach the apex of those structures. Reprinted by special permission of Kirk Anderson.

all men are socialized to desire or expect political participation or leadership. These variations matter significantly in terms of who actually enters/succeeds in politics. But despite hierarchies among men, the consistency of gender stereotypes is so strong that *within* particular groups, more men than women will be associated with public-sphere activities, political participation, and corporate power (see Figure 3.4).

Situational Constraints

Gender socialization produces different male and female orientations toward political participation. And gender stereotyping produces behavioral patterns that result in different concrete living situations for women and men that also constrain women's participation. Hence, we are better able to explain gendered political participation if we look at the *interaction* of stereotypes (for example, how women are assigned domestic and mothering responsibilities) and gender-differentiated living situations (for example, how the gendered division of labor limits women's involvement in traditional or "formal" politics). In masculinist societies, it is women who confront the time and energy demands of having primary responsibility for family care and home care. Family care includes not only child rearing and care of the elderly but also the emotional maintenance work required to sustain intimate and extended family relationships. Worldwide, home care involves ensuring that food is secured and prepared for all and that the household is physically maintained. For millions of women, the latter entails arduous efforts to secure water and fuel. For most women, it means responsibility for cleaning, laundry, upkeep, and seeing that the household functions adequately. Even for affluent women, it means a great deal of shopping, scheduling, and transporting family members. Not surprisingly, because these demands are placed on women more than men, women are constrained in terms of how much time and energy they have for political participation, especially the pursuit of political office.

In most of the world, women's participation in the labor force has increased since 1970.[49] And worldwide, women who earn income are burdened by a **double workday.** They are held responsible not only for work that produces income but also for work that ensures the reproduction of the family unit and the physical maintenance of the household. Moreover, it is not simply the longer workday that inhibits women's participation in politics; it is also women's lack of control over *when* they will be available and whether (or how) family obligations will interfere with political pursuits.[50]

In general, the more demanding the form of political participation (e.g., officeholding versus voting), the more it conflicts with women's mothering responsibilities—though some women, despite these constraints, *are* officeholders. It does appear that women who seek high-level administrative and political careers are more likely than men to remain unmarried, to be divorced, or to enter politics at a later age, when mothering responsibilities have diminished.

These patterns reveal the difficulties *for women only* of combining family responsibilities and political office.[51] Men are typically not forced to make these choices because their political activities are considered separate from their domestic relations. Women, in contrast, are so closely identified with the domestic sphere that when they take on political activities it is considered in combination with, not separable from, their role in the family (see Figure 3.5). It is also important to note that globalization or global economic restructuring for the most part exacerbates this gender imbalance. Men increasingly confront un- and underemployment. But this change in their workday rarely translates into their making greater contributions to family and home care. At the same time, withdrawal of social and welfare services by the state disproportionally hurts women, who (in their role of family and home caretakers) are assigned responsibility for "taking up the slack."

FIGURE 3.5 Double Standards. Men's care for children is viewed as extraordinary and is rewarded, whereas women's domestic responsibilities are viewed as debilitating on the job. Reprinted by special permission of Kirk Anderson.

> Decreased public spending on education, health, and food subsidies means that increased costs must be borne by women, who work longer hours, look for less expensive food, spend more resources on basic health care, make difficult choices about which children will get an education and which will work to sustain the family economy, and face lower wages or fewer job opportunities as the wages in female-dominated industries decline or as the returns to agricultural labor are not sustained.[52]

Hence, insofar as political participation requires time, resources, and control over them, capitalist and masculinist conditions make women's participation exceedingly difficult. And for women of nondominant race/ethnicity and of subordinate classes, the obstacles are multiplied.

Structural Obstacles

Clearly, stereotypes and situational constraints shape the gender of political activism, but the recurring differences in women's and men's participation must also be examined in relation to large-scale, interacting, and enduring social structures. Here we refer broadly to sets of power relations and/or social-cultural institutions that determine the boundaries of individual behavior. Understanding why so few women hold political power requires understanding how social structures and their interaction make it much more difficult for women (than for men) to seek and secure political office. Although primary gender socialization occurs in childhood, the hierarchical dichotomy of masculine-feminine is enforced throughout our lives. The gender dimensions of multiple social structures interact and, in effect, "discipline" individual behavior to conform to stereotypes.

For example, traditional religious belief systems and institutions play an important role in perpetuating images of women that deny them leadership positions. All too frequently, women are portrayed as either the source of evil (the uncontrollably sexual whore) or the model of saintliness (the self-sacrificing virgin). Neither is an appropriate identity for political *leadership*. In addition, the vast majority of religious institutions themselves exclude women from top leadership roles. No matter how this exclusionary practice is legitimized, it in fact sends a clear and unequivocal message that reinforces gender stereotypes: that women are not equal to men and that they cannot be trusted with or lack the qualifications for positions of authority and power.

Religious beliefs interact with and may reinforce other cultural sources of gender stereotyping. This is generally the case in regard to identifying the home/family as woman's sphere and the public/politics as man's sphere. It can also be quite explicit, as in the seclusion of women (*purdah*) practiced in many Islamic countries.[53] The point is that the structural separation of public and private has gendered consequences. Religious, educational, and judicial institutions tend to reproduce the ideological—and gendered—division of public and private. And both informal and formal public-private separations affect women's political participation negatively by identifying women exclusively with the private sphere.

Thus, our expectations of different behaviors for men (appropriate for politics) and for women (inappropriate for politics) make it difficult, first, for women to see themselves comfortably in conventionally defined political roles and, second, for men and women generally to see and accept women as political agents. In the latter case, negative attitudes toward women's political participation are expressed as lack of confidence in and support for female candidates and politicians.[54] In sum, to the extent that we perpetuate the stereotype of "a woman's place is in the home" (or in the bedroom), we ensure that women will be seen as "out of place" in political office.

As indicated in Table 3.2 and Figure 3.6, gender divisions of labor reflect the effects of gender stereotyping. Although the specific jobs assigned to women and men vary cross-culturally, "women's work" worldwide is associated not only with lower status and pay but also with less power than "men's work." As Hilary Lips points out: "Traditional stereotypes work against gender equality in the workplace because they help to promote the idea that women and men are suited for different kinds of

TABLE 3.2   Gendered Employment Patterns: Percentage Distribution of the
Female and Male Labor Force by Major Occupational Group, 1970
and 1990

	Percentage Distribution of the Labor Force, Each Sex							
	Professional and Technical; Administrative and Managerial		Clerical, Sales, and Service		Agriculture and Related		Production and Transport; Workers and Laborers	
Women	1970	1990	1970	1990	1970	1990	1970	1990
Developed regions	13	23	49	48	14	8	20	15
North Africa and West Asia	25	21	26	35	37	27	9	9
Sub-Saharan Africa	5	6	27	23	54	53	7	9
Latin America and Caribbean	13	15	54	55	11	5	15	14
Eastern and South-eastern Asia	8	9	31	38	33	35	20	14
Southern Asia	4	11	8	12	65	44	21	19
Oceania	16	17	22	37	58	21	3	13
Men								
Developed regions	13	20	20	22	15	9	48	43
North Africa and West Asia	7	11	25	29	24	18	38	35
Sub-Saharan Africa	4	5	14	14	48	50	28	21
Latin America and Caribbean	6	11	16	25	44	21	27	36
Eastern and South-eastern Asia	7	9	25	23	32	37	29	29
Southern Asia	2	5	10	20	73	39	13	26
Oceania	7	13	9	15	67	32	17	28

Source: United Nations, The World's Women 1995: Trends and Statistics (New York:
United Nations, 1995), p. 125.

work—and that the jobs for which women are best suited are the least
powerful, lowest-paying ones."[55] The fact that women are most heavily
concentrated in the service sector, constituting the area where they have
made the most "gains" worldwide from 1970 to 1990, is also reflective of
how women are increasingly "serving" globalization. As the global economy becomes more information- than manufacturing-based, more workers are needed in low-level, poorly paid, nonunionized data-entry positions. Gender stereotypes slot women into such positions.

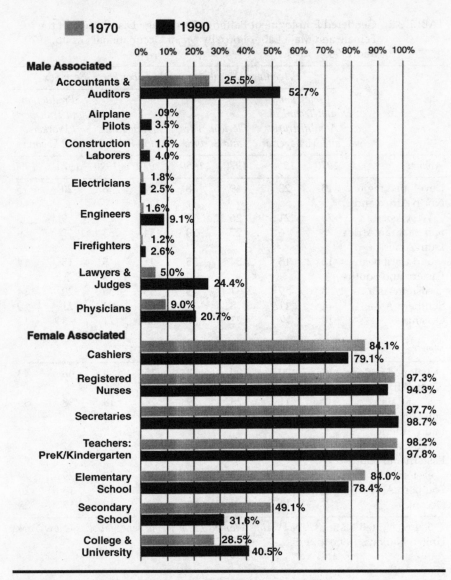

FIGURE 3.6   Gendered Labor Force: Percentage of Women in Selected U.S. Occupations. *Source: Ms.*, September/October 1997, p. 22.

The horizontal and vertical segregation of both men and women in the workforce affects women's access to political power. Horizontally, women are concentrated in fewer occupations than men and in jobs where women are the majority of workers—clerical work, elementary teaching, domestic maintenance, daycare, nursing, waitressing. Moreover, these are not occupations from which political candidates are traditionally recruited. In general, the work women do for pay is an extension of the feminine role assigned to women and replicates work that women are expected to do as mothers and wives: caring for dependents, serving the needs of others, providing social and physical necessities, and being docile, flexible, emotionally supportive, and sexually attractive.[56] Not only are women clustered in certain jobs, but they are also expected to be "feminine" in whatever job they hold.

The workplace is also segregated vertically, with women concentrated in pink-collar jobs (men in blue-collar), in domestic services (men in protective services), and in light industry (men in heavy industry).[57] Vertical gender segregation ("the higher, the fewer") occurs both within and across industries: Women generally are concentrated in part-time, temporary, nonorganized, lower-status, lower-paying, and less powerful positions. As a result, women earn less money, have less secure jobs, and rarely climb into powerful executive ranks. Race, ethnicity, and class discrimination interact with gender discrimination to exacerbate the self-perpetuating cycle of elite males holding onto power at the expense of all other groups.

Gendered divisions of labor affect women's political participation in multiple ways. Most obviously, women's structural disadvantage in the labor market translates into their having fewer resources, less status, and less experience "wielding" power when competing with men for political office. And when it comes to recruiting and promoting people for political office, educational and occupational structures interact to exacerbate women's disadvantage. Women receive not only a *different* education than men but also, in most of the world, a good deal *less* education than men. Because education is so closely related to occupational opportunities, lack of educational training fuels the gender segregation of the workforce and its negative consequences for women. Moreover, certain professions have historically been associated with or appear particularly compatible with achieving and maintaining political power: law, military, career civil service, big business. It remains the case that women are underrepresented in these occupational areas and are especially "absent" at the top levels from which political leaders are often recruited.

Other obstacles to women's political participation are direct and indirect legal barriers. Gaining the right to vote is a first step toward redressing these barriers. France did not legalize women's suffrage until 1944; Switzerland denied women this right until 1971. Black South African women and men did not have voting rights until 1994 after apartheid was abolished. As late as 1995, women were still not permitted to vote in Bahrain, Brunei, Kuwait, Oman, Qatar, Saudi Arabia, and the United Arab Emirates.[58] The right to be elected is a second step. Women did not gain that right until 1952 in Greece, 1961 in El Salvador, and 1974 in Jordan. In the United Kingdom, women were not permitted to run for Parliament until 1918,[59] and married women were barred from the civil service until 1946; in the United States, until 1971, women foreign-service career diplomats were required to resign if they married.

The gender patterns of military service also influence who reaches political office. A strong correlation between military (especially combat) experience and access to political leadership is typical in developing countries under military domination. (Approximately sixty-four countries were so identified in 1990, although that number has been declining as several authoritarian regimes have been replaced by some form of liberal democracy.)[60] But this pattern is not restricted to the remaining militarized states of the Third World. Since the time of George Washington, combat experience—which still excludes nearly all women—has seemed almost a mandatory qualification for those seeking the U.S. presidency. As of 1997, twenty-seven (of the forty-two) U.S. presidents had served in the military, and eleven had held the rank of general; until Clinton's election in 1992, every president since 1944 (Truman) had had military experience.[61]

In the 1992 campaign, opponents of Bill Clinton referred to his failure to serve in Vietnam as a way of challenging his trustworthiness as well as his ability to play the role of commander-in-chief. In the 1984 campaign, vice-presidential candidate Geraldine Ferraro was asked repeatedly whether she "had what it takes" to push the nuclear button; Dan Quayle was rendered suspect by his avoidance of active duty; and George Bush drew on his bailing out of a B-29 to counter the "wimp factor" in his public image.[62] Similarly, it is no accident that as soon as "victories" were reported in the Persian Gulf war, U.S. military leaders were proposed as presidential candidates.[63] For women, who remain a small percentage of the military and are largely excluded from combat, the military path to political power is blocked. In fact, as long as military experience is perceived as the requisite criterion of manliness for high political office, the only way women can "demonstrate" the required militancy is by adopting an *excessively* "tough lady" image (see Figure 3.7). Ironically, the few women in power may feel pressured to "out-macho" their male counterparts and render invisible whatever "feminine" qualities they may have brought to the job.[64] In sum, gender stereotypes and the *interaction* of situational constraints, domestic responsibilities, and religious, educational, economic, legal, and military structures discriminate against women's political participation and, especially, their access to high political office.

From another angle of vision, political institutions themselves can be seen to impede women's participation. Vicky Randall identifies three institutional barriers in her discussion of political recruitment and promo-

FIGURE 3.7 The "Tough Lady" Image. U.S. Secretary of State Madeleine Albright packs a wallop against dictators. Reprinted with special permission of King Features Syndicate.

tion.[65] First, at each level, political advancement requires "appropriate" political, leadership, educational, and/or occupational experience: As noted above, these criteria discriminate against women who are structurally likely to have different and fewer resources and/or who start later in their pursuit of office.

Second, the institutions associated with politics and power and the norms and practices of these institutions are those of "a man's world." Exclusively male until recently and still dominated by men, they are masculinist in the following senses: Behavior traits deemed suitable, sometimes essential, for political success are stereotypically masculine (ambition, leadership, rationality, competitiveness, authority, toughness); meeting times and locations, as well as socializing (networking) activities, are, in practice, convenient for men's (not women's) schedules and geographical mobility; and issues of central importance are not those most immediately relevant to most women's lives ("women's issues" are treated as peripheral to conventional politics).[66]

Randall identifies a third institutional barrier in the direct expression of male prejudice: outright discrimination against women.[67] Forms of discrimination in the workplace vary, but the presence of gender hierarchy and sexism creates a less favorable environment for women, who must then struggle harder than their male counterparts to be successful.[68] As long as the workplace and political office are identified as "male terrain," women constantly confront and must deal with resentment of their unwanted presence. Women are most frequently reminded of their outsider status when they are viewed not as colleagues but in terms of their gender and sexuality. Subtle and not-so-subtle references to women and sexuality produce an atmosphere of male dominance in which women must either become "like men" or become invisible.[69] These are not trivial aspects of power. The pervasiveness of masculinist assumptions, of androcentric worldviews, and of sexist humor poses formidable obstacles. Because we are so saturated with gendered assumptions, these obstacles typically go unrecognized or are not taken seriously as the pillars holding up male privilege and power—at the expense of women's participation.

In 1994 Barbara Nelson and Najma Chowdhury edited an 818-page volume analyzing women's political participation cross-nationally, with case studies from forty-three countries selected to represent a variety of political systems, levels of economic development, and regions. Drawing on the extensive material in this remarkable study, the authors of the first chapter state the following:

> The clear message in the country chapters is that the culture and processes of formal political institutions—especially parties, their affiliated labor or employer groups, their youth wings, and even their women's auxiliaries—are major barriers to women's equal participation in institutional politics. The barriers include the concrete expressions of patriarchal and fraternal privilege found in men's expressive and problem-solving styles, their networks, their workday, their domestic and child-care obligations, and even their traditions of making sexual access to women one of the prerequisites of power.[70]

In short, women's participation requires a transformation not only in gendered divisions of labor and power but also in gendered identities and in gender as a lens that reproduces masculine dominance.

HOW DO WOMEN GET TO THE TOP?

Having identified multiple, interacting factors that impede women's access to office, we will now consider how women, especially those at the apex of political power, managed in fact to get there. Candidates for elite office are traditionally recruited from prior leadership roles in political parties, local or regional government, unions, interest groups, business, civil service careers, and/or the military. We have seen that women are at a disadvantage in regard to these traditional routes to power: In general, they have less access to and leadership experience within the institutions that "feed" candidate pools. Yet women do reach the top. By examining the routes they take, we can learn more about gendered divisions of power.

Most important, both men and women at the apex of national and international power tend to be well educated (the women, often in nontraditional areas), to be affiliated with "political families," and to come from backgrounds of relative wealth and privilege. Some women follow the political party stepping stones to power: advancing through local, regional, and national party activities and building on previous electoral successes (Thatcher, Meir, Cresson, Eugenia Charles). Other women rise to power during transitional periods: when a compromise (and conciliatory) candidate is sought (Chamorro, Aquino) or when grass-roots issues have gained prominence and prompted a search for fresh leadership (Brundtland, Finnbogadottir, Robinson). Finally, some women (Gandhi,[71] Bhutto, Khaleda Zia Rahman, Aquino, Chamorro, Siramovo Bandaranaike, Isabela Perón) acquire office initially through their relationships to politically prominent men and then develop their own claim to political power.[72]

WHAT ARE THE GENDER CONSEQUENCES OF WOMEN IN POWER?

What do these patterns reveal about gender relations? On the one hand, we observe that a frequent route to high office for women is through family connections and, specifically, the death of a father or husband who is in office. Coming from prominent families, acting as "male surrogates," and often symbolizing national unity in conflict-ridden situations, these women must then establish themselves as leaders in their own right. There are several dimensions of gender at work here. Being female is not *always* a disadvantage: When symbols of unity, compromise, or conciliation are sought, women may have an advantage over men. That is, stereotypes of women can work to the benefit of female leaders in situations where crises or transitions require a caring, ameliorative figure. Latin America offers an example: Women there have often deployed the image of "supermadre" to gain political power and, sometimes, to promote alternative political agendas.

At the same time, however, the very effectiveness of the stereotypes serves to reproduce, rather than challenge, gender dichotomies. When women act "like women," even though they are at the helm of national governments, the traditional picture of gender is not disturbed. Similarly, when women assume national leadership as a result of their success in grass-roots activism, their association with "soft issues" (the environment, peace, feminism) can reinforce the traditional *dis*association of women with "hard issues" (national security, economic competition) and the masculine traits assumed necessary for dealing with them (fearlessness, cold reason).

It is not surprising, then, that women who "get there on their own" (Thatcher, Meir) are often identified as especially masculine. Some research suggests that women aspiring to or holding political office play down feminine qualities in order to appear more appropriate for "statesmanship."[73] Certainly Margaret Thatcher conveyed in her attitude and enacted in practice a disdain for feminism. She denied its relevance in her life, and as prime minister she undermined social services for women. During her eleven years of power, she did not appoint even one women to a ministerial post. Moreover, we must acknowledge the instrumental rationality of this behavior: "Those who argue that it should not be necessary for successful women to adopt so-called masculine attributes ignore the fact that, given social definitions of 'male' and 'female' identity traits, this may be the only possible strategy to gain acceptance as a woman in an authority role."[74]

The overall picture remains one of continued gender dichotomies: Women succeed through their identification as "traditional" (feminine) women facilitating male-defined projects, as trivialized "soft leaders," or as manlike by playing down any association with feminine "weakness." It appears that being seen as politically *powerful* in the traditional sense requires that women become "like men." Two points emerge from this brief discussion of women in the highest state offices.

First, as long as female political actors are perceived either as traditional women or "invisible women" (because they are acting like men), gender expectations are not really disrupted. Paradoxically, even when women wield the highest state power, by continuing to behave in gender-stereotypical ways they reinforce rather than challenge the politics of gender. Even though gender is at work here (shaping pathways to and the exercise of power), it remains "invisible" to observers of world politics. In other words, by appearing as traditional women or honorary men, female politicians do not challenge the categorical distinction between femininity and masculinity and do not politicize this gender dichotomy. Their presence in fact works to reproduce traditional gender stereotypes.

Second, and related to the first point, there is no simple, one-to-one relationship between the presence of women in power and the extent of feminist politics. If traditional gender relations remain in place, more women in power need not translate into a politics that is "better" for women in a feminist sense. This is easiest to see when we consider the case of adding women who behave like men: We do not expect feminist action from traditional "men." But the same is true in the case of women who project a traditional image. The promotion of femininity is *not* the same as promoting feminism. As we argue throughout this text, men can be as—and sometimes (given the power of their positioning as males) even more—effective in promoting feminism than women.

Whether and to what extent women in office will promote *feminist* goals is a very complex issue that has generated extensive research.[75] (We discuss the relationship between practical and strategic gender interests in Chapter 5.) One generalization seems to hold: As long as women constitute only a token presence (due to their small numbers and to the cultural isolation of women as "outsiders"), it is unlikely that feminist goals can be effectively promoted. This is true whether or not the women (or men) advocate feminist objectives as part of their campaign commitments. There are simply too many situational and structural obstacles for feminist concerns and projects to gain salience and be taken seriously when promoted by token or marginalized voices.

A 1992 study by the UN Division for the Advancement of Women (UNDAW) determined that a "critical mass" of about 30 to 35 percent women is necessary for women to confidently champion women's needs and priorities.[76] When issues typically relevant to women's lives (child care, parental leave, domestic violence, gendered wage discrepancies, how work and meeting hours are scheduled) are supported by a such a critical mass of parliamentary participants, they are much more likely to get on the agenda and command attention. Similarly, something like this level of participation is required for women to be empowered as agents *for women* (rather than simply being forced to mimic being "men").

Too tellingly, only five countries (Finland, Norway, Sweden, Denmark, and the Netherlands) have reached or exceeded this minimum of 30 percent in national legislatures.[77] Including the Nordic countries, only twenty-two countries reached 20 percent or more in 1997.[78] In the United States and the United Kingdom, where liberal democracy and women's rights have considerable history, women's representation increased only from 11 and 9.2 percent respectively in 1992 to 11.7 and 9.5 percent respectively in early 1997.[79] In view of these numbers, it is no surprise that *feminist* gains are so rare. (We consider what facilitates women's representation below.)

Moreover, we cannot understand the continued invisibility of gender simply by reference to numbers or to the ways in which women politicians "choose" to present themselves (as "masculine" or traditionally feminine). These numbers and choices must be situated within the larger context of "international politics." We begin to do this by examining how international leadership, politics, and power are defined and by locating women as political actors within this context.

WHAT MAKES ACTORS/AGENTS POWERFUL? WHO GETS ATTENTION? FOR WHAT?

Feminists have documented the pervasive bias of androcentrism in political science and international relations. One effect of this bias is the assumption that political actors are men. Another is the narrow definition of politics as exclusively public-sphere or governmental activities. Yet a third effect is the narrow definition of power as the capacity to enforce one's will ("power-over" in contrast to empowerment or "power-to").

These effects are not simply an academic concern because the definitions they take for granted are promoted outside of academic disciplines as well. Consider the focus of television news on "spectacular" (rather than everyday) events: wars, weapons, violence, crises, men as leaders/legislators/protectors and women as dependents/victims. The leaders we see tend to be heads of government of countries that are geopolitically powerful or of foreign policy significance. Otherwise, international news is almost exclusively viewed through the lens of various crises: seemingly hopeless extremities of governmental, military, economic, refugee, population, health, food, water, fuel, and/or ecological breakdown. (The exception is international sports, which foster instead nationalist "ownership" of outstanding performances of individuals and teams—virtually all men except during the Olympics.)

In these accounts, gender issues remain invisible in various ways. Attention to wars and spectacles is at the expense of everyday, maintenance activities that in fact are a precondition of the world's continuing to "work." The latter are largely ignored, yet they are the activities occupying women's—most people's—lives. To the extent that women appear in depictions of politics, they tend to be acting "like men" (Thatcher) or in supporting roles to the main/male actors (for instance, as wives, secretaries). In depictions of crises, women (or what Cynthia Enloe has termed "womenandchildren")[80] are the ever-present victims in need of protection by men or through male-defined programs. Not inconsistent with the crisis picture, women occasionally appear as saints and crusaders (Mother Theresa, Princess Diana), whose model of sacrifice and commitment spurs men on to greater feats of protection (or competitive performance). Here, the "value given to female roles emphasizes gender polarity, thus strengthening male roles as the dominant structure."[81]

Again, not only are women and their activities depicted as secondary to (or merely in support of) men's public-sphere pursuits, but also the *way* in which women make an appearance tends to reinforce rather than challenge conventional gender stereotypes. From manner of dress and demeanor to lifestyle and sexual orientation, we rarely observe any blurring of rigid gender boundaries in the mainstream media. Left in place are androcentric accounts that obscure women as powerful actors/leaders across a spectrum of political activities, that deny the politics and societal importance of ostensibly private-sphere activities, and that mystify the role of masculinism (ideologically and structurally) in the continued subordination of women and perpetuation of multiple social hierarchies. In short, the gender dynamics of politics—especially international politics—remain invisible as long as women "appear" only when they adopt masculine principles *or* epitomize feminine ones.

LOCATING POWER: NATIONALLY AND INTERNATIONALLY

Gender Divisions in Defining and Holding Power

We can begin to see how politics is gendered and how women's choices are structured, if we examine where women are located as political actors. At the national level, as suggested above, women located at the head of governments are typically perceived as "like men" (exceptional women!) or "mothers of their countries." Located at the level of parliamentary/legislative leaders and ministers, women hold significant national power but rarely do so in the most "masculine" areas: defense, foreign policy, finance, justice (see Table 3.3). Although there are individual exceptions, a clear pattern emerges of women's location in areas associated with "social functions" (education, health, welfare).[82] It is difficult to assess to what extent women are forced into these particular areas by gender stereotypes that preclude women's leadership in more "masculine" fields. But however brought about, women's location outside of conventionally defined "power" domains contributes to their invisibility as powerful political actors.

Although consideration of the location of women as political actors within national contexts is illuminating for our discussion, we should not forget that nations themselves are variously located in terms of political tradition, geopolitics, economic development, regional dynamics, religion, and colonial history. We will briefly consider how some of these dimensions, which in fact interact with one another, affect the proportion and visibility of women's political participation.

Gender Dimensions of Varying Cultures, Political Systems, and Regional Distinctions

Women's representation in national legislatures is most favored in countries with liberal-democratic or socialist-communist traditions, and there is considerable evidence that electoral systems based on **proportional representation (PR)**—allotting seats according to the proportion of votes received for a slate of candidates—additionally favor women. "Of the twelve countries with the highest proportion of women in parliaments, all use either proportional representation voting systems, or mixed systems."[83] Proportional representation appears to have made the women's

TABLE 3.3   Gendered Ministerial Power: Percentage of Women in Decision-
Making Positions in Government by Field, 1994

	Chief Executive	Economic	Law and Justice	Social	Political
Developed Regions					
Eastern Europe	3.9	5.1	0.9	10.3	0.6
Western Europe	7.8	8.0	9.7	18.7	7.7
Other Developed Regions	10.9	15.4	15.1	25.1	9.7
Africa					
Northern Africa	5.8	0.0	16.7	1.6	0.0
Sub-Saharan Africa	2.8	4.5	6.9	12.5	4.4
Latin America and Caribbean					
Central America	7.7	9.7	14.6	14.6	6.4
South America	4.9	5.1	5.8	11.5	3.1
Caribbean	7.3	6.7	22.2	22.1	20.5
Asia and Pacific					
Eastern Asia	0.6	1.5	0.0	3.9	0.0
Southeastern Asia	1.9	2.2	0.0	4.9	0.5
Central Asia	0.0	3.9	0.0	9.0	0.0
Southern Asia	5.7	4.9	6.2	4.8	1.0
Western Asia	0.7	1.8	1.5	3.9	0.0
Oceania	8.8	2.2	0.0	5.0	18.3

Source: United Nations, *The World's Women 1995: Trends and Statistics* (New York: United Nations, 1995), p. 154.

breakthrough (exceeding 20 percent representation) possible in the Nordic countries. Among industrialized countries, it has generally translated into the highest ratios of women in parliaments, ranging from a low of 12.8 percent to a high of 38.1 percent (in Sweden). In nonproportional representation systems, by contrast, their ratios range from 5.7 to 13.2 percent.[84]

There is little question that proportional representation and quota systems (voluntary positive party quotas or government-mandated quotas of women candidates) provide institutionalized support that facilitates access for women. But PR alone is insufficient. For the potential of PR to be realized, it must be embedded in a political culture committed to equality (historically associated with social-democratic and socialist systems pursuing equality of outcomes).[85] And it requires strong political leadership and social pressure, which are less likely where conservative (traditional, patriarchal) forces are strong.[86] Methods to supplement PR (and to avoid allowing it to become a way to ghettoize women politically) include the development of gender-sensitive training for political parties, legislators, and bureaucratic managers; women's sections of political parties; women's political organizations that press for the greater participation of women through fundraising, lobbying, and education; and women's political parties (which have been formed thus far in the Philippines, Canada, Germany, Spain, Nigeria, Iceland, and Russia).[87]

Only in the Nordic countries do women fare reasonably well both in national legislatures and elite governmental office (heads of government, ministries). In the former socialist-communist countries, women's representation in national legislatures was quite respectable (as in their unions), but this was not matched by strong representation in elite decision-making. Since the transition, women's proportion of parliamentary seats has declined dramatically. (As Figure 3.2 demonstrates, significant declines are apparent in Asia as well.) From 20 percent in every Eastern European country in 1987, the proportion of women had fallen below 10 percent by 1992.[88] It is worth noting again that what the media refer to as the "democratization" of these countries has had devastating effects on women's political representation and reproductive rights.

The United States has the voting system (single-member-district "winner takes all") that is the least favorable for electing women (and other underrepresented "groups"). In contrast to the strong culture of equality and the weakness of conservative forces associated with social-democratic and socialist systems, liberal democracies emphasize individual freedom, markets, and the principle of governmental noninterference. To put it simply, social democracies seek equality of outcomes whereas liberal democracies—such as the United States, Britain, and France—seek equality of opportunities.[89] In liberal democracies, conservative forces can be particularly effective, not least in shaping political participation. This is especially apparent in the resurgence of conservative forces (promoting so-called traditional family values and anti-immigrant policies) in the United States. The power of conservative forces is relevant worldwide. As Janet Beilstein and Stephen Burgess note, the "third wave of democratization" has promoted not social democracy but liberal democracy, "in which equality of opportunity has prevailed over equality of outcome and in which conservative social forces have not been combatted, but allowed to freely operate."[90]

These points help us to understand what are cast as regional variations in women's political participation, inasmuch as many data sources simply provide aggregate figures by region. For our present purposes, regional comparisons suggest that women's overall political participation is stronger in developed countries (the First World), weaker in Latin American and Asian regions, and least evident in Africa and the Middle East (in short, weaker in those areas referred to as developing, or Third World, countries). It would be misleading, however, to assume that **development** (conventionally measured by a country's degree of industrialization) alone promotes female participation in politics. Reporting to the United Nations, the Division for the Advancement of Women concluded that "level of development as measured by gross domestic product (GDP) is unrelated to percentage of women in decision-making positions."[91] (The **gross domestic product** is a measure of the total output of goods and services produced within a nation's borders.) What matters is the level of and commitment to gender equality rather than the level of development. In brief, there appears to be an interactive effect: "An increase in the general level of equality in a society leads to more women in decision-making which increases policies to promote general levels of equality."[92]

Thus, conventional distinctions between developed and developing countries fail to explain gender patterns. This point becomes clear when we consider that in 1997 women had similar proportions of parliamentary representation in Japan (4.6 percent), Fiji (4.3 percent), and Sudan (5.3 percent); in the United Kingdom (9.5 percent), Angola (9.5 percent), and Bangladesh (9.1 percent); in the United States (11.7 percent), Senegal (11.7 percent), and the Dominican Republic (11.7 percent); in Canada (18 percent), Viet Nam (18.5 percent), and Uganda (18.1 percent); in Switzerland (21 percent), Eritrea (21 percent), and China (21 percent); and in Germany (26.2 percent), Mozambique (25.2 percent), and Seychelles (27.3 percent).[93]

Similarly, it is often assumed that levels of literacy, education, and paid employment are positively correlated with acceptance and promotion of women as equals and with equal rights to political participation. But this easy (liberal) generalization obscures the different ways that religion, colonial history, electoral systems, alliances, militarism, and so forth, interact to generate historically particular gender relations that may or may not enhance women's identification with politics.

Particularly significant are the ways in which cultural belief systems and conservative forces—sometimes based on religion but increasingly on nationalism/ethnicity—shape gender stereotypes and determine "appropriate" gender activities. This is most obvious when cultural beliefs prevent women from assuming roles outside of the family/household sphere: Where women are defined primarily as mothers and wives, and social ideologies *define* their "place" as the private sphere (whether or not women are agents outside of that sphere), opportunities for women's "political" action are severely limited. All religious fundamentalisms—Jewish, evangelical Christian, Catholic, Hindu, Muslim—are masculinist insofar as they promote "traditional" (heterosexist) family structures, privilege the power of males (as heads of families, community leaders, and religious authorities), and reserve the greatest power/sacredness/authority to a definitively male deity or prophet.

Predominantly Islamic countries tend to restrict women to family-oriented activities, so they have less visibility—and power—in public-sphere activities. Women in countries strongly influenced by the Roman Catholic Church are similarly restricted—in this case by expectations that women conform to maternal and/or saintly stereotypes. These are *not* the components of "conventional" political power, though individual women may sometimes take on "moral" leadership by embodying the qualities of saintliness. In sum, the power of fundamentalisms worldwide has significant implications for women's political participation. Democratization that does not address the masculinism promoted by fundamentalisms and nationalisms is not democracy for women.[94]

It is also important to note the negative effects that **colonization** (the imposition of European rule throughout the Americas, Africa, and Asia) and externally imposed **modernization** (industrialization, urbanization, and export-oriented economic strategies) have had on women's status—including, in some cases, the elimination of political rights and power previously held in "traditional" societies.[95] In Norway, which has the most balanced gender representation, a long tradition of legal equality—dating from the Viking period—has facilitated the relatively strong legal position of women and their right to political participation.[96] Nigeria also has a long tradition of women as politically and economically powerful agents, but its colonial experience had negative effects on the power that women previously held through political leadership and/or women's centrality in the marketplace. Eurocentric constructions of masculinity and femininity transformed indigenous political practices and gender divisions of labor in ways that denied the legitimacy of women's public roles and diminished their economic power.

In general, processes of industrialization in the First World and **dependent development** (or **underdevelopment,** by which economies and societies of the First World benefit at the expense of those in the Third World) have two negative gender consequences. First, these processes involve the expansion of monetary exchanges as the basis for social systems, often referred to as the development of cash economies. In contrast to men, women's association with the private sphere restricts their participation in wage labor, especially in high-wage labor. Industrial capitalism's focus on paid labor diminishes the significance of "women's work" and contributes to a deterioration in women's status. The second negative consequence is closely related to the first. Not only paid labor but also public-sphere activities gain in prestige during processes of industrial capitalism.

But the gendered division of public and private spheres tends to exclude women both formally and informally from the sphere of activities that is gaining status. As noted earlier, the public-private dichotomy works in many ways to exclude women from political activities and to minimize the significance of power relations—and therefore politics—in the private sphere. Women lose out as the public sphere of waged labor and political power becomes increasingly distinguished from and considered superior to the "merely" private sphere.

Gender Dynamics and Globalization Forces

Globalization is significantly complicating where power is located. We have focused in this chapter on women as state and interstate actors because, in international relations, power is traditionally assumed to be concentrated in the "public" bodies of states and IGOs. However, as we have indicated, the corporate or "private" sector now exercises an inordinate amount of power in the international system. Numerous commentators on globalization have observed that states and IGOs are increasingly more accountable to corporate interests than to citizens or the world community.[97] Many feminist observers have also noted that just as women are making gains in national legislatures and international parliaments, power is shifting from these politically accountable electoral bodies to largely autonomous, economically driven actors such as the World Bank, the International Monetary Fund, the World Trade Organization, and the European Commission, to which few or no women have been appointed at senior levels.[98] Moreover, the paucity of women at senior levels in corporation boardrooms ensures that women have little influence over either corporate or economic IGO policies.

Under these conditions, the traditional public-private gender dichotomy is somewhat altered. Women remain associated with the "private sphere" of the home and family; however, they are almost completely *dis*associated from the rising power of the "private sector," which is characterized as highly masculinist. In relation to the masculinized private sector, the "public sector" of the state appears more feminized (that is, increasingly beholden to private sector interests), even though women are still not heavily represented in most states. Nevertheless, the state, in the contemporary rhetoric of neoliberal globalization proponents and conservative budget cutters, is increasingly criticized for being economically inefficient and "too soft" on such "domestic" issues as social welfare and crime. In such scenarios, the state or the public sector is characterized as "too feminine" and, thus, must be disciplined by "hard" economic austerity measures. This discipline typically takes the form of **privatization**,[99] in which many activities that have been traditionally state funded and controlled—such as education, social welfare, health care, social security, prisons, and even some forms of law enforcement and national defense—are given over to private corporations to run. It is associated with the erosion of the welfare state, turning public citizens into private consumers and reducing political (and moral) issues to matters of economic efficiency. (The gendered effects of privatization and resistances to it will be discussed further in Chapters 4 and 5.)

This devaluation and diminution of the public sector is a very ominous trend, especially in policy and program areas where women are most heavily concentrated as state leaders, workers, and social welfare recipients. Not only is it creating what many are calling a "democratic deficit," but it also substantially reduces the political space for women to gain power and use it to achieve feminist goals of equity, nonviolence, social and economic justice, and environmental protection.

CONCLUSION

In this chapter we have explored gendered divisions of power by examining the *position of women*—specifically, how women and men are differently located as political actors in state structures. By comparing where men and women are situated, we show both how world politics affects gender and how gendered concepts, practices, and institutions shape who exercises power. By asking gender-sensitive questions—Why are there so few women? How do the few succeed? What effect do they have? What makes actors powerful?—we reveal how gender is rarely acknowledged but always at work in the study and practice of world politics.

The gender dimensions of socialization, situational constraints, and institutional structures pose formidable obstacles to women's participation in formal politics. In large part, for women to acquire state power and be visible as state actors they must conform to gender stereotypes and thus leave gender dichotomies unchallenged. Most women at the helm of governments adopt the gender of state power and state agency: They "become like men," fulfilling androcentric definitions of power and politics. Other women derive legitimacy for their leadership by reference to maternal stereotypes associating women with national conciliation or advocates of "soft issues." Both strategies, however, tend to render gender hierarchy invisible because they reproduce rather than challenge gender dichotomies and their gendered effects.

Adding women as agents of state power certainly changes the position of women in world politics. But how much it changes the power of gender is a more complicated question. Global gender issues are positively affected not just by increases in women's representation but also by decreases in masculinism. Further complicating the issue of how to defuse the power of gender is the shift in power from state to corporate actors. Women's representation in formal politics will be insufficient to bring about positive change as long as masculinism privileges and pervades economic decision-making. In Chapter 4, we continue to explore the position of women by examining the gender-differentiated effects of divisions of violence, labor, and resources. And we continue to reveal how the power of gender interacts with and reproduces these gendered divisions.

NOTES

1. Special Issue, *Time* 136 (Fall 1990): 34.

2. World Commission on Environment and Development, *Our Common Future* (Oxford: Oxford University Press, 1987).

3. James F. Clarity, "Irishwomen Find New Niche (In Politics, Not the Kitchen)," *New York Times,* September 26, 1997, p. A6.

4. United Nations (UN), *World's Women 1995: Trends and Statistics* (New York: United Nations, 1995), p. 153.

5. Naomi Neft and Ann D. Levine, *Where Women Stand: An International Report on the Status of Women in 140 Countries, 1997–1998* (New York: Random House, 1997), p. 18.

6. Barbara Crossette, "French Canadian Is U.N. Chief's First Right-Hand Woman," *New York Times,* January 13, 1998, p. A7.

7. UN, *World's Women 1995,* pp. 153–154.

8. Neft and Levine, *Where Women Stand,* p. 18.

9. UN, *World's Women 1995,* p. 155.

10. Neft and Levine, *Where Women Stand,* p. 19.

11. American Council of Life Insurance and the National Women's Political Caucus, "Fact Sheet on Women's Political Progress," June 1997, p. 7.

12. Ibid.

13. George Gedda, "Albright Backs Fight for Women's Rights," *New York Times,* April 27, 1996, p. A16.

14. UN, *World's Women 1995,* p. 151.

15. Elaine Sciolino, "Top Woman in Iran's Government Once Spoke for Hostage-Takers," *New York Times,* January 28, 1998, p. A6.

16. Neft and Levine, *Where Women Stand,* p. 26.

17. Ibid., pp. 19, 25.

18. David W. Dent, "Women's Political Power," *Christian Science Monitor,* June 22, 1992, p. 9.

19. Joni Seager, *The State of Women in the World Atlas* (New York: Penguin Books, 1997), p. 92.

20. Carolyn H. Becroft, "Military Women: Policies and Politics," *Bureaucrat* 20 (Fall 1991): 10.

21. Ibid., p. 12.

22. Neft and Levine, *Where Women Stand*, pp. 66, 70; Seager, *The State of Women in the World Atlas*, pp. 92–93.

23. UN, *World's Women 1995*, p. 156.

24. Ruth Leger Sivard, *Women . . . A World Survey*, 2nd ed. (Washington, D.C.: World Priorities, 1995), p. 48.

25. Seager, *The State of Women in the World Atlas*, pp. 90, 125.

26. United Nations Development Programme (UNDP), *Human Development Report 1997* (New York: Oxford University Press, 1997), p. 31. As of January 1997, according to the Inter-Parliamentary Union (IPU), women hold 12 percent of seats in single or lower houses and 9.8 percent of seats in upper houses, for a combined percentage of 11.7 worldwide. See IPU, *Democracy Still in the Making: A World Comparative Study. Reports and Documents No. 28* (Geneva: Inter-Parliamentary Union, 1997), p. 82.

27. Vicky Randall, *Women and Politics: An International Perspective*, 2nd ed. (Chicago: University of Chicago Press, 1987), p. 96; United Nations, Division for the Advancement of Women (UNDAW), "Women and Decision-Making," EGM/EPPDM/1989/WP.1/Rev.1 (Vienna: United Nations, 1989), p. 8.

28. IPU, *Democracy Still in the Making*, p. 38.

29. Sivard, *Women . . . A World Survey* (1995), p. 38.

30. Ibid., pp. 37–38.

31. Our discussion here draws on Kristen Timothy, "Women as Insiders: The Glass Ceiling at the United Nations," in Peter Beckman and Francine D'Amico, eds., *Women and World Politics* (Westport, Conn.: Bergin & Garvey, 1995), pp. 85–94; and UN, *World's Women 1995*, pp. 153–156. See also Margaret E. Galey, "The United Nations and Women's Issues," in Beckman and D'Amico, eds., *Women, Gender and World Politics*, pp. 131–140; and Gayle Kirshenbaum, "Inside the World's Largest Men's Club," *Ms.*, September/October 1992, pp. 16–19.

32. UN, *World's Women 1995*, pp. 154–155.

33. Sivard, *Women . . . A World Survey* (1995), p. 48.

34. UNDP, *Human Development Report 1997*, p. 31.

35. The figures and quotation are from David Peterson, "Militant Capitalism II," *Z Magazine*, December 1995, p. 12. He cites the Brussels-based International Confederation of Free Trade Unions (ICFTU) and points out that 90 percent of the murder figure is accounted for by "the somewhat uniquely violent situations in Algeria and Columbia" (p. 12).

36. Randall, *Women and Politics*, pp. 112–115.

37. Marilee Karl, *Women and Empowerment: Participation and Decision Making* (London: Zed Books, 1995), pp. 47–48.

38. Seager, *The State of Women in the World Atlas*, p. 70.

39. Karl, *Women and Empowerment*, pp. 51–52; Susan Bullock, *Women and Work* (London: Zed Books, 1994), p. 133.

40. Women's reported economic activity rates have increased in all regions except sub-Saharan Africa and Eastern Asia, whereas men's economic activity rates have declined everywhere except Central Asia. See UN, *World's Women 1995*, p. xxii.

41. Linkages among underrepresentation, underelection, and underpower (occupying few prestigious posts) are what emerged from the world comparative

study performed in 1996 by the Inter-Parliamentary Union. See IPU, *Democracy Still in the Making*, p. 142.

42. UN, *World's Women 1995*, p. 153.

43. Judith H. Dobrzynski, "Study Finds Few Women in 5 Highest Company Jobs," *New York Times*, October 18, 1996, p. C3.

44. UN, *World's Women 1995*, p. 153.

45. United Nations (UN), *The World's Women: 1970–1990 Trends and Statistics* (New York: United Nations, 1991), p. 35.

46. Randall, *Women and Politics*, pp. 83–94.

47. Hilary M. Lips, *Women, Men, and Power* (Mountainview, Calif.: Mayfield Publishing Co., 1991), p. 191.

48. Randall, *Women and Politics*, pp. 83–94.

49. UN, *World's Women 1995*, p. 109.

50. Randall, *Women and Politics*, p. 125.

51. Kathleen Staudt, "Women in High-Level Political Decision Making: A Global Analysis," EGM/EPPDM/1989/WP.2 (Vienna: United Nations, 1989), p. 11.

52. Najma Chowdhury and Barbara J. Nelson, with Kathryn A. Carver, Nancy J. Johnson, and Paula L. O'Loughlin, "Redefining Politics," in Barbara J. Nelson and Najma Chowdhury, eds., *Women and Politics Worldwide* (New Haven: Yale University Press, 1994), p. 6. Research documenting these additional costs borne by women worldwide is extensive.

53. Shirley Nuss, "Women and Political Life: Variations at the Global Level," *Women & Politics* 5 (Summer/Fall 1985): 67.

54. UNDAW, "Women and Decision-Making," p. 13.

55. Lips, *Women, Men, and Power*, p. 159.

56. Laura Balbo, "The Servicing Work of Women and the Capitalist State," in Maurice Zeitlin, ed., *Political Power and Social Theory*, vol. 3 (Greenwich, Conn.: JAI Press, 1982).

57. Virginia Sapiro, *The Political Integration of Women: Roles, Socialization, and Politics* (Urbana: University of Illinois Press, 1983).

58. Sivard, *Women . . . A World Survey* (1995), p. 32.

59. Equal suffrage with men was not granted until 1928, but women over thirty years of age were permitted to vote in 1918.

60. Ruth Leger Sivard, *Women . . . A World Survey* (Washington, D.C.: World Priorities, 1985), p. 19.

61. Judith Stiehm and Michelle Saint-Germain, *Men, Women and State Violence: Government and the Military* (Washington, D.C.: American Political Science Association, 1983), p. 15. According to *U.S. News and World Report* 111, no. 7 (August 12, 1991), former military personnel serving in the Senate numbered 62 (of 100) and in the House, 219 (of 435).

62. Sheila Tobias, "Shifting Heroisms: The Uses of Military Service in Politics," in Jean Bethke Elshtain and Sheila Tobias, eds., *Women, Militarism, and War* (Savage, Md.: Rowman and Littlefield, 1990), pp. 163–185.

63. *Newsweek* (April 1, 1991, p. 24) acknowledged that Norman Schwarzkopf's "politics are a mystery" but predicted that "[he] could probably win the Democratic nomination if he wanted it and systematically set out to get it." Similarly, even though Chief of Staff Colin Powell lacks formal political experience, he was con-

sidered a serious potential candidate in 1996. The encouraging development in this case is that the candidacy of an African-American was taken seriously.

64. For a fascinating discussion of the role of "warrior queens" throughout history and of contemporary female leaders specifically, see Antonia Fraser, *Boadicea's Chariot: The Warrior Queens* (London: Weidenfeld and Nicholson, 1988).

65. Randall, *Women and Politics*, pp. 92–94.

66. Ibid., p. 93. The "men's club" atmosphere of the U.S. Senate was vividly revealed in televised hearings on the Clarence Thomas nomination for the Supreme Court. Indeed, the Senate stands out as a bastion of male dominance: Including the 9 women serving in 1997, only 26 women have served in the Senate during its entire history, compared to the approximately 1,817 men who have served since 1789. In the House, 165 women have served, compared to more than 10,156 men. (Data from the American Council of Life Insurance and Political Caucus, "Factsheet," p. 3–4, citing U.S. Senate and House historians.)

67. Randall, *Women and Politics*, p. 132.

68. A May 1991 *New York Times* piece described Bush's presidency as an "all-male club" and characterized the inner sanctum as "what one top Republican calls 'a male prep school, locker room atmosphere,'" including "racy jokes" within the exclusively male group (pp. A1, B6). Paternalistic discrimination also shapes women's participation in international politics: As Cynthia Enloe has reported, the Chinese government considers unmarried women (but not men!) too vulnerable and "open to temptations" to be posted abroad (see Enloe, *Bananas, Beaches & Bases: Making Feminist Sense of International Politics* [Berkeley: University of California Press, 1989], p. 113). And the UN has been faulted for continuing to let cultural stereotypes deter it from assigning women to particular countries (see Kirshenbaum, "Inside the World's Largest Men's Club," p. 19).

69. Staudt, "Women in High-Level Political Decision Making," pp. 5–8. Women candidates and ministers in France report "unrelenting ridicule and sexist slurs" on the part of the media, voters, and male candidates and ministers (see Marlise Simons, "Frenchwomen Fight Voter Sexism," *New York Times*, May 23, 1997, p. A6).

70. Chowdhury et al., "Redefining Politics," p. 16.

71. Indira Gandhi, daughter of Jawaharlal Nehru, rose through the ranks of the Congress party, serving briefly as president in 1959. She became prime minister after the sudden death of Prime Minister Shastri and quickly established her own formidable style. A cover story titled "The Changing Woman," in *India Today* (July 15, 1992, pp. 36–43), argued that Gandhi "inspired scores of women politicians" who are now "coming in on their own steam, not as daughters, wives and widows of politicians. . . . [They] are an altogether different breed of politician" (p. 39).

72. Randall, *Women and Politics*, p. 151; Staudt, "Women in High-Level Decision Making," pp. 2–4.

73. Randall, *Women and Politics*, p. 152; Fraser, *Warrior Queens*, pp. 305–322.

74. Betsy Thom, "Women in International Organizations: Room at the Top," in Cynthia F. Epstein and Rose L. Coser, eds., *Access to Power: Cross-National Studies of Women and Elites* (London: George Allen and Unwin, 1981), p. 179.

75. As a model of women's mobilization, Chowdhury and her colleagues ("Redefining Politics," pp. 19–21) suggest relating gender ideologies (beliefs about ac-

tual and preferred gender relations) and their implications for action (advocating acceptance, separate spheres, or system transformation).

76. Karl, *Women and Empowerment*, p. 64.

77. Neft and Levine, *Where Women Stand*, pp. 19, 25.

78. IPU, *Democracy Still in the Making*, compiled from Annex I.

79. These figures are for the House of Representatives and the House of Commons respectively, based on IPU data from 1995 (*Reports and Documents No. 23*) and 1997 (*Reports and Documents No. 28*). On a more positive note, by May 1997, Tony Blair's Labor party victory almost doubled the number of women in the British Parliament—to an all-time high of 120. (See Edith M. Lederer, "Women's Ranks Double," *Dayton Daily News*, May 4, 1997, p. 18A.)

80. Cynthia Enloe, "Womenandchildren: Making Feminist Sense of the Persian Gulf Crisis," *Village Voice*, September 25, 1990, pp. 29ff.

81. Helen Callaway, "Survival and Support: Women's Forms of Political Action," in Rosemary Ridd and Helen Callaway, eds., *Caught Up in Conflict: Women's Responses to Political Strife* (London: Macmillan, 1986), p. 228.

82. UN, *World's Women 1970–1990*, p. 31; Staudt, "Women in High-Level Decision Making," p. 8.

83. Jyotsna Sreenivasan, "Women Still Hold Less Than 12% of Parliamentary Seats Worldwide," *Feminist Majority Report*, Spring 1997, p. 12. See also Randall, *Women and Politics*, p. 141; and Dent, "Women's Political Power," p. 19.

84. Pippa Norris, "Conclusions: Comparing Legislative Recruitment," in Joni Lovenduski and Pippa Norris, eds., *Gender and Party Politics* (London: Thousand Oaks, 1993), p. 314. On improving women's representation in legislatures, see Barbara J. Nelson, "The Role of Sex and Gender in Comparative Political Analysis," *American Political Science Review* 86 (June 1992): 491–495.

85. See Janet Beilstein and Stephen F. Burgess, "Women in Political Decision-Making: Liberalism Versus Social Democracy," paper presented at the annual meeting of the American Political Science Association, 1995.

86. Chowdhury et al., "Redefining Politics," p. 17.

87. Karl, *Women and Empowerment*, pp. 72–78.

88. Beilstein and Burgess, "Women in Political Decision-Making," p. 7.

89. Ibid.

90. Ibid., p. 33.

91. UNDAW, "Women and Decision-Making," p. 11.

92. Ibid., p. 12.

93. Compiled from IPU, *Democracy Still in the Making*, pp. 90–93.

94. See, for example, V. Spike Peterson, "Reframing the Politics of Identity: Democracy, Globalization and Gender," *Political Expressions* 1, no. 1 (1995): 1–16; and Nira-Yuval Davis, *Gender and Nation* (London: Sage, 1997).

95. Nuss, "Women and Political Life," p. 67.

96. *Ms.*, January/February 1991, p. 12.

97. Practically all critics of globalization note this pattern. See, for example, Jeremy Brecher, John Brown Childs, and Jill Cutler, *Global Visions: Beyond the New World Order* (Boston: South End Press, 1993); Malcolm Waters, *Globalization* (London: Routledge, 1995); and James H. Mittelman, ed., *Globalization: Critical Reflections* (Boulder: Lynne Rienner Publishers, 1996).

98. See, for example, Mona Harrington, "What's Wrong with the Liberal State as an Agent of Change?" in V. Spike Peterson, ed., *Gendered States*, pp. 65–82; Drude Dahlerup, "Learning to Live with the State—State, Market, and Civil Society: Women's Need for State Intervention in East and West," *Women's Studies International Forum* 17 (March-June 1994): 117–128; Anne Sisson Runyan, "The Places of Women in Trading Places: Gendered Global/Regional Regimes and Inter-nationalized Feminist Resistance," in Eleonore Kofman and Gillian Youngs, eds., *Globalization: Theory and Practice* (London: Pinter, 1996); and Gita Sen, *Globalization in the 21st Century: Challenges for Civil Society*, University of Amsterdam Development Lecture (Amsterdam: GOM/INDRA, 1997).

99. For two particularly insightful feminist treatments of privatization in its economic, political, and cultural forms, see Janine Brodie, "Shifting the Boundaries: Gender and the Politics of Restructuring," in Isabella Bakker, ed., *The Strategic Silence: Gender and Economic Policy* (London: Zed Books, 1994), pp. 46–60; and Susan Williams, "Globalization, Privatization, and a Feminist Public," *Indiana Journal of Legal Studies* 4 (Fall 1996): 97–105.

FOUR

□ □ □

Gendered Divisions of Violence, Labor, and Resources

The gendered division of power makes possible not only the relative denial of formal power to women in the international system but also the exclusion of women's struggles and "women's issues" from the world politics agenda. To see how the gendered division of power both oppresses women and minimizes their struggles against oppression, we need to explore two interrelated aspects of power: the gendered nature of the concept of power (the lens) and the gendered effects of this concept of power (the different positioning of women and men).

The gendered nature of the concept of power refers to the assumption in world politics of power-over. We argue that this form of power is masculinist because it presupposes the dominant (Western) stereotype of masculine "nature" and behavior—agency, competition, and aggression—often backed by physical or military force. This concept of power keeps most women from being taken seriously as national and international leaders unless they adopt masculine leadership styles while remaining feminine enough to uphold traditional symbols of motherhood and family that undergird the nation. Moreover, because the gendered or masculinist concept of power visualizes it as operating from the top down, women's political struggles—usually carried out at the grass-roots level or from the bottom up—are rendered practically invisible.

The gendered effects of power refer to the ways that men and women are treated unequally in the international system, in which formal top-down power is held largely in the hands of men. These effects have translated into limited access to state power for women and little attention to women's issues by states and international organizations, which perceive "women's issues" as belonging to the private sphere and, therefore, as separate from and inferior to "real political issues" associated with the public sphere. Hence, states and international organizations tend to reduce issues such as reproductive rights, rape, and wife battering to domestic or even personal problems, which then appear irrelevant to the so-called real politics of war and economic competition.

The gendered conception of power produces gendered effects. In a male-dominated world where power-over is valued, those who are neither able nor inclined to engage in aggressive and coercive practices are seen as weak, less important, and even expendable. Because women are associated with feminine characteristics of passivity and compliance, their needs, interests, and even lives have been rendered invisible or unimportant. Broadly speaking, these are the gendered effects of power. They result from the masculinist construction of power as power-over, which gives greater access to power to men, who, then, "overpower" women. In this chapter, to further explain this generalized power imbalance between men and women, we examine other gendered divisions—of violence, labor, and resources—that work to consolidate and reproduce gender inequalities.

Conventional definitions of power stress that to have power, to exercise control over others, one must have certain resources at one's disposal. For an individual, this often means possessing a lot of physical strength, money, and/or property. For a state, this usually means possessing a strong military, a highly industrialized economy, and/or significant natural resources. Persons or states lacking any or all of these attributes are seen as less powerful or even powerless. According to this conventional definition of power, women seem largely powerless.

For example, if we look through the lens of the gendered division of violence, we see that women are stereotyped as smaller and weaker than men and that they represent a very small proportion of the world's formal militaries. Thus, women typically have much less access to most means of destruction and, as a result, are more often victims than perpetrators of direct violence. Through the lens of the gendered division of labor, we see that women's unemployment and underemployment outpace men's in every country, and that women and children constitute the poorest of the poor in every country. In almost every occupational category, women are paid less than men for doing the same job; yet women typically work more hours than men the world over. In short, women lack significant control over the means of production and have too much responsibility for and often too little control over the means of reproduction. Finally, if we look through the lens of the gendered division of resources, we discover that women own only 1 percent of the world's land and have very little private property compared to men. In this sense, women have minimal access to or control over natural resources. In fact, women themselves are often treated as natural resources whose bodies are free or as cheap labor that can be exploited to amass wealth for states, corporations, and individual men.

These manifestations of the gendered divisions of violence, labor, and resources subject women disproportionately to various forms of direct and structural violence and also hinder women from aspiring to or attaining conventional or formal power in homes, communities, workplaces, national governments, and international organizations. Moreover, dealing with the gross inequities created by the gendered divisions of violence, labor, and resources is not high on the agendas of domestic and international policy-makers. In this chapter we will argue that these gendered divisions are not only harmful to women because they produce and reproduce the power imbalance of gender inequality but are also harmful to all of us because they contribute to global crises.

Whereas Chapter 3 examined how the gendered division of power marginalizes women's status in conventionally defined politics, this chapter examines how gendered divisions of violence (security issues), labor (economic issues), and resources (equity and ecology issues) construct and reproduce a gender-differentiated world. To organize the discussion, we identify three interacting components of each gendered division and the issue area it constitutes. The components are (1) the gender dichotomies at work (the underlying assumptions and expectations), (2) the differential effects of these dichotomies on men and women (the roles they are assigned in relation to militaries, economies, and environments), and (3) the systemic consequences of these gender dichotomies (exacerbating global problems). The patterns we identify through the examples we offer (which are, by no means, exhaustive) paint an overwhelmingly negative picture of the gendered effects of world politics; however, it is necessary to understand the full impact of the gendered divisions of violence, labor, and resources and the interactions among them to appreciate the varied struggles against these processes that we document in Chapter 5.

VIOLENCE: WAR AND SECURITY ISSUES

War—its causes and effects—continues to dominate the study of IR. And security continues to be understood in terms of direct violence—in particular, the violence of war. The discipline's focus on direct violence has been at the expense of attending to structural violence and the *insecurities* generated by structural inequalities. In this section we focus on exposing how war, warriors, and militaries are profoundly gendered. At the same time, we remind the reader that direct and indirect (structural) violence are not separate but interdependent. The inequalities of the latter shape the expression of the former. And as dire as the effects of direct violence are, indirect violence shapes the lives of all of us all of the time—and especially injures women and other subordinated people.

Hence, feminists argue that to understand violence and insecurities we must look not only within particular "levels" but also at the linkages among them. In Ann Tickner's words:

> Feminist perspectives on security would assume that violence, whether it be in the international, national, or family realm, is interconnected. Family violence must be seen in the context of wider power relations; it occurs within a gendered society in which male power dominates at all levels. . . . Any feminist definition of security must therefore include the elimination of all types of violence, including violence produced by gender relations of domination and subordination.[1]

Throughout history, women have participated in war, and women fighters exist today. In *Women Warriors: A History*, David Jones provides an up-to-date and comprehensive account "of the female martial tradition in a pan-historical and global perspective."[2] He documents how women warriors have had an important presence across cultures and throughout history. They have led armies, constituted women's battalions, "passed" as male soldiers, rallied the troops as symbolic leaders, defended family and community structures in the absence of men, and exhibited the same courage, loyalty, steadfastness, heroism, and even bloodthirstiness that we associate with male warriors. In stark contrast to modern stereotypes and expectations, Jones argues that "from the beginning women shared the qualitative experience of the warrior; everything men have ever done in warfare, women have also done, and, in many instances, they have done it better."[3] Most of us experience discomfort with—and a desire to reject—this finding, in spite of Jones's well-documented research. Why are we so uncomfortable with the image and, indeed, the reality of *women warriors?*

With modern state-making, gendered divisions became codified in particular ways. Liberalism in political theory favored divisions of power into public-private, government-household, whereas capitalism in economic theory favored divisions of labor into paid-unpaid, productive-reproductive. Interacting with these developments, modern state-making promoted particular divisions of violence. Masculinity involved not only heading the household and earning a "family wage" but also being prepared to defend "home and country." In Jean Bethke Elshtain's words, "[W]ar is the means to attain recognition, to pass, in a sense, the definitive test of political manhood. . . . The man becomes what he in some sense is meant to be by being absorbed in the larger stream of life: war and the state."[4] Femininity involved not only bearing and rearing children and maintaining the home front, but also serving, symbolically and literally, as that which required protection. Whereas men served their country in combat, as "life-takers," women served their country as mothers, as "life-givers."[5]

In recent centuries, most male-dominated societies have constructed elaborate sanctions and even taboos against women as warriors, and especially against women bearing arms and initiating violence. As a result, men have gained almost exclusive control over the means of destruction worldwide, often in the name of protecting women and children, who are either discouraged from or not allowed to take up arms to protect themselves or to be warriors protecting others. It is therefore not surprising that war—which remains the centerpiece of IR—is seen as *men's* deadly business. We argue, however, that war has always involved women as well as the power of gender to promote masculine characteristics—typically at the expense of cooperation, interdependence, and conflict resolution.[6] Moreover, the identification of war with men and peace with women completely unravels in the face of twentieth-century war practices.

In World War 1, 80 percent of casualties were soldiers; in World War 2, only 50 percent. In the Vietnam War some 80 percent of casualties were civilian, and in current conflicts the estimate is 90 percent—mainly women and children . . . In light of these figures, talking of war as if it is something mainly to do with men is a nonsense.[7]

As life-givers, women are not only prevented from engaging in combat but are also expected to restore "life" after a death-dealing war is over. Women are expected to mourn dutifully the loved ones who fell in war and then produce new lives for the nation to replace its lost members. Thus, after the devastation, they must "pick up the pieces" and create the conditions for repopulating society. These conditions include creating more men, who too often serve as soldiers, and more women, who too often bear sons only to lose them through war. The work of men as life-takers thus creates perpetual work for women as life-givers.

In this sense, women are not separate from either the production or the consequences of war, even though they are often prevented from engaging in direct combat. Yet in spite of their participation, women remain associated with war's opposite—peace. By denying history, the characterization of "woman" as passive and submissive is often translated into the idea that women are pacifist by nature. This reinforces the stereotype of women as life-givers and portrays them as insufficiently fit or motivated to be life-takers. The assumption that women have a natural revulsion against war also makes them undesirable partners in combat: How can women be trusted on the battleground if they are unwilling to fight and kill? Men, in contrast, are stereotyped as naturally aggressive and competitive, which presumably prepares them to kill or be killed. In addition, it is assumed that the presence of women on the battlefield will distract men from fighting successfully, perhaps by turning their aggressions away from fighting and toward sexual conquest or by tying them down to protect "weaker" female comrades, thereby endangering the pursuit of body counts. On this view, men might lose the war by pursuing or protecting women on the battlefield rather than fighting successfully to protect their women at home.

After the battle, women are expected to take care of returning soldiers, salving their wounds and psyches as well as meeting needs—for food, clothing, and shelter—previously met by the military. When the "boys come home," women are expected to serve them, and to do so with gratitude for those who fought and took life on behalf of their women and their nation. If women fail in these duties, then male protectors are often given tacit approval for "disciplining" their women, through physical violence if necessary. Such physical violence is learned on the playground when boys play "war" in preparation for their adult roles as potential soldiers. And it is honed when men are actually trained by militaries and participate in "real" wars. Life-takers have no responsibility for "unlearning" these skills during peacetime; global statistics on domestic violence suggest that men may use these skills against the women and children they protected in wartime if the latter do not please them in the home. Thus, those who are denied access to the means of destruction to protect themselves during wartime also have little protection against the wartime protectors who may turn violent in the home.[8]

We now begin to see how gender dichotomies such as the following are at work in reproducing the gendered division of violence: soldiers-mothers, protectors-protected, aggressive-passive, battlefront-homefront, batterers-victims. How are these dichotomies related to the different roles and positions of men and women worldwide? How do they shape our perceptions of war and security issues? How are men and women situated differently in relation to processes of militarization, even when war is absent? And how does a gender-sensitive lens enrich our understanding of systemic militarization as a global problem?

Militarized Masculinity

In societies where masculinity is associated with power-over and violence, men are under constant pressure to prove their manhood by being tough, adversarial, and aggressive. There are, of course, a variety of forms of male aggression that have been deemed unacceptable or illegitimate within civil societies (such as murder, assault, gang warfare, and, at least in terms of the laws of some countries, wife battering and child abuse). However, in one highly legitimated and organized institution within most societies, men not only can but—to be successful—*must* prove their masculinity: the military.

State militaries serve many functions. According to world politics wisdom of the (neo)realist variety, militaries serve to protect the borders of states and the citizens within them from outside aggression, inevitable given the anarchic **interstate system,** which is based on **power politics,** not the rule of law. On this view, militaries are deemed necessary for the maintenance of national security, either as deterrents to would-be aggressors or as effective fighting machines capable of vanquishing actual aggressors.

More critical world politics perspectives see militaries serving other less laudable functions, such as protecting repressive state elites from rebellion by their own people. This is often described as maintaining the **internal security** of states at the expense of nonelite citizens. Also, militaries are implicated in maintaining permanent war economies arising from the infamous **military-industrial complex,** which organizes a state's economy around producing weapons rather than civilian goods. Under such conditions, the military can become one of the few sites for "employment," not only for the poor and least educated who turn to soldiering or working in weapons plants, but also for large numbers of middle-class voters engaged in, for example, research and development activities.

Less appreciated or analyzed, even by many critical world politics observers, is the role that the military plays in reproducing masculinity and femininity as a result of its dependence on these gender divisions. As Cynthia Enloe argues, militaries not only need men to act as "men"—that is, to be willing to kill and die on the behalf of the state to prove their "manhood"—but militaries also "need women to behave *as the gender 'women.'*"[9] In other words, women must be properly subservient to meet the needs of militaries and of the men who largely constitute them.

These needs are enormous. According to Ruth Leger Sivard, "World military expenditures from 1960 to 1990 add up to $21 trillion ($21,000,000,000,000) in 1987 dollars, equivalent in size to the value of all goods and services produced by and for the 5.3 billion people on the earth."[10] Since 1987 (the peak of worldwide military spending) and the end of the Cold War, global military expenditures in 1995 fell to below 3 percent of the world's gross national product (GNP) for the first time since 1960, due largely to the "56 percent decline in military spending by Eastern Europe and the former Soviet republics."[11] With the exception of parts of the Middle East (Israel and Jordan) and the Far East (the "Asian Tigers"), force levels and expenditures are being reduced to various degrees across most developed and developing countries, but the North Atlantic Treaty Organization (NATO) expansion into Central Europe is threatening to reverse these trends.[12] According to Sherle Schwenninger, the estimated cost, over ten years, of this expansion ranges from $35 billion (based on Pentagon figures) to $125 billion (based on U.S. Congressional Budget Office figures).[13] It is further estimated that this expansion will cost the new members in

Central Europe and the extant members in Western Europe $1 billion annually. The U.S. share is pegged at much less (about $200 million annually).

Nevertheless, the United States continues to be the largest military spender in the world, accounting for "41 percent of global defense outlays" in 1995.[14] Representing only 5 percent of the world's population, the United States spends almost $280 billion per year on its military operations (well over five times the amount now spent by Russia, the second highest single-country spender), and about 10–15 percent of that (or $26–39 billion) is spent on its nuclear weapons production and stockpile program.[15] Although a series of nuclear arms "build-down" agreements during the 1990s have reduced the world's nuclear arsenals from 18,000 to 8,000 megatons (the lower amount constituting "727 times the 11 megatons of explosive power used in this century's three major wars which killed 44,000,000 people"),[16] the United States still has almost 8,000 active nuclear warheads and bombs, whereas Russia has about 7,300.[17] As of 1996, the United States had 31,500 tons of stockpiled chemical weapons compared to Russia's 40,000 tons. And since the Persian Gulf war, the United States has become the world's top arms exporter, well exceeding "the total arms exports of *all* 52 other exporting countries combined."[18] The much-hoped-for "peace dividend" is not materializing, given that in 1997, "6 years after the Cold War has ended, the lion's share of [U.S.] income taxes still go[es] to the Pentagon . . . 5 times what [is spent on] education, housing, job training and the environment combined"[19] (see Figure 4.1). Worldwide, "over half the nations of the world still provide higher budgets for the military than for their countries' health needs; 25 countries spend more on defense than on education; and 15 countries devote more funds to military programs than to education and health combined."[20]

Military Women

What effects will military expenses have on the positions of women and men—assuming that militaries will, for the foreseeable future, continue to consume large amounts of resources to the detriment of the civilian population? Although "there were 4.6 million fewer soldiers in 1995 than in 1989 . . . 22.4 million men and women remained under arms, with the developing countries representing 65 percent of the world's total."[21] In 1988 a little over half the world's state militaries, mostly in developing countries ruled by military regimes, excluded women.[22] By 1994 there were more than 500,000 female soldiers serving in regular and irregular armed forces,[23] but women still typically make up less than 10 percent of state militaries. Those countries having the highest rates of female participation in their armed forces include New Zealand (14 percent), Australia (13 percent), the United States (12 percent), Canada (12 percent), and Russia

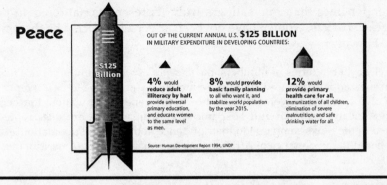

FIGURE 4.1 Life-Taking Takes Priority over Life-Giving. Courtesy of the United Nations Department of Public Information.

(11 percent).[24] Only seven countries allow women to engage in all combat roles (Australia, Canada, Belgium, the Netherlands, Denmark, Norway, and Spain), and only seven more allow women limited combat experience (the United States, the United Kingdom, Israel, Japan, France, Finland, and Ghana).[25] Some women and men are also excluded from state military participation because of bans on lesbians and gays in the military. Most Western European countries lifted these bans during the 1970s and 1980s, as did Canada, Australia, and Israel in the early 1990s; however, they are still in effect in the United Kingdom and the United States.[26]

Given the relatively low rates of female participation in state militaries worldwide, it is obvious that most women are not direct recipients of military spending.[27] Also based on these statistics, few women can claim combat experience, which (as we noted in Chapter 3) has often served as a prerequisite or a test of leadership skills for those seeking high political office. Some feminists, particularly in the United States, have responded to these problems by insisting that the armed forces work to recruit more women by further breaking down discriminatory practices, such as the remaining combat exclusions and the continuing prohibition against homosexual men and women serving in the armed forces. They argue that these steps will balance the gendered division of violence, which currently accords military men more access to formal positions of power and to the resources garnered by military spending.[28]

Other feminists, however, question this strategy. For example, Francine D'Amico argues that in the 1980s state militaries wanted "women to meet personnel needs under conditions of high militarization and to fill the *man*-power shortage, not to promote sex equality."[29] She finds that in the current period of force reductions—referred to in the United States as "the drawdown," which entails a one-third cut in military personnel—the U.S. military is more interested in controlling its composition along racial and gender lines than in creating a truly representational force. In percentage of soldiers, women have not been adversely affected by the drawdown. However,

> it is clear that in terms of numbers, the *presence* of women in the service has been substantially reduced, and this reduction has made the force *less* representative in terms of women's presence in the general population. Further, both African-American and Hispanic-American women are *under*represented in the ranks compared to their presence in the general population *and* compared to the presence of African-American and Hispanic-American men in the ranks.[30]

Far from yielding to feminist and other demands for democratization, the U.S. military is trying to preserve "its racist, androcentric, and heterocentric foundations,"[31] which are responsible for other forms of discrimination against women in the military.

Since the 1991 Tailhook Convention, where women officers of the U.S. Navy were subjected to intense sexual harassment and abuse by male naval officers, many more cases of sexual harassment and rape in the armed services have come to light. A year before the 1996 U.S. Army Aberdeen Proving Ground scandal in which two dozen female recruits charged that they were repeatedly sexually harassed and abused by training officers, the Pentagon surveyed 90,000 female soldiers, sailors, and pilots and found that "nearly 1 in 10 Army women reported being sexually assaulted, and 6 in 10 said they had experienced some form of sexual harassment" by military men, totaling tens of thousands of incidents.[32] To add insult to injury, an investigative report in 1997 revealed that "since 1990 the Army prosecuted 1,329 soldiers for rape and other sexual assaults. Of the 870 convicted, 135—about one in six—got 90 days or less. Ninety-three got no jail time at all."[33] In addition to suffering physical violence at the hands of their own comrades in arms, women in the U.S. military are discriminated against through the following: new "restrictions on deployment of custodial parents" instituted since the Persian Gulf war; the lack of "basic gynecological care or breast cancer detection or treatment" at many military medical centers; the recent discontinuation of "abortion services at military hospitals" by the U.S. Congress; and the concentration of women in clerical/administrative services positions ("pink/khaki collar" jobs).[34] These forms of discrimination, combined with stepped-up attempts to discharge suspected lesbians[35] and continued combat exclusions, constitute formidable barriers for military women (see Figure 4.2).

Based on these findings, women's experiences of discrimination in most state militaries mirror (and are sometimes worse than) those of women in civilian life. Thus, it is not surprising that even when women's participation in the U.S. armed forces was at its numerical peak in 1989

FIGURE 4.2 "Women in Combat." As this cartoon shows, the real war against women extends beyond the battlefield. Reprinted with special permission of United Features Syndicate.

(reaching 229,311 before the drawdown, which reduced women's numbers to 191,399 in 1995),[36] women in general in the United States were experiencing continuous resistance and repeated setbacks to their demands for equality in all spheres of life. Susan Faludi's 1991 bestseller, *Backlash: The Undeclared War Against American Women*, documented the real war most American women faced at that time.[37] She asked, for example, "Why do American women, in fact, face one of the worst gender-based pay gaps in the developed world?" "Why do they represent two-thirds of all poor adults?" "Why are nearly 80% of working women still stuck in traditional 'female' jobs, as secretaries, administrative 'support' workers and salesclerks?" "Why are their reproductive freedoms in greater jeopardy today than a decade earlier?" And given that "battering was the leading cause of injury to women in the late 1980s," why is it that "federal funding for battered women's shelters has been withheld and one third of the one million battered women who seek emergency shelter each year can find none"?[38] Little has changed for the better on this battlefront of structural and direct violence against women, nor is there any evidence so far to indicate that women's military experience is catapulting them into positions of power.

Feminists who question whether it is possible to democratize the military tend also to question whether it should be democratized.[39] An increased presence of women serves to legitimize the institution by giving it a facade of egalitarianism. When women accept the "warrior mystique," they soften the image of the military as an agent of coercion/destruction and help promote the image of the military as a democratic institution, an "equal opportunity employer" like any other (see Figure 4.3), without reference to its essential purpose.[40]

The Wages of War

This essential purpose is organized, direct violence, which, as we and others have argued, depends in part upon the structural violence of organized gender inequality. The only times that women have direct access to the largess that the world's militaries command are during periods of increased militarization, a process that costs most women, children, and men far more than what a few women and a much larger number of men gain from their military participation. And even in this (however brief)

FIGURE 4.3 The Military as an "Equal Opportunity Employer." That is the idea conveyed in this disturbing cartoon. Reprinted by special permission of Clay Butler.

period of military "downsizing," the "peace dividend" is being squandered on reducing budget deficits (produced by the unprecedented military spending of the 1980s) and sustaining unnecessarily high military budgets. This is occurring at a time when social needs, so long neglected during the Cold War, are massive. Worldwide, 1.3 billion people (70 percent of whom are women) are living in absolute poverty; almost 1 billion people (two-thirds of whom are women) are illiterate; and more than 700 million people (mostly children and women) are seriously malnourished.[41] In the United States, one child in five lives in poverty (the highest child poverty rate among eighteen industrialized countries); income inequality is the highest of all industrialized countries (with corporate executives earning about 190 times the average pay of workers, whose wages are about 6 percent lower than in the late 1980s when adjusted for inflation); and welfare reform enacted in 1996 reduces welfare payments (largely to women and children) by $10 billion a year.[42] Meanwhile, the Pentagon received $17 billion more than it requested in both 1996 and 1997.[43] As Sivard observes, "[A]ssigning one-quarter of the military expenditures saved by the end of the Cold War to social programs could implement most of the 'Health For All by the Year 2000' goals,"[44] but there is no movement in that direction. In effect, the gendered division of violence continues to operate to ensure that life-taking activities are still better funded than life-giving ones.

The negative impacts of militarization go far beyond the extraction of public funding from the meeting of basic human needs. Human rights, too, are sorely compromised. At the beginning of the 1990s, when many Cold War–supported military regimes were still in place, Amnesty International released a report[45] that vividly documents examples of military and police forces around the world terrorizing, imprisoning, raping, and torturing women who seek information about family members who have "disappeared" at the hands of government-sponsored death squads or who are active members and/or leaders of peasant land-reform movements, women's rights organizations, ecological groups, community associations, national liberation struggles, and political parties (as shown in Figure 4.4). Since that time, genocidal wars waged under the guise of "ethnic cleansing" (most notably in the former Yugoslavia and in Rwanda and Burundi) and fundamentalist regimes brought to power as a result of Cold War conflicts (such as the Taliban in Afghanistan[46]) have become particularly notorious exemplars of the abuse of women's human rights.

Genocidal rape, which refers to a systematic program of raping women and girls to humiliate (feminize) the enemy and to dilute it as a (biological) nation through the impregnation of the enemy's women,[47] gained worldwide attention when it was revealed that during the war in Bosnia-Herzegovina that began in 1992, up to 60,000 (mostly Bosnian)

126

FIGURE 4.4   Abuse of Women's Human Rights. The poster demands "liberty for prisoners of conscience, impartial trials for political prisoners, abolition of torture and the death penalty all over the world," yet these demands only begin to address the human rights abuses visited upon women. Copyright © Amnesty International. Reprinted by permission.

women had been raped by 1993, largely by Serb forces.[48] The massacres and countermassacres engaged in by the Tutsi and Hutu ethnic groups that began in Burundi in 1993 and in Rwanda in 1994 have left well over a million people dead. It is estimated that more than 250,000 women were raped in the Rwandan conflict.[49] Although sexual assaults have been defined as crimes of war since the 1940s, as Joni Seager notes, it was not until 1995 "that rape was specifically acknowledged as a distinct—and prosecutable—crime of war."[50]

According to Cynthia Enloe, there are "three 'types' of institutionalized militarized rape: 'recreational rape'—the assumption that soldiers need constant access to sexual outlets; 'national security rape'—when police forces and armies use rape to bolster the state's control over a population; and systematic mass rape as an instrument of open warfare."[51] The foregoing discussion spoke to some of the recent sources of the latter two forms. Although "recreational rape" is a feature of most state militaries, it is particularly associated with the U.S. military, in part because the United States sustains the largest number of foreign military bases. This aspect of the U.S. military gained worldwide attention in September 1995, when two marines and a Navy seaman gang-raped a twelve-year-old Japanese girl in Okinawa.[52] The storm of protest and anti–U.S. military feelings on the part of the Japanese that this case evoked has not stopped military bases from also being deeply implicated in the business of prostitution.

Many military men have come to expect sexual servicing not just as a perk but as a right and even a necessity during their stints overseas. Given that "recreational rape" can unleash protest against a foreign military presence (as in the Okinawan case), providing its military men with prostitutes has been a policy of the U.S. government. There are 89,000 U.S. forces stationed in the Pacific area alone,[53] and in countries where there is a large U.S. military presence (such as Japan, South Korea, Guam, Australia, Singapore, Malaysia, and the Philippines), the U.S. government has R&R (rest and relaxation) agreements "that spell out the conditions for permitting and controlling the sort of prostitution deemed useful for the U.S. military."[54] Perhaps the most notorious site was Subic Bay Naval Base in the Philippines. In the late 1980s, Filipino feminist organizations reported that, as a result of high unemployment and extreme poverty, more than 20,000 Filipino women and about 10,000 Filipino children regularly acted as prostitutes for U.S. servicemen at Subic Bay.[55] This situation contributed not only to the spread of acquired immune deficiency syndrome (AIDS) but also to racial tensions and nationalist fervor: Filipinos denounced militarized prostitution as a symbol of their compromised sovereignty. The Subic Bay base was closed in 1991 when the Philippine government revoked its lease, but the nexus between military bases and prostitution continues elsewhere, furthering the gendered division of violence that capitalizes on poverty and leaves despair, disease, and international tensions in its wake. There is also little evidence that militarized prostitution reduces the incidence of rape by military men. Richard Rayner has found that many U.S. military officials and experts believe that rape is a "necessary corollary" to the military's main function—killing.[56]

The logical conclusion of militarization, war, has killed almost 110 billion people over the course of the twentieth century.[57] "The 1990s saw a new peak for the century in the annual numbers of wars (34 in 1992) and in 1994 the highest number of war-related deaths since 1971," 90 percent of which involved noncombatants.[58] (See Figure 4.5.) Robin Morgan argues that killing noncombatants, which "had become a 'legitimate' military tactic in conventional warfare," has invoked what we call **terrorism,** the "random murder of average citizens, including those in no way connected to power."[59] She also notes that whether it is state terrorism or terrorism perpetrated by insurgent groups against states, terrorists are predominantly male. Recent domestic terrorism in the United States perpetrated by right-wing white supremacist groups and militia members fits this pattern. In contrast, the majority of the millions of refugees in the world, fleeing from war or terrorism, are women and children.[60] Moreover, Susan Forbes Mar-

FIGURE 4.5 The Main Casualties of War. As depicted in this horrific "cartoon," the main casualties are civilian "women and children." Reprinted by special permission of Clay Butler.

tin has reported that women, once in refugee camps outside or inside their own countries, frequently are raped by military personnel guarding the camps, insurgent forces who infiltrate the camps, and male refugees:[61] "The problem is so great that the UNHCR (United Nations High Commission for Refugees) recently issued guidelines to its field workers on responding to sexual violence against refugees."[62] Displaced children, both boys and girls, are also preyed upon by armies and guerrilla forces that forcibly conscript them to kill and die.[63]

If all of these consequences are the "essential purpose" of militarization, it is hard to see how participating in it can be liberating for women or men. We still confront the problem of analyzing the recurring linkages between masculinity/violence and femininity/passivity. Judith Hicks Stiehm argued that achieving gender parity in the U.S. armed forces might ultimately force an acknowledgment that war is not "manly" and that women can protect themselves.[64] On this view, women's equal participation might destabilize the ways in which the gendered division of violence and the gender inequality upon which it rests contribute to militarization. However, given the historical patterns during periods of both force increases and force reductions, gender parity seems an unlikely development in any state military. Indeed, even as state militaries are more engaged in the "caretaking" work of peacekeeping, D'Amico finds that the U.S. military, in particular, has largely eschewed this role because "militarized masculinity requires battle glory, not a 'relationship' or long-term commitment."[65]

Moreover, as state militaries begin to privatize many of their functions, we find two further factors mitigating against gender parity in military service. On the one hand, force reductions in the U.S. military, for example, involve shifting clerical and administrative tasks to private contractors, thus reducing the need for female military personnel who are traditionally assigned these duties.[66] On the other hand, large numbers of male military officers and soldiers released from state militaries due to force reductions are creating, in essence, private security forces that offer "military training and related assistance to foreign governments at the bidding of the United States."[67] As Ken Silverstein observes, "[T]he use of private military contractors allows the United States to pursue its geopolitical interests without deploying its own army, this being especially useful in cases where training is provided to regimes with ghastly records on human rights."[68] Such contracting also ensures that the "real" business of war will be kept largely in male hands and remain "manly," regardless of whether state militaries become more "feminized."

Other feminists have pointed out that although comparatively few women are or will be soldiers on the battlefront, many more serve the military on the homefront. "By the mid-1980s, there were an estimated

232,000 women of all racial groups working for American defense contractors."[69] Although the U.S. "military procurement budget, which pays
for new weapons, fell from a peak of $97 billion in 1985 to $44 billion" in
1998,[70] huge contractors, such as Boeing, Raytheon, and Lockheed, still
rely on the cheap labor of women to assemble weapons. One could argue
that this labor contributes more to life-taking than do individual male
and female soldiers on the battlefront.

War has never been an exclusively male enterprise. It depends significantly on female labor, often that of working-class women of color, who
represent over one-third of all enlisted women in the U.S. armed forces.[71]
Add to this the "support" work of millions of military wives, nurses, prostitutes, and defense workers and we begin to see how militaries are dependent on women. The gendered division of violence, however, continues to
obscure this fact through the mechanism of sexism (as well as racism and
classism). In fact, it is the gendered division of violence that separates men
and women into "Just Warriors" who protect and "Beautiful Souls" who
are protected,[72] thus pressing both men and women into serving the
world's militaries in respectively gendered ways. This, in turn, prevents
women and men from questioning the essential purpose and the negative
effects of war, militarization, and violence on their own and others' lives.

LABOR: ECONOMIC ISSUES

Gendered divisions of labor both produce and are produced by stereotypes
of what activities—and corresponding identities—are considered masculine and feminine, and therefore appropriate for men and women. As noted
earlier, gender stereotypes and dichotomies are promulgated by dualistic
categories favored in economic analysis: paid-unpaid work, production-
reproduction, skilled-unskilled, formal-informal. These interact with
other gendered dichotomies that shape how we think about work:
"men's work"–"women's work," labor for profit–labor for love, working-
caretaking, breadwinner-housewife, and family wage earner–"pin money"
wage earner. But for the most part, these divisions are recent. Prior to modern state-making and industrial capitalism, rigid dichotomies were less familiar, and divisions of labor were not codified in strictly male versus female terms. Rather, all able-bodied family and community members were
expected to contribute, and work was a much more communal activity.
"Economics" was not separate from "politics" or "family relations."[73] In
short, the division into public and private spheres was less developed. In
this context, although specific tasks might be gender-coded, the particular
coding has varied greatly over time and across cultures (planting, harvest-

ing, leading discussion, sewing, brewing, and so on, might be the domain of women or men, depending on time and place).

This flexibility is documented in anthropological studies of such diverse, pre-Western-contact cultures as the Igbo of Nigeria, the Hawaiians, and some Native American civilizations, where divisions of labor were fairly elastic.[74] Women participated in productive labor, such as agriculture, creation of artifacts, and trade, and were often allowed to own land and amass wealth in their own right. In addition, women's reproductive functions translated into religious and political authority in many pre-Christian cultures that perceived women's fertility as powerful and sacred. Some women in precolonial cultures became warriors when they had no children or had passed childbearing age. In such cultures, men also transgressed what we, in the "modern" West, have come to define as traditional gender roles. Under conditions of relative equality and elasticity of gender roles, gendered divisions of labor were perceived as complementary, in the sense that those tasks that were gender segregated were viewed as equally valuable to the life of the society.

European state-making, the growth of capitalism, and subsequent Western colonization must be understood as interactive processes. They tend to overlap in institutionalizing more rigid, less equal, and, thus, less complementary conceptions of how labor should be divided between the sexes, between classes, and between nations. This has not totally undermined alternative, more flexible notions of the work that men and women perform, but a more unitary, global, gendered division of labor based on the Western model has emerged in what is now a world capitalist system. In the latter framework, the division of women's and men's work is rooted firmly in patriarchal conceptions of women's and men's "nature" that are inextricable from a liberal-capitalist model of state-based society. Most Western political theorists, from the ancient Greeks to the Enlightenment philosophers, assumed that women's childbearing capacities not only made them more fit for the reproductive work of child care and work in the home, but also made them unfit for the productive labor of business, commerce, and governance occurring outside the home. Moreover, although a few of these theorists saw reproductive work as important to sustaining the good society and the good polity, most viewed productive work as far more important and higher in status. Similarly, they argued that men, who were not identified with the supposedly emotional and irrational realm of biological reproduction, were more fit for high-status work in the economy and the polity. Often displacing more "complementary" arrangements, the Western gendered division of labor set up a rigid separation between women's and men's work and simultaneously devalued women's work.

This rigid separation was justified on the basis of supposedly self-evident "facts" about women's and men's bodies. But this obscures the gender ideology at work, as discussed in earlier chapters—an ideology that projects onto the bodies of men and women a series of fixed and oppositional attributes, traits, and societal positions that have little to do with biology. Indeed, biology itself is never static because bodily functions, abilities, and even meanings change significantly over time in response to different social arrangements and technological interventions. In spite of these fluctuations, the Western gendered division of labor was constructed ideologically and practically on the supposedly "natural" and unchangeable divisions noted above: production-reproduction, public-private, paid-unpaid work, breadwinner-housewife.

Gendered Development

Through colonization, this Western division of labor was imposed on many cultures in the Americas, Asia, and Africa from the fifteenth to the twentieth centuries. As a consequence, the economic status and well-being of many women in diverse cultures around the world were diminished. For example, in her classic study, *Woman's Role in Economic Development*, Ester Boserup found that prior to colonization, farming in many African countries was almost exclusively women's work, and men were largely responsible for clearing fields, hunting, and warfare.[75] Western colonizers first usurped African men's traditional roles by controlling land and then attempted to make these now "lazy African men" engage in farming, which, under Western gender stereotypes, was viewed as men's work.[76] This process involved a systematic transferal of land rights from women to men in many African countries (as shown in Figure 4.6). It also ensured that predominately men, who were deemed heads of households, were schooled in Western agricultural techniques and provided with Western agricultural technologies and access to credit.[77]

This is not to suggest that colonizing practices were generally beneficial to most African and other colonized men. In the wake of Western colonization, many indigenous peoples, both women and men, lost access to ancestral lands for farming and hunting. Giving some men titles to small plots of land not usurped by Western plantation owners and turning men as well as women into farm laborers (either as slaves or minimally paid workers) did not mean **empowerment** (enhanced capacity) for colonized men. However, colonized women became even more marginalized, relative to colonized men, under patriarchal colonial rule. As Gita Sen and Caren Grown observed, "The colonial period created and accentuated inequalities both 'among' nations, and between classes and genders (also castes, ethnic communities, races, etc.) 'within' nations."[78]

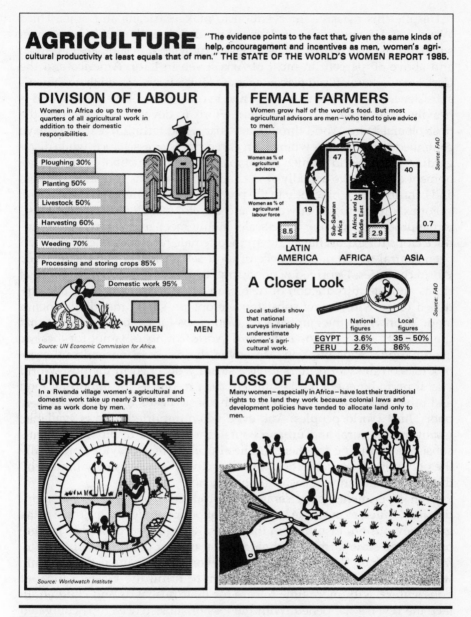

AGRICULTURE

"The evidence points to the fact that, given the same kinds of help, encouragement and incentives as men, women's agricultural productivity at least equals that of men." THE STATE OF THE WORLD'S WOMEN REPORT 1985.

DIVISION OF LABOUR

Women in Africa do up to three quarters of all agricultural work in addition to their domestic responsibilities.

Ploughing 30%

Planting 50%

Livestock 50%

Harvesting 60%

Weeding 70%

Processing and storing crops 85%

Domestic work 95%

WOMEN   MEN

Source: UN Economic Commission for Africa.

FEMALE FARMERS

Women grow half of the world's food. But most agricultural advisors are men – who tend to give advice to men.

Women as % of agricultural advisors

Women as % of agricultural labour force

Source: FAO

LATIN AMERICA — 8.5, 19

AFRICA — Sub-Saharan Africa 47, N. Africa and Middle East 25, 2.9

ASIA — 40, 0.7

A Closer Look

Local studies show that national surveys invariably underestimate women's agricultural work.

Source: FAO

	National figures	Local figures
EGYPT	3.6%	35 – 50%
PERU	2.6%	86%

UNEQUAL SHARES

In a Rwanda village women's agricultural and domestic work take up nearly 3 times as much time as work done by men.

Source: Worldwatch Institute

LOSS OF LAND

Many women – especially in Africa – have lost their traditional rights to the land they work because colonial laws and development policies have tended to allocate land only to men.

FIGURE 4.6   Gendered Development Policies. This series of charts shows how much agricultural work women perform in the Third World, often with the least amount of time and resources. From Jeanne Vickers, *Women and the World Economic Crisis* (London: Zed Books, 1991), p. 21. Courtesy of the United Nations, "State of the World's Women 1985."

Despite this massive intervention to make Africans and other Third World peoples conform to the Western gendered division of labor, women still perform up to 80 percent of all agricultural labor in sub-Saharan Africa and above 50 percent in most of Asia. Even in Latin America and the Caribbean, where official percentages are lower, it is believed that women's subsistence agricultural work there and in other parts of the Third World is heavily underreported.[79] Yet Western efforts to develop or modernize the postcolonial Third World through aid, loans, and technical assistance have continued to favor landowning men as recipients of assistance, while disregarding Third World women's vital role in food production. In fact, development efforts have actually worsened the conditions of female farmers and contributed significantly to the problem of world hunger.

For example, studies of women and development[80] indicate that Western approaches stressing large-scale, highly mechanized farming to produce crops for export have undermined female farming systems that had been central to the maintenance of food self-sufficiency in many Third World countries. Deprived of good, arable land through their loss of land rights and the introduction of cash crops, female farmers have been reduced to growing a few subsistence crops on small, marginal plots of land. Meanwhile, the emphasis on cash crops for export has meant that the majority of food grown in Third World countries is not for local or even national consumption. Moreover, the prices of agricultural commodities on the world market have steadily declined in the post–World War II period, generating insufficient cash resources for importing food and other goods necessary to serve the basic needs of vast numbers of poor Third World peoples. And even when imported food is available, impoverished rural and urban people cannot afford to buy it. Women's subsistence farming for their families in rural areas provides practically the only relief from starvation, yet this activity is increasingly limited by the use of more land for cash crop production.

Even experiments to accelerate food production for national consumption have failed to meet the basic needs of poor people. An example is the **green revolution,** instituted in the 1960s, which relied on highly mechanized, large-scale farming techniques that further displaced subsistence-farming women.[81] Architects of this revolution assumed that moving women off the land would enable them to fulfill the Western ideal of housewifery, with more time to care for their husbands and children. In fact, the reverse happened. With the loss of subsistence crops cultivated by women to feed their families, women were forced into working on "green revolution" farms to supplement their husbands' income so their families could purchase sufficient food. Thus, women's extra household labor increased. Not only were they responsible for reproductive work and whatever subsistence farming they could carry out, but they also became wage laborers, in effect working a triple day, in contrast to men's single responsibility to earn a wage.

The imbalance between women's and men's work was also exacerbated by the urbanization and industrialization resulting from Western approaches to Third World development. Western development agencies assumed that Third World countries could modernize only by following the general pattern of growth in the West—that is, of moving from an agrarian to an industrial economy. Thus, Western-funded development projects in the Third World focused on building large-scale industrial and urban infrastructures often at the expense of developing the agricultural sector. As a result, food was lacking in the cities, where populations were swelling because of the influx mainly of men from rural areas who had left the land in search of more jobs and higher wages.

Most men who migrated to the cities did not make enough money to be the breadwinners for wives and children left behind in rural areas, who in turn had to try to survive through marginalized subsistence farming. Often this situation led to men's abandonment of their families, producing a significant rise in the number of poor, female-headed households. By the early 1990s, one-third of the households in the world were headed by women, and the highest numbers of these were in the Third World (reaching more than 40 percent in parts of Africa and the Caribbean).[82] This systematic impoverishment of rural women and their children produced a marked deterioration in nutrition and health, undermining even further the ability of women to meet basic needs for themselves and their children.

By the 1970s, Western development agencies had begun to recognize the heavy costs of neglecting and even undermining women's roles in the development process. These agencies began to shift their focus from industrial projects to "basic needs" assistance programs, dealing with nutrition, health, housing, education, and home-based income generation. These focused not just on "productive" labor but also on "reproductive" labor and led to the creation of Women in Development (WID) and, later, Gender and Development (GAD) policies and programs within, for example, the U.S. Agency for International Development (USAID), the UN Development Programme (UNDP), the World Bank, and such private agencies as the Ford Foundation. A study of these agencies' performance through the 1980s, in terms of providing direct assistance to women or integrating women into development projects, revealed a very uneven and disappointing record. Nuket Kardam finds that development agencies are, for the most part, not interested in empowering women, but only with providing them, minimally and unevenly, with "welfare and access."[83] In effect, they generally resisted doing anything that might disrupt the gendered division of labor that privileges productive work over reproductive work, that assumes women perform only reproductive

work (which itself is viewed as unimportant to the growth and sustena-
tion of a nation's economy), and, thus, that keeps many women impoverished and relatively powerless. A 1997 World Bank report on its own
progress on mainstreaming gender concerns and actions into its projects
over the preceding three years found that the number of projects that had
such components constituted only 30 percent of the Bank's investment
portfolio over that period, down from 45–50 percent of its projects in the
early 1990s.[84] By its own admission, "integration of gender concerns into
the Bank is not yet systematic" and remains "vulnerable" despite Bank
policy that "gender issues are economic and social issues" and as such,
should "permeate all aspects of the Bank's work."[85]

Gendered Globalization

Unfortunately, whatever gains have been made in getting public and private development lending agencies to begin to recognize the importance
of gender issues to economic development are being eroded as a result of
almost two decades of **structural adjustment programs (SAPs)** instituted
in many Third World countries by the IMF and the overarching process of
globalization, the effects of which have become most visible worldwide
in the 1990s. The institution of SAPs has been in response to the **debt crisis,** which arose in the early 1980s and continues to wreak havoc in the
world economy. The origins and nature of this crisis will not be described
here, but its net effects, negative economic growth in most of the developing world and disruptions of the economies of many developed countries, have been especially injurious to women—particularly poor women
in the Third World. Already suffering significant reductions in real income and employment as a result of the worldwide recession that reduced the price of commodity exports, poor and working-class people in
the Third World faced even harsher treatment when their governments
were forced to accept IMF structural adjustment or austerity programs in
order to qualify for more development loans. Essentially, such programs
require countries to increase productivity and exports while decreasing
government spending on social welfare. Studies show that poor and
working-class Third World women and children bear the brunt of these
policies, which intensify both their labors and their impoverishment
while enabling their governments to make payments on foreign debts.[86]

Globalization, which also has its origins in the unleashing of capitalist
economic forces that brought on the debt crisis, is operating to produce
similar patterns in developed countries, particularly since the end of the
Cold War. Former Soviet-bloc countries, also under pressure from Western governments and lending agencies, have instituted "shock therapy"
programs designed by Western economists to quickly turn socialist

economies into capitalist ones. As with SAPs, these programs drastically cut and/or privatize government services while also privatizing production to increase productivity, exports, and foreign direct investment. And again, working-class women in these countries are disproportionately bearing the costs of this as they face "growing unemployment and the loss of benefits and social protection such as health care, maternity leave and child care facilities."[87] Western countries are also treating themselves with what they have prescribed for others in order to reduce budget deficits and increase economic competitiveness. A mixture of neoliberal and neoconservative policies are cutting and/or privatizing social welfare programs, weakening unions, and restructuring the workforce to produce a lean and mean management system, a smaller core of permanent employees, and a vast pool of temporary, part-time, or contract workers.[88] Women are concentrated in this latter sector of **flexibilized** or **casualized labor,** which provides no job security, few or no benefits, and few regulatory protections with respect to wages and health and safety. Moreover, as social services are slashed, reproductive labor is made even more demanding because women must take on caretaking tasks for which the public sector is abandoning responsibility.

Some women are not disadvantaged by economic restructuring processes, such as women whose knowledge base, skill level, access to credit, management style, and/or social class (as well as racial privilege) enable them to compete in or gain some benefits from the global economy. Moreover, many men, especially in the working class, have lost ground as once high-paid manufacturing jobs are disappearing due to automation and the relocation of assembly plants to areas of the world with cheap, nonunionized labor. Nevertheless, at a time when "85 percent of the world's income is concentrated in the richest 20 percent of the world's people,"[89] women make up the bulk of those who are economically marginalized in both the South and the North. In fact, economic restructuring *depends* upon this economic marginalization, for without the cheap productive and unremunerated reproductive labor that the gendered division of labor assigns to women, it would not be possible for corporations and governments to promote such an unsustainable and inequitable approach to economic growth. As we shall see in the following examples of women's roles in the global economy, women's work "makes the world go round,"[90] but in ways that rarely benefit women.

Sexual Work

Prostitution, which has always been present officially or unofficially around military bases, has now taken the form of big business by being tied to the most lucrative industry in the global economy—international tourism. Jan Jindy Pettman refers to this conjunction between sexual services and economic development as "the international political economy of sex," which "operates in terms of demand—in sex tourism and militarised prostitution—and supply—including the impact of development and restructuring, rural impoverishment and urban unemployment, the low status of women, and poor states' search for foreign exchange."[91] Sex tourism was adopted as a form of economic development in Thailand in the 1970s. In Bangkok alone, more than 250 hotels routinely offered prostitutes to their guests in 1978, and conservative estimates in 1980 indicated that approximately 3 percent of all Thai women were engaged in some kind of prostitution.[92] Tragically, the percentage of children and teenage girls was double this amount. The labor of these women and children is used to provide sexual services to European, North American, and Japanese businessmen and to male tourists, who constituted 73 percent of international visitors to Thailand in 1986.[93] Although some prostitutes working for escort services and massage parlors can make far more than the average semi-skilled woman, the larger number of women and children who work the streets and go-go bars make considerably less than highly paid prostitutes. For the most vulnerable, prostitution may take the form of indentured service.[94] Those who really control and reap the most profits from prostitution are men in the Thai military and police forces, male owners of local and transnational hotel chains, male pimps, and men who run international sexual-slave-trade operations. In 1984, as many as 16,000 Thai prostitutes were "exported" to Japan, Europe, and the Middle East because of the demand for their "special" services.[95]

What makes Thai and other Southeast Asian prostitutes valuable commodities on the world market is a facet of the gendered division of labor. Western gender ideology is infused with racist categorizations that assign different types of "natures" to different types of men and women. In the area of sexuality, white women are construed as prudish and almost asexual, and black women (and men) are seen as wild and even oversexed. Asian women, however, have been marketed as "perfect" sexual playthings for Western or Westernized men. They are described as childlike and virginal and, thus, as appropriately submissive and nonthreatening; yet they are also presented as extremely responsive and sexually experienced. The combination suggests that Asian women want only to please men and, moreover, know how to do it. This ideology "naturalizes" Asian prostitution, effectively hiding the coercive processes of poverty, the state, international capital, and militarization that sentence so many women to the occupation.

Asian women, however, are not the only women now swelling the ranks of the global sex trade. As more and more women are left unemployed or underemployed and governments become more desperate for foreign investment and exchange as a result of SAPs in the South and "shock therapy" programs in the East, sex tourism and sex trafficking have become truly "multinational" enterprises.

> The geographic origins of the women and girls trafficked into Europe have shifted over the past three decades as the global sex industry has made inroads into new parts of the world. During the 1970s, women trafficked into the brothels of Europe were primarily from East Asia, especially Thailand and the Philippines. The roots of this wave of trafficking were the organized prostitution around United States military bases in Vietnam and the Clark and Subic air bases in the Philippines. The 1980s witnessed an influx of women and girls trafficked into Europe's brothels from Latin America and the Caribbean, especially the Dominican Republic, Brazil, and Columbia, but also Ecuador and Chile.
>
> The most recent wave of sexual trafficking involves women transported into Europe from the former Soviet Union and into Western Europe from Eastern Europe.[96]

Prostitution in many parts of Russia has become so widespread, due to women's falling incomes in legal occupations and the rise of organized crime in the context of economic chaos, that government officials in many cities are calling for its legalization in order to collect taxes from it and conduct health examinations to try to stem the huge increases in sexually transmitted diseases.[97] Whether legalized or not, the sex industry has become a major pillar of the global economy, erected literally on the bodies of women.

Domestic Work

In the context of a more globalized economy, migration has swelled to unprecedented levels in the past two decades, with "some 45 to 50 million people 'on the move' internationally each year," half of whom are women.[98] Many of these women are migrating to perform domestic work as part of what has been dubbed the "international maid trade." For Third World women who enter this trade in order to make an income for their families and to service their countries' foreign debts, the largest markets for their work usually lie in places such as North America, Europe, and the Middle East, where there are substantial numbers of middle- and upper-class families. Poor Asian countries such as the Philippines, Indonesia, and Sri Lanka had exported at least 1 million domestic workers to Hong Kong, Singapore, Malaysia, and the Gulf states by 1994.[99] Central and South American states also export maids primarily to North America.

The international maid trade is "a multimillion-dollar transnational business which is closely related to other agencies that facilitate the migration process, such as banks, money-lenders, hotels, airlines, illegal money-changers, translation services, medical clinics, and training institutions," all of which profit far more than the domestic worker whose weekly wages average only about US$100.[100] This trade in cheap domestic labor is also economically beneficial for the sending country and the host families, but domestic workers themselves typically face multiple hardships that include separation from their children; loneliness and homesickness; lack of control over earnings that they send home; religious and familial pressures to migrate for money, "behave" while away, and conform to traditional customs upon return; and sexual abuse by their employers, against whom they usually have no recourse as noncitizens in foreign countries.[101] Thus, the gendered division of labor operates to produce domestic servants who will remain subservient wherever they go.

Domestic and sexual services have also reached new heights of commodification through the multimillion-dollar transnational mail-order bride industry. It is estimated that there are now up to 250 companies in the United States that specialize in marketing women primarily from Asia, Latin America, and, more recently, Russia and Eastern Europe as potential wives for American men, who pay up to $15,000 for these companies' services. One such company advertises 3,500 women on its website and portrays "Russian women as 'traditional' and 'family-oriented,' untainted by Western feminism,'" thus playing "to men's desires for women who are white—yet exotic."[102] This patriarchal (and racist) desire for subservient wives constitutes the "pull factor," and the economic desperation of women in the South and East produces the "push factor," which make this highly exploitative and lucrative industry possible. And like other domestic and sexual services industries, it is proving quite dangerous to women as cases of battering and murder by unsatisfied male consumers (who are not screened for histories of abuse by "introduction" agencies) mount up.[103] This outcome should come as no surprise to an industry that thrives on promoting gender inequality and oppression.

Informal Work

Various forms of sexual and domestic work constitute only part of what is referred to as the **informal sector,** which includes a whole range of legal and extralegal economic activities that lie largely "outside national accounting, labour legislation, and social protection" mandates and are typically performed in the contexts of self-employment, family businesses, and insecure wage work.[104] As we have seen, informal work is "directly linked to the consumption and production of the so-called formal sector" consisting of more secure, protected, and officially counted wage labor.[105] It is estimated in the 1990s that the informal sector contributes between 12 and 51 percent to total production in Third World countries,[106] accounts for 40 to 66 percent of Third World urban employment, and is a growing feature of industrialized economies.[107] The sheer size and growing economic significance of this sector has led many to question why it is devalued by the label *informal*. The fact that women are more often found working in this sector "because of lack of opportunities or other obstacles to wage employment"[108] offers one explanation for this devaluation.

The most prevalent forms of women's informal work, beyond sex and domestic service, are "petty" trading of mostly small, inexpensive commodities ranging from vegetables to handicrafts and subcontracted, home-based piecework. Such work has become vital to the survival of poor and working-class families as wages in the formal sector have plummeted due to SAPs and other forms of economic restructuring. Although there is a long tradition of strong and independent "market women" in West Africa and parts of the Caribbean who wield power in open-air market settings and make good incomes from their work as traders, many more women make supplementary incomes as street vendors for male merchants who control the market. These women are often subjected to sexual and police harassment as well as to merchant exploitation, and typically have to hand over their incomes to their husbands.

Home-based piecework, or "homework," although usually associated with the early industrial development and assumed to be a thing of the past, is, in fact, on the rise the world over in the age of globalization. This increase is attributable to several factors: corporate desires to cut labor and overhead costs by "outsourcing" production tasks, such as sewing and light assembly work, that can be performed by subcontracted laborers in their homes anywhere in the world; large pools of migrant and immigrant workers who are drawn into homework because of racist/sexist discrimination and restrictive immigration laws that prevent them from working in the formal sector; and increasing pressures on women to make money to support their families, despite a lack of access to child care.[109] The same factors are also associated with the reappearance of "sweatshops" in the North as well as the South, where (immigrant) women and children toil at sewing machines, under unsafe and "hidden" conditions, to produce designer-label clothing.

Women currently constitute about 90 percent of all homeworkers,[110] and their work is arduous, isolating, and poorly paid. Consider the 100,000 to 200,000 lace makers of Narsapur, India, who "work 6–8 hour days for an average payment equal to 19 percent of the minimum wage for women" in India. Male traders and exporters have become rich selling this handicraft on the world market.[111] The gendered division of labor has ensured that these lace makers are viewed and view themselves as "housewives" rather than as "workers," and their labor is not even counted in their country's official statistics.[112]

The increasing reliance of the formal economy on the informal economy to produce goods and services under poor working conditions and at extremely low pay rates begins to explain why it is that, at a time when women are entering the formal workforce in record numbers, the global phenomenon of the "feminization of poverty" is increasing.

Formal Work

The **feminization of poverty** is strongly linked to the **feminization of labor.** Although the former refers to the exceptionally high numbers of (especially Third World and minority) women within the ranks of the poor, the latter has several dimensions. On one level, the feminization of labor means that there is now a preference for women workers in a globalized economy. As a result of the decline in heavy manufacturing (at least in the West) and the increase in high-technology, information-based industries (a process that is variously referred to as de- or post-industrialization or post-Fordism), service and light-industry jobs are the fastest-growing occupations in the world economy. Women are in high demand to fill these positions, which, whether in the formal or informal economy, are typically low paying, nonunionized, and relatively unregulated in terms of health and safety requirements. Gender stereotypes account for why women are sought for these jobs. Through them, women are perceived as particularly compliant workers who need only make "pin money" to supplement their families' income. Although many women are the sole support of their families and have been active in agitating for better working conditions, the ideology of the gendered division of labor is used to rationalize the use of women as cheap labor. This ideology also typically construes women as either unskilled or particularly good at detail work that requires manual dexterity, thereby "ghettoizing" them into pink-collar service occupations, light-industry assembly work, or "sweatshop" jobs. The rise of these occupations has translated into increasing rates of female labor-force participation but, as shown in Figure 4.7, has not necessarily led to livable wages for women and their families.

A second meaning of the feminization of labor relates to the degradation of work, reduction in incomes, and decline of labor unions in the formal sector—processes that affect both women and men. The informalization of once-formal jobs discussed earlier is deeply implicated in these processes. Responsible, too, is trade liberalization. Since the 1980s, neoliberals have touted "free trade" as the "way to foster economic growth by internationalizing domestic economies."[113] One result has been a spate of

Doonesbury   BY GARRY TRUDEAU

FIGURE 4.7 "Doing It" for Nike. This is just one of a series of cartoons in this well-known strip that highlights the poor working conditions of women in Nike factories in Asia. Reprinted with special permission of Universal Press Syndicate.

free trade agreements, ranging from the completion of the Uruguay Round under the General Agreement on Tariffs and Trade (GATT) and the creation of the World Trade Organization (WTO) to a series of regional trade compacts such as the North American Free Trade Agreement (NAFTA). Another result has been the formation of the European Union (EU), which goes beyond the much earlier formation of the European Economic Community by integrating member countries not just economically but also politically and monetarily.

Free trade agreements require countries to substantially reduce all tariff and nontariff trade barriers to open up their economies to foreign competition on the assumption that the most efficient industries will survive and pass on lower prices to consumers. But the costs of this for workers (and for the environment, which we will discuss in the next section) can be quite high. These costs include the loss of jobs when "inefficient" businesses close down or move elsewhere for cheaper labor to better compete; the loss of workplace protections such as those provided by health and safety regulations, which can be either construed as nontariff barriers to be done away with in the name of foreign competition or relaxed to cut domestic business costs to better enable them to compete; and the loss of income when wages are cut as companies "race to the bottom" in order to compete with one another.[114]

Although this competition negatively affects many working-class (and even some middle-class) men and benefits some women who work in sectors that are the "winners," an even larger number of women are the biggest "losers." Women workers are concentrated in the sectors made most vulnerable by trade liberalization: "clerical, service, retail, textiles and light manufacturing."[115] **Free trade zones (FTZs)**—transnational corporation (TNC) manufacturing enclaves, also known as export-processing zones (EPZs) created to escape trade barriers—are notoriously dependent on women's labor. For example, 85 percent of the workers in the world's seventy-nine light-assembly and manufacturing FTZs operating in thirty-five countries in the mid-1980s were women. Pressed to work at a much faster pace and 50 percent more hours than Western workers, these women earned 20 to 50 percent less than men doing comparable work and received as little as 40 cents an hour.[116] As one Mexican worker observed, a person can work in the *maquiladoras,* or Mexico's FTZs, for ten years and still live in abject poverty, complete with cardboard roofs, no electricity or safe drinking water, and little to eat.[117] It is rare, however, that women last ten years working in FTZs. The typical female worker is between sixteen and twenty-five years of age. By the time she reaches her mid-twenties, she is "burnt out" by the pace of the work, the long hours, and the toxic chemicals that are heavily present in such unregulated industries.

She also may be losing her eyesight from the unabated close work required to sew intricate garments or from looking through a microscope for as long as twelve hours a day to assemble microchips (see Figure 4.8). Moreover, during her "productive" years, she will be subjected to sexual harassment by supervisors—"the 'lay down or be laid off' policy"[118]—and will be responsible for supporting and doing the reproductive labor for her family, as a single parent or as a daughter. If she rebels against her lot through labor organizing, she is pressured into submissiveness by her employers, her government, and even her male family members who rely on her for this meager, but often singular, wage.

Despite this high degree of exploitation, women's wages in FTZs are usually higher than the wages made by women (and many men) not working in FTZs in Third World countries. However, two factors further threaten women's access to these wages. First, free trade agreements may eventually make FTZs obsolete, for the very trade barriers that FTZs are set up to circumvent are lessened by such pacts.[119] This would result in massive FTZ job losses for women. Second, a 1997 investigation conducted by the U.S. Labor Department, which was prompted by worker complaints to the WTO, found that in Mexico "thousands of border assembly plants administer medical tests to weed out pregnant applicants and harass pregnant workers to coerce their resignation."[120] This is done to ensure that U.S. corporations that own most of the 2,700 *maquiladora* plants do not have to pay for maternity benefits. Firing and not hiring women because state-mandated maternity benefits are viewed as too costly by corporations are becoming common practices in China and much of Eastern Europe and Russia as well.[121]

A final dimension of the feminization of labor is related to the growth of the financial sector at the expense of the manufacturing sector. As Saskia Sassen observes, "Finance allows superprofits by maximizing the

FIGURE 4.8   Women on the Global Assembly Line. Shown here are workers in a *maquiladora* in Tijuana, Mexico. Photos courtesy of the American Friends Service Committee. Photographer: Gary Massoni.

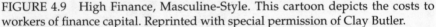

FIGURE 4.9   High Finance, Masculine-Style. This cartoon depicts the costs to workers of finance capital. Reprinted with special permission of Clay Butler.

circulation of money (e.g., securitization, multiple transactions over a short period of time, selling debts, etc.) in a way that manufacturing does not."[122] Thus, investments are increasingly used for market speculation and drawn away from the production of jobs and goods (see Figure 4.9). It is also creating a new class of cosmopolitan elites who rely on low-paid service labor to sustain their jet-setting lifestyles. This situation is resulting in a new twist on the gendered division of labor:

> Westernized men and women—e.g., executives, managers, bankers, investors—are given the masculinized traits of autonomy, authority, resourcefulness, and control. Traditionalised men and women—e.g., waiters/waitresses, hotel staff, airline attendants, peasants, hawkers, guides—are assigned the feminized characteristics of dependency, contingency, subsistence, and subservience. They are qualified only to serve or barter, not to compete with or dominate, others.[123]

In short, the gendered division of labor ensures that the restructuring of the world economy, which reaps huge profits for the international elite at the expense of the vast majority of the world's population, is made possible, in large measure, by the superexploitation of poor and working-class women. Moreover, the rise of globalization is putting into sharp relief how deadly the intertwining of the gendered divisions of violence, labor, and resources can be for women, children, men, and the planet.

RESOURCES: EQUITY AND ECOLOGY ISSUES

At first glance, the issue of the use and abuse of the global environment and its natural resources seems to have nothing to do with gender. At one level, it can be argued that all human beings have an impact on the natural environment and that all human beings are affected by the degradation of the environment by "man-made" pollution. At another level, we have come to think of natural resources as the property of states (and corporations), whose relative power in the international system depends upon the extent of the resources under their control and their ability to both exploit and preserve them for economic purposes. Through these lenses, there is no room for seeing or thinking about what we call the gendered division of resources. However, if we look more closely at the way in which resources are divided within and between states, which resources are valued, how resources are used and by whom, and where pollution is most concentrated, we begin to see gendered patterns. Looking still deeper, we also begin to see that the very relationship that "man" has with nature in the late twentieth century throughout the world has been formed, in part, by a Western (neoliberal and capitalist) gender ideology that is becoming increasingly global and quite harmful to the earth and its inhabitants.

The Indian physicist and ecofeminist Vandana Shiva argued that before the rise of Western colonization and Western science, indigenous peoples throughout the world had close and relatively harmonious relationships with the natural world, viewing it as sacred and alive with spirituality.[124] Typically, natural forces were seen as feminine because they represented to these cultures the generative power of fertility and birth. Many of these pre- or non-Christian cultures worshiped female deities who were embodied in all manner of natural objects, ranging from volcanoes and bodies of water to trees and animals. What Shiva called the **feminine principle** ensured that people used, but did not abuse, the natural environment. In fact, the "feminine principle" was itself a reflection of women's particular relationship with nature through the productive and reproductive work they performed in these cultures. Not only did women bring new life into the world through childbirth, but they were also responsible for gathering and cultivating the staple foods consumed for the perpetuation of life.

As we noted earlier, in many places the rise of Western colonization undermined communal land use and women's land rights. This disrupted carefully balanced and ecologically sound relationships between peoples and their lands. In addition, the rise of Western science transformed peoples' notions of nature, and a worldview that saw nature strictly as a resource for "man-made" projects replaced belief systems in which nature was revered as the manifestation of divinity. Early Western science, coupled with Christian ideology, turned the feminine principle upside down. Nature was still thought of as feminine; but rather than powerful and goddesslike, nature was seen as a passive resource from which men could take anything they needed or wanted without care for the effects of their interventions. This reversal in gender ideology and environmental thinking paved the way for rapacious land-use patterns and technologies, which have led to numerous ecological crises since the advent of the industrial revolution.[125] Western gender ideology construes nature as a passive resource to be controlled, used, and even abused. As this ideology has become increasingly widespread, environmental crises have followed, ranging from the problems of acid rain and global dumping to ozone depletion and global warming.

Gender ideology is by no means the sole cause of these problems, but if we look through the lens of the gendered division of resources, we see that gender ideology contributes to the growth and perpetuation of these problems. Although there are still cultures that retain some reverence for the feminine principle of nature, the increasingly global aspects of the gendered division of resources rest upon the following dualisms: culture-nature, active-passive, subject-object, users-resources, advanced-primitive, and exploitation-stewardship. These dualisms are manifested in the contemporary situation, where women have a great deal of responsibility for caring for the environment but little say in how it will be used and for what purposes.

Gendered Resource Depletion

Denying women any appreciable role in decision-making about use of the environment has led directly to what Gita Sen and Caren Grown call the **food-fuel-water crises** in the rural areas of the Third World.[126] These crises result from resource depletion that threatens the survival of people in subsistence economies. Women's displacement from the land by large-scale agricultural development for export has contributed to high levels of famine, particularly in Africa. But there are additional consequences of this displacement, contributing not only to continued hunger but also to deforestation and desertification. Women are the main food producers and processors in most of the rural areas of the Third World, and they must have access to clean water and firewood for fuel. As their land is lost to corporate farms and as water sources are polluted by agricultural runoff from fertilizers and pesticides, rural women are forced to travel farther and farther in search of clean water, sometimes as far as twenty kilometers (about twelve and one-half miles) from their home. Because the amount they can carry is limited, they may have to fetch water several times a day, adding more hours to their hard labor to sustain the meager diets of their families (see Figure 4.10).

Similarly, as forests are cut down for large-scale agricultural enterprises, women must go farther afield to look for the firewood needed to cook and to boil water, making it safe to drink. When water and fuel sources are being depleted, not only does food become scarce, but also the basis for ecologically sound agricultural practices is eroded. First, female subsistence farmers are forced to cultivate small plots of land over and over again rather than engage in crop rotation. This depletes vital soil nutrients and can eventually even lead to small-scale desertification. Large-scale desertification is the result of the overuse of crop lands by corporate farmers who do not rotate crops, and who overwater and salinate the soil and/or grow crops using methods that destroy fragile topsoil.

Second, when the soil is too depleted to produce crops, rural populations are reduced to consuming the seeds for future crops, destroying their capability to produce their own food. Another alternative is to seek food, as well as fuel and water, farther away from their homes. This pushes rural peoples into marginal and therefore sensitive ecosystems, even conservation areas and parks. Different interests motivate poor rural peoples, who have few alternatives for survival in the short term, and ecologists, who take the longer view toward saving the environment but who do not work on remedies for the unequal distribution of land and resources that forces poor people to seek food, fuel, and water in protected areas.

This unequal distribution of land and resources arises not just from class status but also from gender divisions in a world in which women own only 1 percent of the land. The Western assumption that women are not farmers has led both to the loss of women's land rights and to the failure to provide technological assistance to women who work the land. As we have learned from the unforeseen consequences of high-technology experiments such as the green revolution, not all technology is good or appropriate for every socioeconomic and environmental context. Development mistakes (mistakes for the large number of people impoverished by them) might have been avoided if women, who are the most reliable "natural resource managers," had been consulted about how best to use the land and what technologies are most appropriate.[127]

Most women agricultural workers are not formally educated in modern, Western agricultural techniques. However, they work closely with and on the land and have developed significant informal knowledge

FIGURE 4.10   Gendered Ecology. (*top*) This photo of a Chadian refugee woman in Sudan shows how deforestation results from pushing people off their land. UNHCR/S. Errington. (*bottom*) A view of a workers' shantytown outside a *maquiladora* in Tijuana, Mexico, shows the degraded environment in which women workers and their families must live as a result of the industrial pollution surrounding these "homes." Photo courtesy of the American Friends Service Committee. Photographer: Diane Shandor.

about ecosystems and appropriate land-use patterns. As farmers, women often know which plants have the most nutritional value and what forms of cultivation lead to the least soil erosion and water consumption. As traditional healers, women often know which plants have medicinal value and what practices sustain the biodiversity of an ecosystem to ensure that such healing vegetation is preserved. As fuel gatherers, women know they are dependent on forests to provide renewable sources of firewood.[128] International and national development planners and agencies that ignore women's knowledge and introduce inappropriate technologies can do much more harm than good.

Globalization forces are constituting an even more serious threat to ecological sustainability and biodiversity as capitalist expansion spreads industries and enterprises into areas that previously were untouched by economic development. Trade liberalization policies, such as Trade-Related Intellectual Property Rights (TRIPs) that were codified in the most recent GATT agreement, are essentially allowing transnational pharmaceutical companies to take out patents on seeds and plants that may be used in the industrial production of medical drugs. Shiva argues that, because "intellectual property rights are recognized only as private rights," which exclude "all kinds of knowledge, ideas, and innovations that take place in the 'intellectual commons,'" such as "in villages among farmers and in forests among tribals," rural women, who most often are the custodians of seeds and plants for community medicinal use, not only lose control over these plant materials but also are dispossessed of their knowledge as profit-making enterprises monopolize how this material will be used.[129] The privatization of even genetic materials undermines both public accountability for how the earth and living things on it are used (and abused) and women's capacity for developing more sustainable practices.

Gendered Resource Destruction

Of course, women are not always kind to the environment, especially when they become members of consumer-oriented cultures, which are increasing in number as a result of globalization. Western gender ideology encourages women to adopt a consumer lifestyle through which they can beautify their bodies (according to Western standards), dress fashionably (as defined by male fashion designers), and stock their homes with modern "conveniences" (some of which actually create work). Beauty products are implicated in all manner of ecological harm, ranging from inhumane animal testing of makeup and shampoos to ozone depletion from aerosol spray use. Fur coats are products of the brutal destruction of animals for their pelts. Finally, "keeping up with the Joneses" keeps women (and men) enamored of the idea that they must have more cars, dish-washers, laundry machines, microwaves, refrigerators, and other devices that require much energy to produce and operate, result in a great deal of air and water pollution, and create a significant amount of garbage when they are thrown away to make way for new, improved models.

Whereas middle- and upper-class consumers in "throw-away" societies are heavily implicated in resource waste and environmental pollution, poor and working-class women worldwide suffer the effects of environmental degradation and pollution. The poor and working class are concentrated in crowded and often highly polluted residential areas and largely unregulated, toxic workplaces. For example, women working in Mexico's *maquiladoras* report high levels of illness-causing dust in unventilated garment-industry sweatshops and open trays of cancer-causing chemicals next to them in electronic-industry workrooms.[130] In the rural villages of the Third World, women have the greatest exposure to the harmful gases released from their cookstoves.[131] And given the rise in poor, female-headed households, a large number of women and children live in remote rural areas and urban slums, where toxic-waste dumps are common. This situation occurs frequently in Third World countries that accept toxic refuse from the First World in order to earn foreign exchange. Indeed, Joni Seager reports that there were "at least 1000 attempts to export more than 160 million tons of toxic waste from rich countries to poor since 1986."[132]

Women's reproductive organs are harmed by exposure to industrial toxins in workplaces and residential communities, resulting in ovarian cancer, infertility, miscarriages, and birth defects.[133] Recognition of women's susceptibility to industrial toxins has led to some restrictions on where women are allowed to work. However, data on sterility, cancers, and genetic damage indicate that men's reproductive health is also put at risk by working in toxic environments. This suggests that the gendered solution of barring women from certain workplaces is simply an "industrial protection racket" that draws attention away from polluting industries as the real problem.[134] Similarly, women's reproductive failures have called attention to the hidden effects of nuclear testing and nuclear power plant emissions and accidents. Yet, it is rare that states and industries are held accountable for the extensive reproductive harm and genetic damage their nuclear programs have produced.[135]

Militaries are the worst polluters in the world, according to Seager, who has catalogued the many and extensive harms done to the environment by military installations. This list includes such practices as the production and dumping of toxic wastes from chemical weapons programs, the appropriation of land equal to the size of Turkey in thirteen industrialized countries, the consumption of huge quantities of oil, the emission of large amounts of carbon dioxide and chlorofluorocarbons (CFCs) that cause global warming and ozone depletion, and the destruction of thousands of animals each year in weapons and other tests. The shroud of "national security" in combination with masculine privilege, however, ensures that in "virtually every country, military facilities are exempt from environmental regulations and monitoring requirements."[136] The "war on drugs," too, which the U.S. government uses to justify continuous and widespread spraying of carcinogenic herbicides throughout the countrysides of Central and South America and Southeast Asia, is causing untold numbers of birth defects and reproductive disorders in rural women who live in these areas.[137]

Women as Damaged Resources

Just as women have little control over the systematic poisoning of their bodies, they are also denied choices as to whether or not they will have children. In a world where the global population will reach 8 billion by 2020 if present demographic rates continue, only 57 percent of couples of child-bearing age practice some form of family planning.[138] States, the many men (and a few women) who run them, and various fundamentalist religious groups who enjoy state support must be held accountable for the denial of reproductive rights to women around the world. About 62 percent of the people of the world live in places where access to safe and legal abortion is either severely restricted or not available at all.[139] Even in many developed countries with liberalized abortion laws, there are significant restrictions ensuring that only middle- and upper-class women can afford abortions. The denial of reproductive rights is directly related to environmental and equity issues, most visibly in regard to population pressures and health crises for women.

The World Health Organization estimates that more than 500,000 women die from pregnancy-related causes every year, and 99 percent of those deaths occur in the Third World. Of the approximately 50 million women who have abortions each year, half undergo illegal abortions; and of those women, between 70,000 and 200,000 die from these clandestine operations.[140] For Third World women, the risk of dying from pregnancy-related causes is exponentially greater than that for women in the developed world, as Figure 4.11 illustrates. Clearly, there are significant costs for women, their families, and their societies resulting from the gendered division of resources that denies women reproductive rights and services. In economic terms alone, this denial entails staggering medical, nutritional, and welfare service costs.

For example, by spending $412 million on family-planning services in 1987, the United States saved $1.8 billion in costs associated with danger-

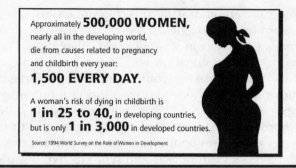

Approximately **500,000 WOMEN,**
nearly all in the developing world,
die from causes related to pregnancy
and childbirth every year:
1,500 EVERY DAY.

A woman's risk of dying in childbirth is
1 in 25 to 40, in developing countries,
but is only **1 in 3,000** in developed countries.

Source: 1994 World Survey on the Role of Women in Development

FIGURE 4.11   Reproductive Health. Childbirth can be deadly when women are denied access to reproductive services, as this graphic depicts. Courtesy of the United Nations Department of Public Information.

ous pregnancies, unsafe abortions, and unwanted children.[141] Such savings are even more critical in the Third World, which has few and overburdened health-care facilities. Freeing up these services from mostly preventable maternity-related illnesses and deaths would translate into more resources for treating other catastrophic illnesses such as AIDS.

Women are now contracting the AIDS virus at a higher rate than any other group, not only in the Third World but also in North America. "WHO projects that by the year 2000, more than 13 million women will have been infected by the AIDS virus, and about four million will have died from it."[142] The gendered divisions of violence, labor, and resources have conspired to make this so, putting young women, especially, at tremendous risk through prostitution, rape, poverty, poor health care, and lack of contraceptive services and "safe sex" education. These factors, along with a host of other health threats to women ranging from domestic violence and female circumcision to forced sterilizations and preferences for male children in many parts of the Third World,[143] have minimized women's power to control their own bodies, making them highly susceptible to contaminants and disease, which they end up passing on to their children, who, in turn, become damaged global "resources."

In short, under the gendered division of resources, women not only have little access to resources that might make their lives longer and easier but also are treated as resources themselves, to be used and abused when it suits the purposes of powerful men, states, and industries. What women need and want is rarely considered in the calculus of how resources are defined, divided, and used. As a result, not just women but the entire planet and its other inhabitants suffer from this far-from-benign neglect.

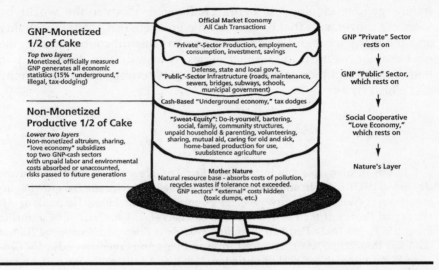

FIGURE 4.12   The Industrial Cake. This graphic of the "Total Productive System of an Industrial Society (Three-Layer Cake with Icing)" depicts how dependent the male-dominated formal economy is on exploitation of women's productive and reproductive labor and on degradation of the planet. Copyright © Hazel Henderson from *Building a Win-Win World* (1991, 1995, Berrett-Koehler Publishing Company, San Francisco, CA). All rights reserved.

CONCLUSION

The gendered divisions of violence, labor, and resources are interrelated and reinforce one another. The global forces of militarization, capitalist accumulation, and resource extraction and exploitation both produce and depend on these gendered divisions, which, in the final analysis, benefit only the most privileged members of global society (see Figure 4.12). Although more men than women are among those most privileged, the vast majority of men worldwide are susceptible to violence perpetrated by other men who are proving their "masculinity," relegated to receiving wages commensurate with those of underpaid women in the global economy, and are subject to deteriorating health as a result of environmental degradation and the destruction of the "feminine principle." Thus, women and men ultimately share similar interests in confronting and struggling against these global forces and the gendered divisions on which they depend.

Unfortunately, gender ideology sustains inequalities between women and men and obscures the common causes that should unite them. In effect, it divides women from men and weakens the struggles of us all against global violence, world poverty, and planetary destruction. Fortunately, gender ideology is being challenged all over the world by women's movements that have made the link between gender inequality and the many local and global problems to which it contributes. In the next chapter, we turn to these struggles, whose success depends upon both women and men making the connection between gender hierarchy and global crises.

NOTES

1. J. Ann Tickner, *Gender in International Relations* (New York: Columbia University Press, 1993), p. 58. In addition to Tickner's excellent text, there is a growing literature on "gendering security." See, for example, Cynthia Enloe, *The Morning After: Sexual Politics at the End of the Cold War* (Berkeley: University of California Press, 1993); Jan Jindy Pettman, *Worlding Women: A Feminist International Politics* (London: Routledge, 1996); Jennifer Turpin and Lois Ann Lorentzen, eds., *The Gendered World Order* (New York: Routledge, 1996); and Miriam Cooke and Angela Wollacott, eds., *Gendering War Talk* (Princeton: Princeton University Press, 1993).

2. David E. Jones, *Women Warriors: A History* (Washington/London: Brassey's, 1997), p. xiv.

3. Ibid., p. xiii.

4. Jean Bethke Elshtain, "Sovereignty, Identity, Sacrifice," in V. Spike Peterson, ed., *Gendered States: Feminist (Re)Visions of International Relations Theory* (Boulder: Lynne Rienner Publishers, 1992), p. 143.

5. See Jean Bethke Elshtain, *Women and War* (New York: Basic Books, 1987).

6. For example, Rebecca Grant argues that "marshalling a heightened national image of the feminine role was part of the process of legitimizing the military and cultural foundations of America's superpower status." The feminine mystique was thus integral to broader processes cultivating a new postwar role for the United States, as military and economic superpower in a Cold War context. (See Grant, "The Cold War and Feminine Mystique," in Peter R. Beckman and Francine D'Amico, eds., *Women, Gender and World Politics: Perspectives, Policies, and Prospects* [Westport, Conn.: Bergin & Garvey, 1994], p. 122.)

7. Pettman, *Worlding Women*, p. 89.

8. See, for example, Isidora Sekulic, "Inside Serbia: The War at Home," *Ms.*, March/April, 1994, pp. 18–19; Simona Sharoni, *Gender and the Israeli-Palestinian Conflict* (Syracuse, N.Y.: Syracuse University Press), p. 127; and Verna Nikolic-Ristanovic, "War and Violence Against Women," in Turpin and Lorentzen, eds., *The Gendered World Order*, pp. 195–210.

9. Cynthia Enloe, *Does Khaki Become You?* (Boston: South End Press, 1983), p. 212.

10. Ruth Leger Sivard, *World Military and Social Expenditures* (Washington, D.C.: World Priorities, 1991), p. 11.

11. Ruth Leger Sivard, *World Military and Social Expenditures 1996* (Washington, D.C.: World Priorities, 1996), p. 11.

12. Ibid.

13. Sherle R. Schwenninger, "The Case Against NATO Enlargement: Clinton's Fateful Gamble," *The Nation*, October 20, 1997, pp. 24, 26.

14. Sivard, *World Military and Social Expenditures 1996*, p. 40

15. Ibid., pp. 21, 40.

16. Ibid., p. 23.

17. Ibid.

18. Ibid., p. 41.

19. National Priorities Project, "The Ohio Story," *America-at-a-Glance Series*, 1 (1997): 3.

20. Sivard, *World Military and Social Expenditures 1996*, p. 39.

21. Ibid., p. 8.

22. Francine D'Amico, "Women as Warriors: Feminist Perspectives," paper presented at the 32nd Annual Convention of the International Studies Association, Vancouver, British Columbia, March 20–23, 1992, p. 29.

23. Dan Smith, *The State of War and Peace Atlas* (London: Penguin Books, 1997), p. 64.

24. Ibid., p. 65; Joni Seager, *The State of Women in the World Atlas* (New York: Penguin Books, 1997), pp. 92–93.

25. Seager, *The State of Women in the World Atlas*, pp. 92–93.

26. Pettman, *Worlding Women*, p. 151. The supposedly more benign policy of "Don't Ask, Don't Tell, Don't Pursue" instituted by the Clinton administration has actually resulted in higher gay and lesbian discharges than ever before. Moreover, discharge rates are higher for women than men. See C. Dixon Osburn and Michelle M. Benecke, "Conduct Unbecoming: Second Annual Report on 'Don't Ask, Don't Tell, Don't Pursue,'" in Laurie Weinstein and Christie White, eds., *Wives & Warriors: Women and the Military in the United States and Canada* (Westport, Conn.: Bergin & Garvey, 1997), pp. 151–178.

27. As wives of soldiers, women may receive part of their husbands' military salary and other "benefits" that militaries provide to families. However, they pay high prices in terms of sacrificing their own careers and doing unpaid labor for the military. (See Weinstein and White, eds., *Wives & Warriors*.)

28. See Lucinda Joy Peach, "Behind the Front Lines: Feminist Battles over Women in Combat," in Weinstein and White, eds., *Wives & Warriors*, pp. 99–135.

29. See D'Amico, "Women as Warriors," p. 27.

30. Francine D'Amico, "Policing the U.S. Military's Race and Gender Lines," in Weinstein and White, eds., *Wives & Warriors*, p. 216; emphasis in original.

31. Ibid., p. 200.

32. Jim Weiner, "Army Expands Sex Inquiry: One Sergeant Pleads Guilty," *New York Times*, November 13, 1996, pp. A1, A16.

33. Russell Carollo, Jeff Nesmith, and Elliot Jaspin, "Army Treated Rape as Lesser Crime," *Dayton Daily News*, January 12, 1997, p. A1.

34. D'Amico, "Policing the U.S. Military's Race and Gender Lines," pp. 220–221, 222.

35. Many women are accused of being lesbians after they file charges of sexual harassment and rape. See Osburn and Benecke, "Conduct Unbecoming," p. 154.

36. D'Amico, "Policing the U.S. Military's Race and Gender Lines," p. 216.

37. Susan Faludi, *Backlash: The Undeclared War Against American Women* (New York: Crown Publishers, 1991).

38. Ibid., pp. xiii–xvi.

39. See Peach, "Behind the Front Lines," pp. 106–109.

40. D'Amico, "Women as Warriors," p. 31.

41. Sivard, *World Military and Social Expenditures 1996*, pp. 30, 31, 36.

42. Ibid., p. 42.

43. National Priorities Project, "The Ohio Story," p. 3.

44. Sivard, *World Military and Social Expenditures 1996*, p. 8.

45. Amnesty International, *Women in the Front Line: Human Rights Violations Against Women* (New York: Amnesty International Publications, 1990).

46. When the Taliban came to power in Afghanistan in 1996, they issued a series of decrees that included forbidding women to work and closing all schools for girls. See John F. Burns, "Afghanistan's New Rulers Soft-Pedal Their Hard Line," *New York Times*, October 2, 1996, p. A3; and Jan Goodwin, "Afghan Women Under the Taliban," *On the Issues* (Summer 1998): 25ff.

47. Euan Hague, "Rape, Power, and Masculinity: The Construction of Gender and National Identities in the War in Bosnia-Herzegovina," in Ronit Lentin, ed., *Gender and Catastrophe* (London: Zed Books), p. 10.

48. Charlotte Bunch and Niamh Reilly, *Demanding Accountability* (New York: UNIFEM, 1994), p. 36.

49. Asoka Bandarage, *Women, Population, and Global Crisis* (London: Zed Books, 1997), p. 286.

50. Seager, *The State of Women in the World Atlas*, p. 116.

51. Ibid.

52. Richard Rayner, "The Warrior Besieged," *New York Times Magazine*, June 22, 1997, p. 29.

53. Sivard, *World Military and Social Expenditures 1996*, p. 41.

54. Enloe, *The Morning After*, p. 158.

55. Cynthia Enloe, *Bananas, Beaches & Bases: Making Feminist Sense of International Politics* (Berkeley: University of California Press, 1989), p. 66.

56. Rayner, "The Warrior Besieged," p. 29.

57. Sivard, *World Military and Social Expenditures 1996*, p. 7.

58. Ibid., p. 17.

59. Robin Morgan, *The Demon Lover: On the Sexuality of Terrorism* (New York: W. W. Norton, 1989), p. 45.

60. The UN estimated that by 1995, 75 percent of all refugees and displaced people were women and children. See Noleen Heyzer, "A Woman's Development Agenda for the 21st Century," in Noleen Heyzer, ed., *A Commitment to the World's Women* (New York: UNIFEM, 1995), p. 3.

61. Susan Forbes Martin, *Refugee Women* (London: Zed Books, 1991), p. 19.

62. United Nations (UN), *The World's Women 1995: Trends and Statistics* (New York: United Nations, 1995), p. 47.

63. Bandarage, *Women, Population, and Global Crisis*, p. 285.

64. Judith Hicks Stiehm, *Arms and the Enlisted Woman* (Philadelphia: Temple University Press, 1989).

65. D'Amico, "Policing the U.S. Military's Race and Gender Lines," p. 203.

66. Ibid., p. 222.

67. Ken Silverstein, "Privatizing War," *The Nation*, August 4, 1997, p. 12.

68. Ibid.

69. Enloe, *The Morning After*, p. 47.

70. Leslie Wayne, "The Shrinking Military Complex," *New York Times*, February 27, 1998, p. C6.

71. D'Amico, "Policing the U.S. Military's Race and Gender Lines," p. 220.

72. Elshtain, *Women and War*.

73. See Anne Sisson Runyan, "Of Markets and Men: The (Re)making(s) of IPE," in Kurt Burch and Robert A. Denemark, eds., *Constituting International Political Economy* (Boulder: Lynne Rienner Publishing, 1997).

74. See, for example, Ifi Amadiume, *Male Daughters, Female Husbands* (London: Zed Books, 1987); Jocelyn Linniken, *Sacred Queens and Women of Consequence* (Ann Arbor: University of Michigan Press, 1990); and Harriet Whitehead, "The Bow and the Burden Strap: A New Look at Institutionalized Homosexuality in Native North America," in Sherry B. Ortner and Harriet Whitehead, eds., *Sexual Meanings* (Cambridge, Eng.: Cambridge University Press, 1981), pp. 80–115.

75. Ester Boserup, *Woman's Role in Economic Development* (New York: St. Martin's Press, 1970), p. 19.

76. Ibid.

77. See ibid., ch. 3.

78. Gita Sen and Caren Grown, *Development, Crises, and Alternative Visions: Third World Women's Perspectives* (New York: Monthly Review Press, 1987), p. 24.

79. UN, *World's Women 1995*, pp. 113–114; Susan Bullock, *Women and Work* (London: Zed Books, 1994), p. 22.

80. See, for example, Sue Ellen Charlton, *Women in Third World Development* (Boulder: Westview Press, 1984); Sen and Grown, *Development, Crises, and Alternative Visions;* Irene Tinker, *Persistent Inequalities* (Oxford: Oxford University Press, 1990); and Janet Momsen and Vivian Kinnaird, eds., *Different Places, Different Voices* (London: Routledge, 1993). See also Marianne H. Marchand and Jane L. Parpart, eds., *Feminism, Postmodernism, Development* (London: Routledge, 1995), for contemporary feminist thought on women and development, which critiques some earlier feminist work in this area.

81. Charlton, *Women in Third World Development*, pp. 88–91.

82. Seager, *The State of Women in the World Atlas*, pp. 20–21, 105.

83. Nuket Kardam, *Bringing Women In: Women's Issues in International Development Programs* (Boulder: Lynne Rienner Publishers, 1991), p. 119.

84. World Bank, *Mainstreaming Gender in World Bank Lending: An Update, Report No. 16490* (Washington, D.C.: World Bank, 1997), p. 6.

85. Ibid., p. 43.

86. See, for example, Jeanne Vickers, *Women and the World Economic Crisis* (London: Zed Books, 1991); and Bullock, *Women and Work*, pp. 5–6.

87. WIDE, NAC-Canada, Alt-WID, and CRIAW, "Wealth of Nations—Poverty of Women," framework paper for "Globalization of the Economy and Economic Justice for Women," ECE Regional NGO Forum, Vienna, 1994, p. 6.

88. Ibid., p. 3.

89. Sivard, *World Military and Social Expenditures 1996*, p. 31.

90. Enloe, *Bananas, Beaches & Bases*, p. 1.

91. Pettman, *Worlding Women*, pp. 197–198.

92. Thanh-Dam Truong, *Sex, Money and Morality: Prostitution and Tourism in South-East Asia* (London: Zed Books, 1990), p. 167.

93. Ibid., p. 173.

94. Ibid., p. 185.

95. Ibid., p. 182.

96. Dorchen Liedholdt, "Sexual Trafficking of Women in Europe: A Human Rights Crisis for the European Union," in Amy Elman, ed., *Sexual Politics and the European Union* (Providence, R.I.: Berghahn Books, 1996), pp. 87–88.

97. Ibid., p. 88; Alexandra Stanley, "With Prostitution Booming, Legalization Tempts Russia," *New York Times*, March 3, 1998, pp. A1, A8.

98. Pettman, *Worlding Women*, p. 66, 68.

99. Geertje Lycklama à Nijeholt, "Women in International Migration," in Heyzer, ed., *Commitment to the World's Women*, pp. 59–60.

100. Ibid., pp. 61, 63.

101. Ibid., pp. 62, 63.

102. Lena H. Sun, "Here Comes the Russian Bride," *Washington Post National Weekly Edition*, March 16, 1998, p. 10.

103. Ibid., p. 11.

104. Bullock, *Women and Work*, p. 57.

105. Ibid.

106. UN, *World's Women 1995*, p. 116.

107. Bullock, *Women and Work*, pp. 59–60.

108. UN, *World's Women 1995*, p. 116.

109. Bullock, *Women and Work*, pp. 63–65. See also Eileen Boris and Elisabeth Prugl, eds., *Homeworkers in Global Perspective* (London: Routledge, 1996); and Sheila Rowbotham and Swasti Mitter, eds., *Dignity and Daily Bread* (London: Routledge, 1994).

110. Bullock, *Women and Work*, p. 63.

111. ISIS: Women's International Information and Communication Service, *Women in Development* (Philadelphia: New Society Publishers, 1984), pp. 98–99.

112. Chandra Talpade Mohanty, "Women Workers and Capitalist Scripts: Ideologies of Domination, Common Interests, and Politics of Solidarity," in M. Jacqui Alexander and Chandra Talpade Mohanty, eds., *Feminist Genealogies, Colonial Legacies, Democratic Futures* (New York: Routledge, 1997), p. 21.

113. Lourdes Beneria and Amy Lind, "Engendering International Trade: Concepts, Policy, and Action," in Heyzer, ed., *Commitment to the World's Women*, p. 69.

114. See, for example, Jeremy Brecher and Tim Costello, *Global Village or Global Pillage* (Boston: South End Press, 1994).

115. WIDE, NAC-Canada, Alt-WID, and CRIAW, "Wealth of Nations—Poverty of Women," p. 4.

116. Rachel Kamel, *The Global Factory: Analysis and Action for a New Economic Era* (Philadelphia: American Friends Service Committee, 1990), pp. 10–11.

117. Ibid., p. 35.

118. Ibid., p. 10.

119. Beneria and Lind, "Engendering International Trade," p. 78.

120. Sam Dillon, "Sex Bias at Border Plants in Mexico Reported by U.S.," *New York Times*, January 13, 1998, p. A6. In addition, more than 100 *maquiladora* workers have been raped and murdered since 1993 in Cuidad Juarez. See Sam Quinones, "The Maquiladora Murders," *Ms.*, May/June 1998, pp. 11–16.

121. Beneria and Lind, "Engendering International Trade," p. 75.

122. Saskia Sassen, "Economic Globalization: A New Geography, Composition, and Institutional Framework," in Jeremy Brecher, John Brown Childs, and Jill Cutler, eds., *Global Visions: Beyond the New World Order* (Boston: South End Press, 1993), p. 65.

123. Lily M. H. Ling, "White Man's Burden or Dark Irony: Conquest and Desire in Western Political Thought," paper presented at the *Millennium* 25th Anniversary Conference, London School of Economics, U.K., 1996, p. 12.

124. Vandana Shiva, *Staying Alive: Women, Ecology, and Development* (London: Zed Books, 1989). Other ecofeminists have criticized Shiva's too simplistic historical view and are concerned that her idea of "the feminine principle" suggests a "natural" tie between women and nature. See Rosi Braidotti, Eva Charkiewicz, Sabine Hausler, and Saskia Wieringa, *Women, the Environment and Sustainable Development* (London: Zed Books, 1994).

125. See Carolyn Merchant, *The Death of Nature: Women, Ecology and the Scientific Revolution* (New York: Harper & Row, 1980).

126. Sen and Grown, *Development, Crises, and Alternative Visions*, pp. 44–52. The specter of ecological crisis appears in the First World as well. For example, oil spills, fuel shortages, and unreliable and/or unsafe water supplies are increasingly widespread threats.

127. See Annabel Rodda, *Women and the Environment* (London: Zed Books, 1991).

128. In Mali, for example, certain trees are designated as "women" trees. This means that they are reserved for firewood, which is typically harvested from dead branches, and thus, the trees are not to be cut down. (See ibid., p. 75.)

129. Vandana Shiva, "GATT, Agriculture and Third World Women," in Maria Mies and Vandana Shiva, eds., *Ecofeminism* (London: Zed Books, 1993), p. 238.

130. Kamel, *The Global Factory*, p. 35.

131. Sivard, *World Military and Social Expenditures* (1991), p. 37.

132. Joni Seager, *Earth Follies* (London: Routledge, 1993), p. 150.

133. Lin Nelson, "The Place of Women in Polluted Places," in Irene Diamond and Gloria Feman Orenstein, eds., *Reweaving the World: The Emergence of Ecofeminism* (San Francisco: Sierra Club Books, 1990), pp. 177–179.

134. Ibid., p. 179.

135. See Rosalie Bertell, *No Immediate Danger* (London: Women's Press, 1985); and Seager, *Earth Follies*.

136. Seager, *Earth Follies*, p. 37.

137. Ibid., p. 30.

138. Naomi Neft and Ann D. Levine, *Where Women Stand: An International Report on the Status of Women in 140 Countries, 1997–1998* (New York: Random House, 1997), p. 111.

139. Ibid., p. 122.

140. Ruth Leger Sivard, *Women . . . A World Survey* (Washington, D.C.: World Priorities, Inc., 1995), p. 28.

141. Joni L. Jacobson, "Coming to Grips with Abortion," in Lester R. Brown, ed., *State of the World 1991* (New York: W. W. Norton, 1991), p. 130.

142. Sivard, *Women . . . A World Survey* (1995), p. 29.

143. These ominous aspects of family planning arise from coercive tactics on the part of states, population planners, and patriarchial cultures, such as the one-child-per-family rule in China and abortions performed in India when the fetus is determined to be female. As a result of such tactics, there is now a ratio of 93 females to every 100 males in India. (See Neft and Levine, *Where Women Stand*, p. 127.)

FIVE

□ □ □

The Politics of Resistance: Women as Nonstate, Antistate, and Transstate Actors

The gendered division of power and its subsets, the gendered divisions of violence, labor, and resources, severely restrict the effects that women can have on world politics. As Chapter 3 indicated, with a few notable exceptions, women who have made it into the corridors of power as state actors have done little to dispel prevailing gender ideologies and divisions. Too typically, they have adopted masculine leadership styles for themselves without disrupting feminine stereotypes more generally. These "steel magnolias" simply combine and, thus, reinforce the gender divisions of masculine and feminine. They rarely challenge such divisions, unless there is a critical mass of women within formal power structures who support the development of feminist politics and more feminist leadership approaches.

Most often, critical masses of female political actors who *do* challenge gender dichotomies are found outside of formal power structures. Because they typically organize outside of state apparatuses, these actors tend to be invisible through the state-centric lens on world politics that prevailed until recently. Now that market forces, in the form of private firms and international financial institutions (IFIs), are challenging and complicating traditional state prerogatives in world politics, IR has begun to direct attention to what is frequently referred to as **civil society.** Neoliberals and neoconservatives tend to conceptualize civil society in terms of the private sector defined as corporate and individualist interests that are in tension with and seek to maintain autonomy from the state. Critical perspectives tend to view civil society in terms of social movements that resist both state domination and capitalist market exploitation.[1] This latter definition of civil society is making women more visible as actors in

163

world politics. However, only feminist perspectives highlight the central roles that women play in social movement activism.

Women are found in large numbers in social movements for peace, human rights, economic justice, and environmental protection as members of both "mixed" organizations (which include men and women) and "separate" organizations (which are women-centered in terms of leadership, focus, and membership and, thus, are referred to as women's movements). Until recently, the activities of such social movements have been concentrated below the level of the state and confined within state boundaries. However, as economic, environmental, and social issues increasingly cut across state boundaries due to globalization forces, social movements are becoming more transnational in focus, organization, and impact, thereby also raising their profiles in world politics.

This chapter focuses on women in their social movement roles as nonstate, antistate, and transstate actors who, to varying degrees, do challenge the gendered divisions of power, violence, labor, and resources within local, national, and international contexts. We examine the multiple political roles that women play in women's and other social movements as well as the systemic effects of their political activities. Hence, our discussion shifts attention away from "fitting women into" traditional IR frameworks and toward an understanding that accommodates and empowers women's struggles against the hierarchical consequences of practicing "world politics as usual." We also highlight the fact that women's activism not only resists oppressive state and market forces but also often seeks to transform civil society.

Indeed, their emphasis on the transformation of civil society is what makes women's movements somewhat distinctive among social movements. Feminists tend to go beyond many critical formulations of civil society by arguing that civil society is not that autonomous from the state and the market, nor does it always resist the negative effects of these forces. All ideals and social movements have potential for variously regressive as well as progressive consequences. Just as there are progressive aspects to civil society, there are also regressive dimensions insofar as civil society reproduces oppressive structures (such as the patriarchal family) and ideologies (such as sexism, racism, ablism, and homophobia). If these oppressive dimensions of civil society are not confronted and changed, it is unlikely that progressive, inclusive, and democratic social movements will flourish or that the negative effects of states and markets (reflecting problematic aspects of civil society) will be thoroughly challenged. Thus, as we document the liberating aspects of social movement struggles in which women significantly participate as members and leaders, we are reminded that movements can perpetuate at the same time that they challenge gender dichotomies. This caution is especially warranted when there is insufficient attention given to the transformation of civil society in the context of struggles to change states and markets.

WOMEN'S MOVEMENTS

No woman is born—and not all women become—feminist, but some women *and* men do. How one becomes a feminist varies with each individual, but the impetus for developing a feminist consciousness often arises when a person experiences a contradiction between who that person thinks she or he is and what society wants her or him to be. It may arise out of a contradiction in the opportunities a society says it offers to an individual and what that individual actually experiences. In advanced (post)industrial societies, women are typically told that, under the law, they have equal opportunities (in the liberal democratic sense) to compete for political and economic power. In fact, however, indirect or structural barriers to full political and economic participation reduce most women's rights and choices. In more traditional societies, particularly those that experienced some kind of colonial or neocolonial rule, externally imposed laws and certain cultural and religious traditions combine to deny equal opportunities to women, even under the law. The gendered division of power in both cases circumscribes women's (and men's) choices to be and do things deemed outside of their assigned gender roles.

Throughout history, women—individually, collectively, and sometimes with men—have struggled against direct and indirect barriers to their self-development and their full social, political, and economic participation. In the modern era, they have often done so through organizing women's movements that have addressed many issues and, thus, taken many forms (see Figure 5.1). People associate women's movements with campaigns to gain equal rights for women under the law. But women have often sought more transformative changes in social, political, and economic systems because prevailing masculinist systems undermine women's struggles for gender equality despite formal equal rights. As a result, it is sometimes difficult to separate women's movements from other political movements agitating for social, political, and economic transformation. In this text, we regard as feminist those political movements in which participants self-consciously and deliberately link gender inequality and oppression with other forms of social, political, economic, and/or ecological injustice in order to transform civil society as well as states and capitalist markets. In the following sections we review feminist orientations (introduced in Chapter 2) in terms of their implications for movement strategies for social, political, economic, and ecological justice.

FIGURE 5.1 Feminisms in Action. (*top left*) The National Organization for Women Rally to Stop Violence Against Women was held in Washington, D.C., in 1995. Courtesy Rick Reinhard, Impact Visuals. (*bottom left*) Palestinian women fast in 1991 in Gaza City to protest conditions inside Israeli prisons for Palestinian political prisoners. Courtesy Paul Dix, Impact Visuals. (*top right*) A woman demonstrates against political repression in Chile in 1986. The protest sign reads "For life and for peace, stop the murders." Photo courtesy of Amnesty International. (*bottom right*) Women members of UNITE Local 23–25 show their unity with sweatshop workers at a rally protesting working conditions in a midtown Manhattan garment shop in 1995. Courtesy Earl Dotter, Impact Visuals.

Liberal Feminists

Feminists engage in many kinds of strategies to erode or explode gender dichotomies. Liberal feminists, who are most active in equal rights movements, seek to eliminate these dichotomies by eliminating the emphasis on gender *difference* and replacing it with an emphasis on sameness. They argue that women are equal to men because they do not categorically differ from men in regard to capacities for aggression, ambition, strength, and rationality. This argument is at odds with the idea that women are naturally the opposite of and inferior to men. But the problem is that this perspective too often accepts masculine traits as the norm to which women can and should aspire. As a result, it challenges the gendered *division*, but not the gendered *notion*, of power. It leaves intact and even reinforces the idea that power equals masculinist aggression, ambition, strength, and rationality. A system of power-over is thus perpetuated, ensuring that women and men who appear lacking in these traits will not be admitted to the corridors of power. Instead, they will remain the objects of power to be manipulated and coerced.

In short, the question that liberal feminists must grapple with is "Equal to whom and for what?" As our earlier discussion indicated, this question is particularly pertinent with respect to the issue of women in the military. Even if women were to be admitted into state militaries in numbers equal to men's and as equals of men (neither of which is likely in a power-over system), the problem still remains that state militaries are organized hierarchically and for the purpose of engaging in direct violence and/or "backing up" systems of indirect violence.

Similar points can be made in regard to the goal of female-male parity in senior management positions in the private sector (which the UN estimates will take 475 years to realize at present rates).[2] Corporations, too, are organized hierarchically and according to power-over principles. There is no guarantee that a critical mass of women at the top would fundamentally change these principles. Moreover, it matters *which women* constitute that critical mass. If women reaching positions of power are those already privileged by race/ethnicity, class, sexuality, and nationality—and not necessarily supportive of feminist principles—it is unlikely that capitalist exploitation will cease. In short, gender equity in power structures is necessary, but not necessarily sufficient, to transform these hierarchical structures.

Radical Feminists

Radical feminists are particularly difficult to characterize, because the label encompasses a variety of commitments. On the one hand, radical feminists are distinguished from liberal and socialist feminists by their greater attention to the role of culture in denigrating women's experiences and ways of knowing, objectifying women's bodies, and devaluing that which is associated with the feminine. In contrast to liberal feminists, who seek equality in male-defined terms, radical feminists typically celebrate the distinctiveness of women and the cultural superiority of female ways. In a key sense, radical feminists see masculinity not as a solution but as the problem, due to its emphasis on aggression, competition, and violence, directed by men against women *and* feminized men. Thus, for some radical feminists (often referred to as cultural feminists) a primary strategy is to revalue previously denigrated aspects of femininity, making them the norm to which all people should aspire in pursuit of a better world.

For example, cultural feminists seek to remove the negative connotations from such feminine traits as passivity, nurturance, emotionalism, and dependence and to redefine them more positively. Women's purported passivity—destructive if it keeps them from acting politically against their oppression—is positive to the degree that it promotes a desire for accommodation and thus a nonviolent resolution of conflicts. Similarly, women's supposed proclivity to nurture—problematic when it comes to tying women exclusively to reproductive labor—is positive as an ethic of care that extends to children, the poor and victimized, and the planet as a whole. Indeed, radical feminists, many of whom are also known as ecofeminists, generally argue that the near worship of masculine rationality has promoted an instrumentalism that threatens the very life of the planet and its inhabitants. They point out that (inter)dependence, not autonomy, is essential for human and planetary survival. People and nature are bound up in webs of interdependency that entail responsibility and care for others. Thus, radical feminists insist that interdependence be revalued and redefined in a way that promotes the establishment of mutually respectful relationships among women and men, among peoples, and with nature—a mutual respect that recognizes the inescapable interdependence of all life. Some ecofeminists and cultural feminists go on to theorize that women's greater tendency toward emotion and intuition offsets the rationalistic calculus that has no feeling for life and, thus, no concern for the destructiveness of instrumentalism.

On the other hand, for many radical feminists the politics of sexuality is paramount. They argue that a fundamental source of women's oppression is male domination of women's bodies, both ideologically (through pornography, demeaning stereotypes, sexist jokes) and practically (through androcentric marriage and property laws, denial of women's reproductive rights, sexual violence). Here the personal is political in the sense that even women's most "private" and intimate experiences are shaped by institutions and structures that privilege male-defined pleasures and masculinist principles. As a corollary, these radical feminists are critical of heterosexism, which assumes heterosexuality is the only "normal" and therefore legitimate pattern of sexual and social relations. Heterosexism insists on a rigid dichotomy of masculinity-femininity, demonizes all but heterosexual desire and intimacy, denies legitimacy to homosexual family life, and fuels the hatred and violence of homophobia. Not surprisingly, some radical feminists advocate separatism from men—sexually and otherwise—as a basic strategy.

The activist work of radical feminists is often geared toward intervening in destructive relationships through the establishment of rape crisis centers and battered women's shelters in many parts of the world. They are also active in peace, ecology, reproductive rights, antipornography, and gay and lesbian rights movements. Their aim in all these movements is to undermine masculinist systems of power-over and replace them with systems of empowerment.

In short, radical feminists have no interest in being equal to men, if being equal means becoming like or the same as male oppressors.

Thus, some radical feminists reject the liberal feminist strategy of supporting the entry of women into state militaries. They argue instead that neither women nor men should enter the military, which, in their view, is a patriarchal institution designed to exaggerate masculinity, oppress women, and destroy human and planetary life. Similarly, they may criticize efforts to bring women into positions of corporate power, preferring to create alternative lifestyles that rest upon the formation of women-centered, collective, nonhierarchical, self-sufficient, small-scale, and environmentally responsible economic enterprises and political and social communities.

Socialist Feminists

Socialist feminists, while supporting many of the goals of liberal and radical feminists, typically highlight economic issues and their relationships to power and culture. They also question the continued use of problematic gender categories. Like radical feminists, they argue that the divisions between private and public, reproduction and production are patriarchal constructions, but they believe that the answer is not to revalue the private sphere and reproductive work but, rather, to show how the private, reproductive sphere and the public, productive sphere are not only interrelated but also less distinctive than they seem. For the majority of people in the world—that is, non-Western, poor and working-class women and men of color—a rigid distinction between who can and cannot work in the public, productive sphere is impossible. Poor and working-class women have never had the dubious luxury of being confined to the private sphere of home and family.

In addition, socialist feminists argue that it serves only masculinist interests to separate productive and reproductive labor and give no value to the latter, as has been the case under capitalism (and in states' calculations of the gross domestic product [GDP]). Reproductive labor, including the labor that women perform in the informal, home-based economy, is productive work and should be counted as such. If it were, then attention would be drawn to the impoverished circumstances under which most women labor and which affect the overall productive capacities of societies. It would also expose the costs to society extracted by capitalist reliance upon women's cheap or free labor to make a profit. In other words, if capitalist industries had to pay the actual costs of women's reproductive labor (based on the prices charged for providing equivalent services, such as day care and housecleaning), we would see how these industries, as currently organized, are not in fact efficient or competitive, but wasteful and expensive.

Under the current system, workers' wages can be kept artificially low because they do not have to be used to pay for women's reproductive labor in the home. This permits resources and wealth to be concentrated at the top of corporate hierarchies, where the least productive (and reproductive) work is done. Hence, if women's reproductive labor is to be taken seriously, the very nature of corporate organization and production would have to change. First, the wage structure would have to be adjusted to ensure that more money and resources are distributed to productive and reproductive workers. Second, there would be greater demand for the production of things that meet the basic needs of households rather than luxury items that can be consumed only by the few. States, too, would have to shift their orientation, focusing programs on assisting reproductive labor rather than subsidizing exploitative, luxury-oriented industries.

In sum, socialist feminists encourage us to rethink, rather than embrace, gender dichotomies. In the process, work and welfare are redefined by expanding the idea of work and exonerating the notion of welfare. The latter would no longer be a system of meager handouts but a societal priority to increase all people's productivity in equitable, healthful, mutually respectful, and life-affirming ways. Thus, socialist feminists are interested in undermining the power-over system of capitalist patriarchy through empowerment. However, they believe this can be accomplished best by a societal and global redistribution of power, as opposed to placing their hopes in the empowering capacity of feminine traits. As a result, socialist feminists are most active in socialist revolutions and women's economic movements, organizing around such issues as women on welfare, women in development, and the effects of economic globalization on women.

Through this work, socialist feminists, like radical feminists, have also criticized state militaries. However, socialist feminists tend to emphasize that the military-industrial complex impoverishes women by extracting resources from state and global economies that should go to meet basic needs. Women entering the military in greater numbers will not change this imbalance of resources between the military and the civilian economy. As socialist feminists further observe, the ongoing privatization of the public resources of the state acts to divert moneys away from basic needs provision in order to enhance corporate profits.

Postcolonial Feminists

Postcolonial feminism arises from the experiences of women of color, whether as Third World inhabitants, immigrants, or indigenous minorities. Postcolonial feminist analyses include socialist feminist critiques of capitalist patriarchy, but they also expose how the ideologies and practices of racism, colonialism, and neo-colonialism (or imperialism) decisively contribute to the oppression of women of color. They also draw attention to the economic, political, and cultural forces of contemporary recolonizations and to nationalist and/or religious fundamentalisms, which they argue are the twin features of globalization.

Postcolonial feminists understand globalization as largely a continuation of the centuries-long process of colonization, which has always depended upon the superexploitation of the reproductive and productive labor of Third World women living in the South and North. The main difference, at this historical juncture, is that many white women (as well as men of color and even some white men) in the First World of the West and the former Second World of the East are increasingly being brought under the yoke of global capitalist expansion through restructuring processes. The fall of the "socialist alternative" that the East however problematically represented (especially for the South), coupled with technological advances in information and production systems that have allowed corporate and financial institutions to bypass state regulations, have left all workers more vulnerable at the present time. These processes have also made states in the North more responsive to corporate interests than to citizens, whereas states in the South—at the expense of their peoples' basic needs—are made more beholden to IFIs and more reliant on foreign direct investment (FDI). Thus, postcolonial feminists use the term **recolonization** to refer to both the intensification of colonization in the South and the extension of colonizing practices to the North, brought about under the banner of globalization.

Recolonization is not only an economic and political process but also a cultural one. Transnational corporations produce largely Western products and services for global consumption, leading to what many globalization commentators call the "MacDonaldization" or homogenization of cultures the world over. Indigenous food, clothing, customs, and beliefs are either swept away or debased by the twin processes of Western homogenization and the commercialization of "exotic" cultures for tourist consumption.

A major response to this cultural "contamination" and degradation has been the rise of nationalist and/or religious **fundamentalisms** to supposedly regain and reassert "authentic" national identities, cultural traditions, and belief systems. As postcolonial feminists observe, fundamentalist movements and regimes, whether secular nationalist, Christian, Jewish, Hindu, Confucian, or Islamic, are dominated by men and base their programs for national and cultural "sanitization" on controlling "their" women's bodies. Since women in patriarchal cultures are assigned the role of being "culture bearers" for present and future generations, they are the most targeted, often brutally through enforcement of dress codes and private and public behavior edicts, in fundamentalist campaigns to restore national and cultural "authenticity." Moreover, "[s]ex is seen as the vulnerable link in maintaining group boundaries, so it is especially important for colonising—and, if they can, colonised—men to control same-group women's sexual behavior and domestic lives."[3] This confirms the postcolonial feminist insight that gender is always raced and race is always gendered.

These observations lead postcolonial feminists to contest Western feminist assumptions about the nature of and split between public and private space that supposedly mark all women's lives. As we noted earlier, most women of color in the South and North have never been confined to the private sphere of the family, since they have had to labor outside of their homes out of economic necessity. Their participation in the public sphere has been far from liberating due to the nature of the work they are typically assigned as a result of the matrix of sexism, racism, and classism, whereas the private realm of family does represent an escape from at least racist behavior. Moreover, their experience of sexism in the private sphere derives not just from patriarchal familial ideologies but also from racial/ethnic, nationalist, and religious ideologies that prescribe that women must look and behave in culturally "authentic" ways. Thus, when we look through the lens of the lives of women of color, we see that the private is always constructed by public forces and, in fact, is never truly private.

We also see through this lens that what is assumed to be public space, the state, is, in fact, not public space, especially for immigrant and migrant women. As Anannya Bhattacharjee explains:

Immigration laws have *privatized* the nation; it is now bounded space into which only some people can walk some of the time. A man's control over his wife or an employer's control over the domestic worker in the home extends to controlling her recognition as a member of what constitutes the public—in this case, being a legal resident of a national community (in itself a private concept).[4]

Analyzing gender oppression as multilayered leads postcolonial feminists to also challenge the categorical distinction between the local and the global. Rather, they argue, global forces of domination are produced and sustained by varying local practices of domination (in families, communities, and nations), and, thus, local resistances can contribute significantly to destabilizing global power structures.

Accordingly, postcolonial feminists engage in and foster the development of grass-roots women's movements, which work to subvert local practices of domination, make connections between these local practices and global forces, and ally with other grass-roots women's groups across borders to form transnational feminist resistance networks. This type of organizing enables diverse women to articulate their own experiences of oppression and identify its multiple and overlapping sources. It also avoids "the old sisterhood model of missionary work" in which white, middle-class, Western feminists spoke for all women and purported to know what all women should do to end oppression.[5]

Inderpal Grewal and Caren Kaplan speak to the difference it makes when this imperialist model of feminism is abandoned:

For example, when the United States gave billions to General Zia of Pakistan to fight the Soviets in Afghanistan, the United States propped up a regime that was inimical to women. U.S. feminists need to fight against this kind of aid on their home ground instead of abstractly condemning Islam as the center of patriarchal oppression. Simultaneously, we need to examine how the importance of Christian fundamentalism within the Republican party in the United States affects the lives of millions of women worldwide through funding and development practices that structure reproductive and other politics. Transnational feminist approaches link the impact of such policies on women on public assistance in the United States and women who have little agency in their dealing with U.S.-sponsored clinics and health centers that have been established in the so-called peripheries.[6]

Thus, postcolonial feminists insist that feminist strategies to undermine militarism, capitalism, and fundamentalism must be undergirded by commitments to anti-imperialism, solidarity work, and democratic practices. This requires that "local" women's movements around the world, including white Western ones, listen to one another and share their analyses of how militarization and globalization are produced and reproduced in their own national and local contexts. This has the potential effect of multiplying and intensifying solidarity and resistance strategies.

Postmodernist Feminists

Postmodernist feminists, found most often in academic circles, but also in feminist political movements, partake of many forms of feminist analysis and have been particularly influenced by postcolonial feminist thought. These feminists are critical not just of gender dichotomies and categories but also of the concept of gender itself, as it is typically used within other feminisms. Their concern is that the concept of gender, like that of sex, still contains within it traces of biological determinism and "essentialism." They argue that other feminisms, even when they criticize how gender is constructed and used by capitalism, militarism, and other power-over systems, tend to speak of gender as if it stems from women's and men's essential natures and seemingly unalterable roles. This residual essentialism risks leaving gender dichotomies intact.

They worry, for instance, that the cultural feminist tendency (within radical feminism) to glorify feminine traits does not alter masculinist assumptions that women must nurture and must be protected. By the same token, they argue that socialist feminist proposals to improve the conditions of women's reproductive labor leave intact the idea that only women do reproductive labor by virtue of their roles as wives and mothers. They also question the use of such homogenizing terms as *Third World women*, which may be useful to describe shared material conditions but also problematically assume a singular shared identity.

Postmodernist feminists extend their critique of gender categories by challenging us to rethink our use of the even more basic terms *woman* and *man*. Their point is that we are all more complicated beings than these unitary labels suggest and our experiences of being gendered—as woman or man—vary along dimensions of race, class, nationality, ethnicity, sexuality, and so on. All these identities with which we are labeled, either individually or in hyphenated form (such as white-poor-French-woman), are social constructs that are created, given meaning, and reproduced by the differing, yet interlocking, systems of power in which we are embedded. That is, these identities do not arise from our genitals or skin color (although, historically, physical attributes have been made politically salient). Rather, the identities arise from and are perpetuated by social and psychological interpretations of physical differences among people—interpretations that are used to organize people hierarchically all over the world. Postmodernist feminists do not question the existence of pervasive sexism and racism. But they urge feminists and other political movement activists to avoid speaking of women and men, blacks and whites, and so on, *as if* they were unitary, essential categories that do not change in meaning over time and across cultures.[7]

Because postmodernist feminists are concerned with complicating rather than reproducing gender (and even sex) categories, they, like postcolonial feminists, are wary of feminisms that posit a natural sisterhood of women, presupposing a universally shared experience of oppression. They argue, instead, that women have different experiences of oppression (according to their socioeconomic, cultural, and political locations) and that any solidarity women may develop should arise from women's (and men's) consciously choosing to work together on an issue. They do not expect that such coalition building will be free of conflict among different women (and/or men) working together—or that it should be. Whatever consensus is built will arise from a struggle to see and value one another's perspectives, and whatever actions are taken may apply only to the specific context of the struggle.

In short, the point is not that there can be no large-scale, transnational movements to address global problems but, rather, that all struggles must be understood in context and strategies for change must be sensitive to specific differences. Hence, local and localized solutions, geared for subverting power-over in the multiple sites where it is developed and deployed, might produce the most just outcomes in the struggles against multiple global problems. For example, postmodernist feminists, although generally critical of state militaries for the violence and economic impoverishment they have visited upon most women, recognize that women are no more inherently peaceful than men are inherently aggressive. They also recognize that peace does not always bring justice. Thus, many postmodernist feminists believe that women should have the maneuvering room to "fight" in their struggles for a peace predicated on equality and justice. However, the meanings of peace, equality, and justice are always contestable for postmodern feminists. We (meaning diverse movements with diverse perspectives) cannot know in advance what these look like as if there were a preexisting blueprint. Rather, we can only engage in daily struggles against power-over systems and among ourselves to constantly give new meanings and more substance to these terms.

Indeed, a central strategy of postmodern feminists is politicizing or "deconstructing" language. As we discussed in Chapter 2, all languages are rife with gender symbolism and thus are productive of dichotomous thinking and naturalize oppressive ideologies, structures, and actions. In short, language is political. Postmodern feminists take on terms used in everyday parlance, popular culture, and disciplinary/professional discourses; deconstruct them to reveal gendered assumptions; and contest their dominant meanings so they no longer hold such power. In IR, post-modern feminists have deconstructed such terms as *sovereignty, security, dependency, nationalism*, and, most recently, *globalization*. For example, Julie Graham and Katherine Gibson[8] argue that globalization is too often represented as an inexorable force by commentators on both the right and the left. Within this framing, resistance appears futile. Indeed, Graham and Gibson draw a parallel between the representation of globalization as inevitable and the "rape script" wherein men's desire to rape and women's victimization are taken as givens. Hence, terms such as *capitalist penetration* evoke the image of inexorable processes: a rape that cannot be avoided or resisted. This conceptual box prevents us from seeing that global capitalism is far more vulnerable than it has been made to appear; like all systems or processes, capitalism is not inexorable but depends entirely on decisions and actions taken by people. The violence of rape and the violence of capitalist exploitation *can* be resisted because their agents are flesh-and-blood people. But to be systemically effective, resistance must be collective as well as individual.

PRACTICAL AND STRATEGIC GENDER INTERESTS

Women, feminist or not, who become involved in political activities often do so as a result of what Maxine Molyneux calls "practical" or "strategic" gender interests.[9] In Molyneux's words, **practical gender interests** "are usually in response to an immediate perceived need, and they do not generally entail a strategic goal such as women's emancipation or gender equality."[10] By contrast, **strategic gender interests** are derived from a more general analysis of women's subordination and involve the formulation of system-transforming, or strategic, objectives to overcome that subordination.[11] According to this distinction, women who organize spontaneously to protest food shortages, low pay in the workplace, or lack of adequate health care for their families are generally acting upon their practical gender interests. That is, they are seeking a change in conditions without insisting on a change in the larger system of gender dichotomies. Stated differently, even though practical gender interests do in fact arise out of gendered divisions and hierarchy, they are distinguished from strategic gender interests by not fundamentally challenging those divisions and hierarchy.

When women participate in political movements as a result of their practical gender interests, they may develop an awareness of their strategic gender interests by self-consciously confronting their subordination as women. This involves recognizing how practical and strategic interests are related. That is, practical gender interests are often not being satisfied because strategic gender interests are being thwarted. With this insight, women are able to *link* systemic gender inequalities and the more immediate problems—often of sheer survival—that they face in everyday life.

The distinction between practical and strategic gender interests has been criticized by postcolonial feminists who argue that they tend to reproduce hierarchical dualisms that divide the personal from the political, the private from the public, and feminine from feminist consciousness, while also privileging the latter in each dyad.[12] We share this criticism and use these conceptual categories to represent a "continuum"—emphasizing relationships—rather than a "dichotomy."[13] In Jennifer Schirmer's words, women have "*multiple* 'strategic' and 'pragmatic' interests that change over time and that they themselves do not deem separate."[14]

This means that movements arising out of women's practical gender issues should not be viewed as constituting only reformist politics, any more than movements arising out of strategic gender interests should be viewed as always constituting transformative politics. Strategies and movements are not simply *either* reformist *or* revolutionary, but are always more complex in their effects. Movements arising out of practical gender interests can have revolutionary, or transformative, consequences; and movements arising out of strategic gender interests may result only in reform, and only for a few women. Moreover, we must remember that both reformist and transformative politics are necessary—not only to ameliorate the oppressive conditions under which most women live but also (eventually) to eliminate these conditions altogether. They are also both feminist in that they challenge, in varying degrees, gender oppression.

We further note that women can and have engaged in reactionary politics, often in response to their practical gender interests, but sometimes in pursuit of their strategic gender interests. Women who become fundamentalist, antifeminist, and/or militarist may do so because they think that their traditional roles of wife and mother, from which they gain a certain amount of protection and esteem, are threatened (whether by atheists, feminists, or Communists). Some feminists alienate others by actions that have tended to exclude rather than include. For example, women of color and poor women have accused white, Western, middle-class women of failing to work with them to place the critique of *all* social hierarchies at the center of feminist theorizing and activism.

By referring to practical and strategic gender interests, we hope to show not only that these are intertwined but also that there are relationships among local, state, and global feminist movements. Most political resistance is a response to local and immediate conditions that are perceived as obstacles to the realization of practical interests. But oppressive conditions at the local or state level are often a manifestation of more encompassing systems of hierarchy (racism, capitalism, sexism). As activists become aware of the relationship between local struggles and larger systems of hierarchical relations, some pursue system-transforming strategies. In this way, participation in local resistance actions can lead to participation in (or at least support for) larger and sometimes global social movements.

There is no perfect or universal formula for eradicating women's global subordination arising out of gendered divisions of power, violence, labor, and resources. And there is no *guarantee* that pursuing gender interests, whether they be practical, strategic, or both, will promote entirely progressive effects in relation to other hierarchies. Nevertheless, in the sections that follow, we look at a variety of women's nonstate, antistate, and transstate struggles that attest to the fact that women all over the world are political, are active, do challenge gender dichotomies, and do change world politics by their political agency—even though very few women are state actors.

ANTIWAR AND PEACE MOVEMENTS

The discipline of international relations, which essentially began after World War I—the war that was supposed to end all wars—has been preoccupied with the question of how to prevent or stop war. With the rise of peace studies during the Vietnam era, IR also began to ask what peace is, because surely it must be more than simply the time between wars. Women have long been involved in analyzing how to stop war and how to create peace, though they have received no attention for these activities in past and most contemporary international relations literature. Instead, their peace efforts have been ignored or trivialized—largely by men who stereotype women as soft-headed, irrational pacifists. This characterization is political because it excludes women's perspectives from the study of war and peace. Instead, that subject is reserved for and addressed by "realists": ostensibly hard-headed, rational men, especially those with military experience.

In addition, the gendered division of violence positions women as life-givers, expected to mourn the toll of war quietly, pick up the pieces when it is over, and not undermine the war effort by asking For whom? and For what? Women who do ask questions are seen as ungrateful for the protection courageously delivered by men and states through their military might and actions. Yet despite this gendered state of affairs, women have protested loudly and often against war and for a more just and peaceful world (see Figure 5.2).

FIGURE 5.2   Women for Peace. This graphic, which appeared outside the Peace Tent at the NGO Forum during the final conference of the UN Decade for Women in 1985 in Nairobi, Kenya, quotes British novelist and essayist Virginia Woolf. Writing between World Wars I and II, she believed that women had common cause, enabling them to transcend borders and end wars. Courtesy of the International Women's Tribune Centre, Inc. Illustrator: Anne S. Walker.

Examples extend from the fifth-century B.C. Athenian play *Lysistrata,* in which women refused to sleep with men who went to war, to the International Women's Gulf Peace Initiative in 1991 against hostilities in the Persian Gulf. However, it was not until the rise of the first wave of feminism, during the latter part of the nineteenth century, that the political linkage between peace and women's emancipation was made. This pre–World War I period is considered the golden age of peace movements in the West. Predominantly white, middle-class women formed a variety of peace societies (such as the Union Internationale des Femmes, the Ligue des Femmes pour Desarmament, the Alliance des Femmes pour la Paix, and the Société d'Education Pacifique in France), which were used as models for women's peace societies elsewhere in Western Europe, the United States, and even Japan.[15] Liberal feminist peace activists made their presence known at major international peace conferences, including the first and second Hague conferences in 1899 and 1907, respectively.[16] And socialist feminists organized their own international conferences, such as the First and the Second International Conference of Socialist Women, held in 1907 and 1910, respectively, at which they endorsed resolutions against the militarism of imperialist powers.[17]

In 1915, predominantly white, middle-class feminists in the United States under the leadership of Jane Addams formed the U.S. Woman's Peace Party (WPP). The WPP tapped both practical and strategic gender interests by calling for women's suffrage (the right to vote) and arguing that the role of women as mothers gave them a special moral responsibility to oppose war. Not all suffragists supported a platform of peace, especially after World War I had broken out. But in 1915, 1,136 delegates from twelve countries made a dangerous wartime journey to The Hague to attend the International Congress of Women to protest against the war. The congress passed twenty resolutions on the destruction of humanity, the use of sons for cannon fodder, and the victimization of mothers/women that war inflicted.[18] The congress also founded the Women's International League for Peace and Freedom, which continues to exist, with headquarters in Geneva and thousands of chapters all over the world (see Figure 5.3).

During the interwar years, white, middle-class women in large numbers joined organizations such as the British Peace Pledge Union and, within these organizations, formed their own women's committees and peace campaigns.[19] As World War II loomed, such organizations collapsed when both women and men were drawn into the war effort by their governments. Governments appealed to women's practical and strategic gender interests. They encouraged women to support their "boys" by mothering the nation through rationing, buying war bonds, and doing volunteer work for the duration. They also offered women jobs in wartime industries that had previously been closed to them.[20] Yet this combination was not entirely liberating. Even though women went out to work in large numbers, they were still expected to fulfill the maternal role for servicemen and the nation.[21]

As a result, when men came home from war, most women were laid off from higher-paying jobs in wartime industries and were expected to go back to being full-time homemakers. This was, however, a "luxury" affordable only to white, upper-middle-class women: In actuality, 84 percent of all U.S. women working during 1944–1945 were doing so out of economic necessity,[22] and only 600,000 women had left the paid workforce by 1946.[23] Nevertheless, 58 percent of U.S. women in 1943 felt that they could "best help the war effort by staying at home."[24] The onerous task of combining work with family led many married women to leave their jobs readily, albeit under pressure from husbands, unions, and bosses who were hostile to their presence in the workforce when the war ended. In this sense, the disruptions of World War II did not really chal-

FIGURE 5.3 "Are These Your Priorities?" Activists from a coalition of groups, including the Women's International League for Peace and Freedom, Citizens for Participation in Political Action, and the Massachusetts Common Agenda, handed out leaflets in downtown Boston on April 15 (tax day), 1992. They provided information on current federal spending of tax dollars and sought greater public awareness of the need to reduce military spending and reapportion money to domestic areas such as education, housing, health care, and the environment. Courtesy Marilyn Humphries, Impact Visuals.

lenge or undermine gender roles and dichotomies, which were ultimately deepened and reinforced.

At the same time, the fact that women—especially white, middle-class women—were encouraged to take their role as wives and mothers as definitive during the 1950s led some of them into antimilitary movements from the 1960s through the 1980s. For example, the 1960s saw the rise of Women Strike for Peace in the United States and the Voice of Women in Canada, which organized to "End the Arms Race, Not the Human Race."[25] Women Strike for Peace organized a one-day strike on November 1, 1961, in which 50,000 women left their homes and workplaces to protest the arms race. So threatening was this action to Cold War orthodoxy that in 1962 the House Committee on Un-American Activities accused leaders of this grass-roots women's movement of being Communists.[26]

FIGURE 5.4   Peace Encampment. On December 12, 1983, 30,000 women from all over the world surrounded the military base at Greenham Common in the United Kingdom to protest the deployment of cruise missiles. Courtesy Catherine Allport, Impact Visuals.

During the 1980s, a host of women's antinuclear groups emerged in response to the post-détente resurgence of the arms race and the U.S. testing and deployment of cruise missiles. These groups ranged from the Oxford Mothers for Nuclear Disarmament (U.K.), Women Opposed to Nuclear Technology (U.K.), and the Women's Pentagon Action (U.S.), to women's peace camps set up outside nuclear installations throughout Europe and North America. These women's peace encampments, including Greenham Common (see Figure 5.4) and "Molesworth in England, Comiso in Italy, Hunsruck in West Germany, Seneca and Puget Sound in the United States, Nanoose in Canada, Soesterburg in Holland, Pine Gap in Australia, and others,"[27] attracted many thousands of women who insisted that life on the nuclear precipice was intolerable to them, their children, and their grandchildren. This perspective encouraged many women to demand an end to East-West hostilities by staging "peace walks" from Stockholm to Moscow and organizing international women's peace conferences such as the one called "The Urgency for True Security: Women's Alternatives for Negotiating Peace" held in Halifax, Nova Scotia (Canada), in 1985 and the subsequent Women's "Peace Tent" experiment at the Non-Governmental Forum for the end of the UN Decade for Women Conference in Nairobi, also in 1985.[28]

At the same time, groups such as the Mothers of the Plaza de Mayo in Argentina and Mothers of El Salvador organized to bear witness to brutal regimes that had made their children "disappear." Women in Northern Ireland, such as Mairead Corrigan and Betty Williams, who won the Nobel Peace Prize in 1977, rallied to stop the bloodshed between Protestants and Catholics. The Mothers of the Heroes and Martyrs in Nicaragua cried out against the U.S.-sponsored contra war against the Sandinista government and its people; the Shibokusa women of Mount Fuji in Japan protested the expropriation of land by the U.S. and Japanese militaries; the Sri Lankan Voice of Women for Peace was calling for the end of the civil war between Sinhalese and Tamils; women of Fiji appealed to the French government to stop nuclear testing in the South Pacific; and black South African women were still struggling against the violence of apartheid.[29]

The end of the Cold War has not brought the end of peace movements as civil and regional conflicts rage on, military budgets are still bloated, huge nuclear stockpiles remain in place, and attempts to institute a comprehensive nuclear test ban treaty have so far failed. On the positive side, 1997 saw the signing of treaties to ban chemical weapons and landmines. And in the same year, Jody Williams, a woman from rural Vermont in the United States, won the Nobel Peace Prize for forming and leading the International Campaign to Ban Landmines, which, after six years of struggle, convinced 122 countries (with the notable exception of the United States) to sign the December 1997 treaty banning these weapons that kill at least 26,000 people per year.[30] This makes her the seventh woman in the twentieth century to receive such an honor, and one of three to receive it in the 1990s. Daw Aung San Suu Kyi, the democratically elected leader of Myanmar (formerly Burma), who was prevented from taking office and put under house arrest by the current dictatorial regime, won it in 1990. Rigoberta Menchu, a Guatemalan Indian peasant, was awarded it in 1992 for her struggles to end the persecution of her people during the thirty-six-year civil war in Guatemala, which tentatively ended with the signing of the first truce in December 1996.

Women have also been instrumental in bringing about the Middle East peace process. Palestinian women were major organizers of and participants in the *intifada* (uprising) that began in 1988 against Israeli occupation. Israeli women, operating in solidarity with Palestinian women, engaged in many forms of peace activism, the best known of which were the weekly vigils of Women in Black (see Figure 5.5). These city streetcorner

FIGURE 5.5   Women in Black. This vigil took place in Jerusalem in 1993.
Courtesy Olivia Heussler, Impact Visuals.

vigils, which bore witness to the occupation and demanded an end to it, began in 1988, were interrupted briefly during the Persian Gulf war, and ended in 1993 just after the Israeli-Palestinian peace accord was signed in Oslo.[31] With the subsequent assassination of Israeli Prime Minister Rabin by a Jewish fundamentalist and a harder-line government coming to power, the peace process is now seriously faltering. Women are again taking to the streets.

As Cynthia Enloe observes, "Wars—hot and cold—are like love affairs. They don't just end. They fizzle and sputter; sometimes they reignite. Mornings after are times for puzzling, sorting things out, for trying to assess whether one is starting a new day or continuing an old routine."[32] For most women, the so-called end of war means that the struggles for peace and justice are just beginning. The 20,000 South Korean women who were used as sexual slaves, or "comfort women," by Japanese soldiers during World War II have been struggling for compensation for this war crime for more than fifty years.[33] It was only in 1998 that three such women were awarded the equivalent of US$2,300 each by a Japanese court.[34] Meanwhile, Japanese women continue to protest the U.S. military presence in Okinawa, which has been responsible for so many rapes there. MADRE, a U.S.-based international human rights organization, is working with Rwandan women and girls—who constitute 70 percent of the remaining population of that country and almost all of whom have been raped—to try to heal themselves and rebuild their society. MADRE has been doing similar work with women in Haiti, the former Yugoslavia, and parts of Central America.[35]

The motivation of much of this past and contemporary peace building and peace organizing by women has been their identification with and assigned responsibility for mothering. For many of these women, an interest in protecting their children and future generations from the ravages of war and war preparation has been paramount. But they also call attention to the fact that reproductive work in terms of providing food and shelter for their families is made much more difficult—and even impossible—by war machines that eat up people and resources. Thus, women's political action on behalf of peace often arises from "practical" gender interests emerging from women's assigned roles in the so-called private sphere.

On the face of it, these women's struggles for peace do little to disrupt gender dichotomies because they leave in place the image of men as aggressive and bellicose life-takers/killers in contrast to women as pacifist life-givers/reproducers/mothers. However, these struggles are feminist in that they do call into question other aspects of gender hierarchy produced by the gendered division of violence. For example, by the very act of "leaving home" and taking on so-called public-sphere institutions and issues—often at the risk of death and imprisonment or, at the very least, censure by governments and mainstream societies—these women challenge the idea that women are weak, passive victims who can only mourn their fate on the homefront. Similarly, such actions belie the idea that it is only men who suffer from the ravages of war and war preparation and that war-related deaths occur only on the battlefield. In fact, women's protests against war and all other kinds of state violence reveal generally hidden and unfamiliar costs of modern total warfare.

Moreover, the horrors that women identify completely undermine the notion that men are protectors and that women are protected. Insofar as the male-dominated state security apparatus is the cause of their suffering and that of their children, many of these female peace activists ask, Who is going to protect us, or how are we going to protect ourselves, from the protectors? It is in the struggle to answer this question that many women have become "soldiers for peace," a contradiction in itself that forces us to rethink gender categories, identities, and practices.

Within these movements as well are women struggling on behalf of their strategic gender interests. Peace activists who most readily identify themselves as feminists are more wary of tactics that promote or celebrate motherhood as the basis for women's peace activism.[36] Socialist feminists are aware that women's responsibility for mothering has often brought them into the struggle for peace (a connection that cultural feminism highlights), yet they and other radical feminists warn us that until reproductive labor is no longer the sole or major responsibility of women, there will be no real change in the priorities of states, international organizations, and the mostly elite men who run them. Moreover, as long as women remain tied to the currently devalued "private sphere," their protests will be marginalized by those in power, who will continue to expect the women to "pick up the pieces" in the wake of continual destruction. Indeed, these feminists ask whether there can be any peace worth having in the absence of gender, race, and class justice.

Finally, postmodern feminist peace activists argue that neither women nor mothers are innately peaceful or necessarily life-givers. On the contrary, women, like men, have always served militaries and supported wars—as spouses, workers, soldiers, government officials, and parents. When we dispel the notion that the struggle for peace is not some innate feminine attribute that is "soft" and available only to women, the way will be opened up for many more to join the struggle for peace *and* justice such that world politics will enhance, rather than undermine, the survival and equality of all.

NATIONALIST AND ANTINATIONALIST MOVEMENTS

The fact that women take up arms in national liberation struggles contradicts the stereotype that women are naturally peaceful (see Figure 5.6). As noted in Chapter 3, women have participated as leaders and followers in

FIGURE 5.6 Taking Up Arms. A female guerrilla fighter in the Zapatista revolutionary army in Chiapas Mexico in 1994. Courtesy Fred Chase, Impact Visuals.

populist struggles and violence throughout recorded history. For every female revolutionary leader such as Joan of Arc, Olympes de Gouge, Rosa Luxemburg, Alexandra Kollantai, Dora Maria Tellez, and Winnie Mandela, there have been millions of women who took action in countless uprisings, guerrilla movements, and revolutions—ranging from the French, American, Russian, and Chinese revolutions to more recent revolutionary struggles throughout Latin America, the Caribbean, Africa, and the Middle East.[37] Not all these women have taken up arms. More typically they have worked in underground movements to hide and heal guerrilla fighters, pass information and weapons, and organize communities in support of the revolution. Still, most revolutionary women have advocated armed struggle as a necessary, although not the only, facet of revolutionary action.

Although often motivated by the same concerns as men—a desire to overthrow corrupt regimes, to fight colonialism and imperialism, and to build nationalism and a national economy not controlled and impoverished by foreign elites—women also join or are encouraged to join revolutionary struggles on behalf of their practical and strategic gender interests. In the testimonial literature that chronicles women's experiences in nationalist struggles, we find women revolutionaries who were drawn into the struggle both as mothers responsible for providing for their families and as women seeking greater equality with men, first on the battlefield and then in the government of the new state-to-be. Consistent with the pattern observed in peace movements, women tend to become involved initially because of their practical gender interests. But as they encounter sexism in nationalist and revolutionary movements, women often begin to recognize and work toward strategic gender interests.

An example is the role of women and women's associations in the revolutionary struggle against the Somoza regime in Nicaragua. Gloria Carrion was active in the Association of Nicaraguan Women Confronting the Nation's Problems (AMPRONAC) and became the general coordinator of the Luisa Amanda Espinosa Nicaraguan Women's Association (AMNLAE) after the victory of the Sandinista National Liberation Front (FSLN). Lea Guido was also an organizer with AMPRONAC and, later, the minister of public health in the National Reconstruction government. In interviews, both Carrion and Guido reported that women were drawn into the struggle on the basis of their family and maternal roles.

Carrion described women as "the centres of their families—emotionally, ideologically and economically"—who do not see themselves "'simply' as housewives" subordinated to husbands.[38] Guido told of a women's campaign around the slogan "Our Children Are Hungry, Bring Down the Cost of Living." She argued that the parties of the traditional left had failed to mobilize women because they did not address women's practical gender interests. The women's campaign was successful "because we learned how to involve women in the national struggle while at the same time organizing around problems specific to women."[39] AMPRONAC and, later, AMNLAE brought many women into nonviolent aspects of revolutionary struggle on the basis of their practical gender interests. Engaging in revolutionary violence generated particular problems for women. By becoming guerrilla fighters, women transgressed their traditional gender roles and were often seen as threatening to revolutionary men. Confronting the sexism of their comrades, many women were awakened to strategic gender interests. Monica Baltonado, a guerrilla commander of the Nicaraguan Revolution, pointed out that the extent of sexism among men of the FSLN varied:

> Some comrades were open to dealing with sexism while others remained closed. Some said women were no good in the mountains, that they were only good "for screwing," that they created conflicts—sexual conflicts. But there were also men with very good positions. Carlos Fonseca, for example, was a solid comrade on this issue. It's been a long struggle! We won those battles through discussions and by women comrades demonstrating their ability and their resistance.[40]

Women, who constituted over 30 percent of guerrilla combatants, did prove their mettle in the insurrections against Somoza's regime.[41] However, after the triumph, they made up only 6 percent of military officers in the Sandinista People's Army (EPS), which discouraged women's participation on the basis that women's first obligation is to motherhood.[42] After protests from AMNLAE, three women's *reserve* battalions were set up. The majority of women who wanted to defend the revolution were active in two organizations: the Sandinista Popular Militias (MPS), designed to defend farms and factories against sabotage by U.S.-supported contra forces, and the Sandinista Defense Committees (CDS), which organized neighborhoods to create better living conditions. The MPS and the CDS were viewed—by male leaders and often by women themselves—as more consistent with women's mothering roles and family responsibilities. Indeed, although AMNLAE's symbol was a picture of a young woman with a rifle on her back and a baby in her arms, in actuality most Nicaraguan women were encouraged to put down the gun and pick up their baby after the triumph.

That mothering was incompatible with violent revolutionary action was recognized by women fighting for the independence of Zimbabwe in the 1970s. One young female guerrilla reported that women were able to convince their male comrades to accept the use of contraceptives by arguing that "to be sent back to Mozambique for five months to have a baby was a setback to the war."[43] The women who made this "practical" argument, however, had undergone deeper transformations that tapped their strategic gender interests, especially in regard to reproductive rights: "Our attitudes to contraception and abortion changed during the years of struggle. The girls really adopted a new way of living after what they've seen in the bush, the contacts they've had with other people from European countries, from the books they've read."[44]

Revolutionary struggles, indeed, create "new women" who transgress proscribed gender roles, but these women remain disadvantaged in terms of the gendered division of power and resources when the revolution is over. A spokesperson for the Omani Women's Organization, which was active in the People's Front for the Liberation of Oman in the mid-1970s, put it this way: "Many men had received education and political experience . . . before they joined the Front, while women had their first education and political experience when as young girls they joined the Revolution."[45] Because women had less formal training than men before the revolution, they were again left out of the picture when military demobilization proceeded. In sum, women are more easily demobilized and sent back home, whereas men assume positions of power in new regimes when revolutions are successful.[46]

A "successful" revolution is, conventionally, one in which a dictator or ruling regime is toppled and a new regime is put in its place. Rarely is a positive change in the condition and status of women viewed as a key measure of a revolution's "success." Nevertheless, there have been instances where conditions that intersect with women's practical gender interests have improved. Not infrequently, socialist revolutions brought improvements in meeting basic human needs. For example, delivery of improved health care reduces rates of infant mortality, provision of education expands work opportunities, and better nutrition supports a generally healthier population. Such gains particularly benefit the large numbers of poor women who are finally provided some assistance in meeting their assigned responsibility for sustaining the family.

In the area of women's strategic gender interests, some socialist revolutionary movements and later governments instituted reforms intended to break down sexual stereotypes and inequalities. For instance, Cuba's revolutionary government wrote a new Family Code that afforded women equal rights in marriage and divorce and called for equal responsibilities in the household, including shared housework.[47] Nicaragua's Sandinista government passed similar legislation in 1981.

Unfortunately, these and other such measures, although progressive in comparison to measures in many other countries, were not motivated solely or primarily by feminist concerns. More typically, the governments wanted to get more women into the productive labor force to increase the country's gross domestic product (GDP). Moreover, the shared-domestic-responsibility clauses in both the Cuban and Nicaraguan family codes were rarely enforced, which meant that men ultimately have had no obligations to participate equally in reproductive labor. Finally, the gains women made as a result of socialist revolutions—of either the practical or strategic variety—have been seriously eroded. This is a consequence of both internal and external dynamics: the economic, political, and social turmoil created by foreign military intervention and economic embargoes, civil wars, and the overthrow of socialist regimes in Eastern Europe, the Soviet Union, and Latin America. In Nicaragua, where the Sandinista government lost power in 1990, this has meant huge setbacks for women. Despite protests by thousands of women, the current right-wing regime of President Arnoldo Aleman is setting up a Ministry of Family that reestablishes and enforces patriarchal family relations and undermines services relating to single mothers, reproductive health care, and combating domestic violence.[48]

The so-called velvet revolutions that ended the communist regimes in Eastern Europe and the Soviet Union, in which women participated in great numbers, ushered in not just "democratizing" regimes but also "shock therapy" capitalism. As we discussed in Chapter 4, the latter has seriously undermined women's practical gender interests in terms of employment and access to formerly free public goods and services, such as health and child care. The former, as noted in Chapter 2, has ironically translated into precipitous declines in women's formal political representation. However, the greater freedom of expression available to women in these post-communist countries has led to the formation of autonomous feminist movements that are responding to the assaults on women arising from the unleashing of the forces of globalization, nationalism, and religious fundamentalism in such contexts. As a result of the years of betrayal that women experienced under state socialism, they are wary of both Western liberal and socialist feminist strategies that call for greater participation in the state and greater state intervention to redistribute resources. Since communist systems completely controlled and surveilled all public space, women under these systems had more maneuvering room in the private realm. Thus, post-communist feminist strategies focus more on changing civil society where control over women is now being exerted. As Nanette Funk puts it:

Reassertion of control over women's bodies and returning women to the home signifies men's regaining control over what was "theirs," a reappropriation of (male) collective identity and a symbol of having wrested control away from a dead state socialism. It similarly signifies the reinstituted power of the church. At the same time, the symbol of woman as mother is a useful instrument in nationalist conflicts.[49]

Socialist, post-communist, and older liberal democratic regimes rest on this **gendered nationalism,** which involves the manipulation of gender identities and symbols as well as gendered divisions of power, labor, and resources to build and maintain national unity. Struggles for economic and political justice have typically been framed within the context of national self-determination and autonomy—concepts that have a decidedly masculinist cast and, up to the present period, have largely translated into self-determination and autonomy for men and, especially, male leaders. As we have seen, this lauded self-determination has been made possible largely through women's undervalued and unheralded reproductive labor, which "frees" men for the seemingly greater heroics that shape *the* national identity. As Enloe observes, "The notion of what 'the nation' was at its finest hour—when it was most unified, most altruistic—will be a community in which women sacrificed their desires for the sake of the male-led collective."[50]

Under this construction of the nation, women's feminist aspirations are forced into conflict with their national allegiance, thus enabling old and new regimes to ignore and even vilify feminist demands. An extreme example of gendered nationalism infused the 1978 Iranian Revolution, in which large numbers of women contributed to the downfall of the shah, only to become the primary targets of sexual "purification" campaigns to limit their autonomy under the right-wing Islamist regime of the Ayatollah Khomeini.[51] But the pattern of gendered nationalism is in fact widespread. Virtually without exception, women have been used—as symbols of national morality and purity, as behind-the-scenes support workers, as guerrilla fighters—to win nationalist struggles. But with victory, the practical and strategic interests of women are subordinated to masculinist priorities in the name of national consolidation and continued unity. Nevertheless, women continue to participate in nationalist projects. This may implicate them as xenophobes in nationalist fundamentalist movements or, more positively, as those resisting global capitalist (re)colonization.

These points alert us to many vexing questions that feature in contemporary feminist debates regarding the relationship between nationalism and feminism: Is a feminist nationalism possible, or is this a contradiction in terms? Is there such a thing as a nonviolent, nonstatist, and nonexclusivist nationalist project? How do nationalist projects both unite and divide women? Can feminist identity politics transcend nationalist identity politics? How would the world be organized differently in terms of priorities and boundaries if feminist identities supplanted nationalist ones? There are no firm answers to these questions because, as Jan Jindy Pettman observes, "the nation never just is, anymore than the state just is. Nationality and citizenship, like race and ethnicity, are unstable categories and contested identities."[52] In Benedict Anderson's words, the nation is "an imagined community,"[53] or an ever shifting construction, which Pettman notes can evoke images of "the people" in terms that are either "racist and exclusivist" or "inclusive and multicultural."[54] But in all its forms to date, the construction of the nation has rested on constructing women as "the markers, reproducers and transmitters of the nation."[55] This makes women central to nationalist projects but ensures that they are given little political space to redefine what those projects could or should be or what alternative forms of identity could or should form the basis of a just political community.

ECONOMIC MOVEMENTS

Women's protests in regard to economic conditions are perhaps the most durable and pervasive example of their being political actors. As we have seen, women are at a disadvantage owing to the gendered division of labor within the home and family (the unpaid labor force), the gendered division of labor in the workplace (the paid labor force), and the gendered international division of labor (the global economy). These processes have relegated large numbers of women, especially those with children, to poverty and have given most women few options for earning a living wage or for moving up the economic ladder. The struggle to provide for themselves and their families on a day-to-day basis limits women's time and energy for political activism. But it has also served as a motivating force for even the poorest of women to leave their homes to protest the unfair economic straits in which they find themselves. These economic protests take many forms and sometimes bring women into related struggles, such as women's, peace, revolutionary, and ecological movements. Like their participation in other movements, women's participation in economic movements often emerges from practical gender interests.

The gendered division of labor within the home holds women primarily responsible for the well-being of the family. As a result, women are often quick to challenge authorities when the mainstays of life are threatened. It is the gender stereotype of women as life-giving and life-sustaining that positions women as primary caretakers and makes them the first to protest when economic conditions keep them from providing that care.

There are many examples of women taking to the streets collectively—in "bread riots," seizures of grain or foods, protests against the sale of overpriced goods, and/or demands for a just price for market products.[56] For instance, in the Flour War of 1775 that precipitated the French Revolution, women "took positive and often violent action to rectify intolerable conditions—conditions threatening to family and community stability."[57]

In 1929 women in Nigeria responded in force against colonial taxation and marketplace policies: "Tens of thousands of Igbo women marched, dressed in symbolic war attire, danced, chanted, sang, 'sat on' offending men, destroyed courts and prisons, freed prisoners, cut telegraph wires, set up their own courts and offices, closed down markets, collected money to sustain their actions, and set up or revived organizations for mutual support."[58]

Such actions are especially common in nonindustrialized contexts where the marketplace is dominated by women as producers, exchangers, and consumers of basic goods. There, traditional gender assignments make the provision of basic goods women's domain and serve to legitimize women's acting on behalf of family and community to protest against basic goods shortages. Also in these contexts, traditional gender assumptions that women are vulnerable and in need of protection serve, to some degree, to inhibit violent reprisals directed by authorities against their unauthorized demonstrations. However, women's participation is no guarantee that officials will not act swiftly and violently against economic protests, as the killing of fifty women in the Igbo "women's war" makes clear.[59]

In industrialized contexts, where most poor, urban women cannot produce basic goods and are made dependent on state welfare systems, women's protests against the impoverishment of their families often take the form of welfare rights movements. For example, from 1966 to 1970, the Brooklyn Welfare Action Council (B-WAC) organized thousands of welfare recipients to fight for minimum welfare standards that would guarantee the right of every family to have the essentials for survival and modern life. B-WAC members staged a number of visible and theatrical protests outside welfare offices and inside shopping complexes. They demanded supplemental payments and department store credit for welfare recipients who could not live from check to check. For a brief period of time, B-WAC succeeded in getting more funds to welfare recipients to pay for such modern essentials as "costs of laundry; graduation; layettes; confirmation, camp, gym, and spring clothes; and washing machines."[60]

These cases and many more like them suggest that women's struggles against the consequences of the gendered division of labor in the home—women's practical gender interests—are primarily local and short-term engagements. Because women are acting in their traditional roles as family caretakers, they are focused upon their most immediate economic needs and usually seek only relief, not social transformation. As a result, their gains are typically temporary. The basis of their struggles does not challenge—but rather reinforces—their gender roles, leaving them still responsible for reproductive labor, even under the worst economic conditions. The point is that as long as reproductive labor is viewed as a private matter to which women are assigned, neither men as individuals nor the agencies of the state are under any obligation to do more than provide temporary—and usually insufficient—relief in response to women's economic protests.

In the face of meager and grudging assistance to women responsible for "unpaid" reproductive tasks, some women are challenging the notion that women's reproductive labor is just a private matter that does not even constitute "work." Some women's economic movements emphasize the fact that reproductive labor is the precondition of all other human activities: We cannot exist without the work that women do in food production and preparation, emotional and physical caretaking, and maintenance of the material and psychological dimensions of what we think of as home. Domestic work is essential, yet we deny its value to ourselves (as individuals whose emotional and material "basic needs" must be met) and to our societies (which would perish without this unpaid labor). Just how extensive and valuable is this labor? According to Ruth Leger Sivard, the "value of women's work in the household alone, if given economic value, would add an estimated one-quarter to one-third to the world's GNP."[61]

Denying the centrality and value of domestic labor has various consequences for women's and men's lives. The most basic reality is that women, who spend more time working than men, are accorded less status for what they do, and men increasingly accumulate control over cash resources. "Tilting first under rules that say women must do all domestic work, the scales are tipped further by men's greater opportunities to earn wages. Advantage builds on advantage until today they are tilted so steeply that almost all of the world's wealth is on man's side, while most of the world's work is on woman's."[62]

Women have protested the devaluation of domestic work and men's increasing economic control in diverse ways. The risk of divorce, loss of economic support, and threat of violence (against themselves and/or their children) make going on strike in the home a risky option for women. But women do resist by following strategies of "refusing to cooperate." For example, men grow maize (corn) and women grow groundnut (peanuts) in Zambia. When maize profits soared, women did not shift production in their fields to the more lucrative maize "because they—and not their husbands—kept the money from sales of groundnut."[63] Women also challenge the devaluation of their domestic work by insisting that they be paid for it. In the past several decades, "wages for housework" campaigns have been a feature of feminist debate and political action, especially in Europe and North America.

In a parallel vein, feminists have challenged national and international (UN, World Bank, IMF) accounting methods that keep women's domestic

FIGURE 5.7   National Accounting. This graphic represents the Women's Budget Initiative in South Africa in 1996, which calls for all government departments at all levels to determine budget impacts on and priorities for women. Courtesy of International Women's Tribune Centre, Inc. Illustrator: Anne S. Walker.

work invisible by according it no value in estimating national productivity. For example, the Sisterhood is Global Institute sponsors census projects conducted by women's organizations in many countries to make this time and effort visible, thereby pressuring international and national agencies to start counting it.[64] As Carol Lees points out, the effects of national accounting are not gender neutral: "As a result of the exclusion of women's labor from information gathering we are denied proper access to programs and policy at every level of government in every country"[65] (see Figure 5.7).

These actions extend beyond women's practical gender interests because their goals are not only better conditions for women to perform reproductive labor but also equity in the cash resources available to women and men. By redefining women's reproductive labor as work on which the public sphere depends and by demanding payment for this work, women are attacking the ideological and structural barriers that impoverish them relative to men. However, revaluing domestic work does not necessarily challenge the stereotype that only women should do it, nor does it disrupt the idea that men are better suited for more highly paid jobs in the public sphere.

The gendered division of labor in the workforce has stirred many women to join trade union movements in the hope of improving general working conditions and wages as well as receiving pay equity relative to men in the same or comparable jobs. Berenice Carroll reminds us that it was women who initiated the earliest industrial labor strikes during the first half of the nineteenth century and a strike by women was the first of the rebellious actions that culminated in the Russian Revolution.[66] From the 1909 uprising of female shirtwaist factory workers in New York that inspired the formation of the International Ladies Garment Workers Union, to the Women Workers Movement founded in 1984 in the Philippines to protest labor conditions for women in free trade zones, to the creation of the Homeworkers' Association in Toronto, Canada, in 1992, women have been active organizers. And their efforts have had international implications. However, as these examples suggest, women often have created their own trade unions because they were marginalized or silenced by male-dominated unions concentrated in heavy industries, where women workers are in the minority.

Because of most women's locations within the wage labor market—in low-wage, light-industry, and service jobs as well as in the so-called informal labor force of street vendors and subsistence agricultural producers—their labor organizing is more difficult, but also more varied, than the typical workplace-centered organizing that occurs in male-dominated industries. For example, in India, women street vendors formed the Self-Employed Women's Association (SEWA) to demand better wages from commodity suppliers. Because traditional trade unions did not organize such workers until very recently, SEWA, which began in 1972, had to develop a pioneering and imaginative strategy. Women street vendors organized other women street vendors by visiting them on the street and in their homes and providing literacy training so that they could participate more fully and equally in decision-making. The Honduran Federation of Peasant Women, another group that was overlooked by industry-based union movements, sought not better wages from their employers (multinational, or transnational, corporations that were paying them the equivalent of US$2.00 a day) but, rather, alternative income-generating opportunities that would release them from having to work for MNCs.[67]

These examples show women's labor organizing to be oriented toward increasing women's autonomy as workers. Seeking more control over their working hours and workplaces reflects their practical gender interests in having more time and energy to perform their reproductive labor. However, the strategies employed to achieve these ends often lead women to challenge a host of institutions and policies that traditional labor organizing fails to confront. For example, in order to promote healthier and safer conditions for women workers in the Philippines, the feminist organization known as the General Assembly Binding Women for Reform, Integrity, Equality, Leadership, and Action (GABRIELA) has organized women and men around such issues as "International Monetary Fund and World Bank intervention, U.S. military and economic intervention, government land reform policies, government budget allocations, establishment of a nonalignment policy and a nuclear-free-zone provision for the Philippines."[68] GABRIELA also promotes income-generating activities, community development, vocational-training and educational programs, opportunities for feminist research, and transnational linkages with other women's movements. In this way, the strategic gender interests of women are awakened and mobilized in the process of fighting for working conditions that better meet their practical gender interests.

These national and local women's struggles in the waged labor force are linked through transnational women's economic movements that challenge the international gendered division of labor that shores up the current capitalist global economy. Formed in 1974, the Women's International Information and Communication Service (ISIS/WICCE), at different times based in Switzerland, Uganda, Italy, the Philippines, and Chile, has connected more than 10,000 women's groups in 130 countries. Among the many issues and strategies ISIS/WICCE deals with is the organizing of women's groups against economic development policies that marginalize and exploit women workers.[69] Since 1978, the American Friends Service Committee, through its Women and Global Corporations Project, has linked workers, activists, and researchers worldwide who are promoting legislation to stop TNC practices that are reducing jobs and wages for women workers in the North and exploiting women's cheap labor in the South.[70]

The debt crises and structural adjustment programs imposed by international lending institutions have had particularly negative consequences for women. Accordingly, a variety of global and regional women's and development organizations have focused on combating these gender-differentiated effects. Such groups include Development Alternatives with Women for a New Era (DAWN), founded by Third World and First World women researchers and activists, which produced its first analysis of development strategies and their gendered consequences for the Nairobi meeting that concluded the UN Decade for Women.[71] Since then, DAWN's Latin American Region Research Group has connected Latin American women's groups developing alternative economic strategies with poor women and their local organizations. This networking includes "the Centro de Estudios de la Mujer in Chile and in Argentina; La Morada, also in Chile; Flora Tristan in Peru; CIPAF in the Dominican Republic; IDAC in Rio de Janeiro; the Rede Mulher in São Paulo, CEAAL throughout Latin America; the SOS Corpo in Recife and innumerable other groups."[72] DAWN is also working with the Women and Development Unit (WAND) in the Caribbean and the African Association of Women for Research and Development (AAWORD) in West Africa "to evaluate standard macro- and micro-economic analyses, document their negative impact on women, and develop alternative frameworks."[73]

As globalization forces have intensified worldwide in the 1990s, DAWN has also formed a coalition with feminist organizations in the North working on gender and global restructuring issues. The Women's Global Alliance for Development Alternatives includes DAWN, Women in Development Europe (WIDE), Alternative Women in Development (Alt-WID), in the United States, the National Action Committee on the Status of Women (NAC), in Canada, the Canadian Research Institute for the Advancement of Women (CRIAW), the Center for Women's Global Leadership, in the United States, the Society for International Development/Women in Development Program (SID-WID), in Europe, the Eurostep Gender Working Group, and the Women, Environment and Development Organization (WEDO), in the United States. This alliance, which was forged through a succession of UN conferences on sustainable development, human rights, population issues, and women's rights through the first half of the 1990s, made its debut at the World Summit for Social Development held in Copenhagen in 1995. Recognizing that globalization has produced poverty in both the South and the North, while enriching only a few in either region, this alliance came together to insist that "development alternatives must come from the international women's movement working alongside other progressive movements."[74]

Several such alternatives were outlined in Ottawa at a 1994 meeting of international feminist academic and activist experts on gender and global restructuring in preparation for the 1995 Fourth World Conference on Women in Beijing.[75] The following measures were recommended: that Western Banks and IFIs forgive the debts owed to them by Third World countries in order to stop imposing unsustainable austerity programs; that a transaction tax on all international financial flows be imposed to generate funding to increase social welfare spending and aid and to increase access to credit for women; that representation on the governing boards of IFIs and the leadership councils of trade unions be gender balanced; that TNC labor and environmental practices be regulated; that social and environmental clauses appear in all trade agreements; and that all International Labor Organization (ILO) conventions to protect workers be ratified and enforced by all national governments.

Such demands are also emerging from regional cross-border women's organizations. Mujer a Mujer, for example, mobilized Mexican, American, and Canadian women workers initially to resist the imposition of NAFTA and later to monitor the enforcement of and further extend its social and environmental clauses. Women's organizing within traditional trade unions has prompted the American Federation of Labor and Congress of Industrial Organizations (AFL-CIO), the Trade Union Congress (TUC), in the United Kingdom, the International Ladies Garment Workers Union (ILGWU), and the International Confederation of Free Trade Unions

FIGURE 5.8 Women Workers Mobilize. Shown here are Asian-American women at an anti-NAFTA rally during an AFL-CIO convention in San Francisco in 1993. Courtesy Rick Gerharter, Impact Visuals.

(ICFTU) not only to increase efforts to organize women workers in all sectors but also to support these demands, including bringing women (especially women of color) into union leadership positions (see Figure 5.8). Finally, organizations of poor women on welfare and recipients of foreign aid are linking transnationally to stop the erosion of the welfare state in the North and the developmental state in the South. This, however, raises feminist questions and debates about whether the state, in the North or South, can be sufficiently stripped of its patriarchal or gendered underpinnings to be an equitable redistributor of resources to women and a reliable partner in resistance to global capital.

In sum, women in many countries are engaging in unprecedented global and regional organizing efforts to confront a host of economic exploiters—from IFIs and development agencies to transnational corporations to sex tourism operators. Women's nongovernmental organizations are committed to grass-roots organizing by poor and working-class women, whose struggles are given support by the research of, but not led by, more privileged academic women. Although the immediate goal of these struggles is to meet the practical gender interests articulated by poor and working-class women, the analysis that informs these struggles goes to the heart of every woman's strategic gender interests—interests that many men increasingly disenfranchised by globalization are beginning to share. That analysis exposes the gendered division of labor in all its forms and shows that this division prevents most women from having an equitable share of local, national, and global wealth, despite the fact that they are now the primary breadwinners the world over. Because women have so many economic responsibilities but few rights and resources, they have become primary actors in the struggles to reform and transform markets and states, calling for, in Valentine Moghadam's words, a "new gender contract" that is "predicated on women's full citizenship, recognition of their economic contributions, and entitlement to social benefits."[76]

ECOLOGY MOVEMENTS

Perhaps the newest form of women's political action is in the area of saving the environment. From the tree-hugging Chipko Movement in India to the tree-planting Greenbelt Movement in Kenya and the nature-worshiping ecofeminist movement in North America, women are on the move to stop the rape of Mother Earth. For Third World rural women, saving the environment is crucial to economic survival. As the primary gatherers of food, fuel, and water, these women have particularly strong interests in reversing deforestation, desertification, and water pollution (see Figure 5.9). When these processes threaten women's abilities to draw upon natural resources for themselves and their families, the women act in the only way available to them—putting their bodies on the line:

> In 1974, village women of the Reni forests of the Chamoli district in Uttar Pradesh decided to act against a commercial enterprise about to fell some 2,500 trees. The women were alone; the menfolk had left home in search of work. When the contractors arrived, the women went into the forest, joined hands and encircled the trees ("Chipko" means to hug). The women told the cutters that to cut the trees, they would first have to cut off their heads. The contractors withdrew and the forest was saved.[77]

Like women's struggles against immediate economic threats posed by the gendered division of labor, creative responses to the gendered division of resources may be effective in the short term, but they fail to address long-term systemic issues. In the Chipko case, the responses confronted but did not undermine forces of global capitalism that are among the ma-

Women in the landscape

Women as fetchers of water, collectors of firewood, tillers of the land and as mothers are usually the first to feel the effects of environmental degradation in the developing world. They are also in the best position to manage the environment but their role is frequently ignored by policy makers and planners.

In Africa, women are responsible for 75% of all subsistence agriculture and 95% of domestic work.

FIGURE 5.9   Women for the Land. This illustration shows how close women's work is to the land and how responsible women are for its preservation. Originally from "The State of the World's Women 1985." Courtesy of United Nations Department of Public Information.

jor causes of deforestation, nor did they challenge the idea that only women need be the stewards of the environment because they are closer to nature than men. These spontaneous strategies also typically fail to redistribute in favor of women the resources necessary for more effective long-term organizing.

The Greenbelt Movement in Kenya, formed by Wangari Maathai of the National Council of Women, has begun a resource-generating process through which women can become more effective stewards of the environment. After instituting an effective national tree-planting campaign, the movement established a tree nursery. "Women are involved in rearing the seedlings, planting and marketing; in addition to becoming expert foresters, they also earn a cash income. The Greenbelt Movement is not only restoring the environment, but also enables women to benefit from environmental education, and to practice professional forestry techniques, while at the same time they are developing their status."[78] This kind of organizing not only meets women's practical gender interests but also creates conditions under which women can fight for their strategic gender interests.

This holistic strategy is also evident in such movements as the Calcutta Social Project, started by middle-class Indian women in the 1960s. The Calcutta Social Project was designed to change the lives of the poor who were forced to live on and around the city's massive waste dumps. "They began with literacy and recreational classes for young garbage pickers in an abandoned shed. Then vocational training in carpentry, masonry, and sewing were added. A primary health care clinic now flourishes."[79] Such projects not only reduce the misery experienced by people living in extreme poverty but also give them the tools to change their landscape and their work. Once again, however, such projects do not directly counteract the economic, political, and social forces that construct and perpetuate a "throw-away" society.

For Western ecofeminists, the key to confronting systemic forces that despoil the environment is questioning the treatment of both women and nature as resources to be used and abused by men and industries. This orientation gained momentum in 1980 following the Three Mile Island nuclear power plant accident in Pennsylvania. Shortly afterward, 600 women gathered for a weekend meeting on "Women and Life on Earth: A Conference on Eco-Feminism in the Eighties." Ecofeminist Ynestra King opened this conference, proclaiming: "We're here to say the word ECOLOGY and announce that for us as feminists it's a political word—that it stands against the economics of the destroyers and the pathology of racist hatred. It's a way of being, which understands that there are connections between all living things and that indeed women are the fact and flesh of connectedness."[80]

In 1980 this U.S. movement spawned a similar one in the United Kingdom, which became known as Women for Life on Earth. Ecofeminist activists on both sides of the Atlantic were prominent in the 1980 and 1981 Women's Pentagon Actions and in the encirclement of the Greenham Common nuclear base on December 12, 1980. These actions were based on the premise that "we see the devastation of the earth and her beings by the corporate warriors and the threat of nuclear annihilation by the military warriors as feminist concerns."[81]

From this ecofeminist perspective, if patriarchy, capitalism, racism, industrial development, and militarism are the sources of environmental degradation, then women are the solution to it. Rather than questioning the gender stereotypes that associate women with nature and stewardship, most ecofeminists insist that women are closer to nature because of the reproductive and productive work they do and, thus, are in the best position to care for the environment. Ecofeminists use this argument in an attempt to counter other gender stereotypes about women and nature as objectified and passive resources, which powerful men may manipulate for their own purposes.

Just as mainstream environmentalist movements in the West have been accused of racism, sexism, and elitism,[82] Western ecofeminist views have been criticized for their essentialism. Insisting that women have a closer relationship to nature because their bodies are more attuned to it is actually the result of patriarchal ideologies that fuse women with nature. A more effective strategy would emphasize

> that women and nature are simultaneously subjugated, and that this subjugation takes historically and culturally specific forms. If women take themselves seriously as social agents and as constitutive factors in this process, their praxis to end this double subjugation can be rooted not so much in women's equation with nature, but in taking responsibility for their own lives and environment.[83]

This approach developed out of international organizing around women, environment, and development (WED) issues that culminated in the Women's Action Agenda 21, which was drafted at the "Women and the Environment—Partners in Life" global women's conference held in Miami in 1991. This agenda was brought forward to the UN Conference on Environment and Development (UNCED), also known as the Earth Summit, in Rio de Janeiro in June 1992. In the agenda,

> global development and environmental problems were summarized as wasteful overconsumption in the developed world, inappropriate development leading to debt and structural adjustment in the South, increased poverty and continued land and forest degradation, environmental damage, pollution, toxic wastes, population growth, creation of ecological refugees and last but not least, excessive war and military spending associated with environmental damage.[84]

In response to these processes that undermine both the earth and women, women demanded in Miami and Rio de Janeiro that they should have

> the right to bring their perspectives, values, skills, and experiences into policy-making at all levels and to be on equal footing with men in UNCED and beyond. They called for a "Healthy Planet" in which participatory democracy, open access to information, accountability, ethical action, justice and the full participation of women are realized. They challenged the present development model with its economistic conception of sustainability and suggested a more holistic notion of politically, socially and culturally sustainable development, that is, sustainable livelihoods for all.[85]

Unfortunately, the UNCED conference produced few binding agreements and little change in the use and abuse of the environment and women. If anything, globalization forces since then have conspired to reverse what few agreements were reached. For example, although at UNCED industrialized countries pledged to reduce greenhouse gases to their 1990 levels by the year 2000, it was acknowledged at the 1997 UN conference on global warming in Kyoto that the United States was "likely to increase emissions of carbon dioxide by 13 percent" by the end of the 1990s as a result of "an economic boom that has overwhelmed steady improvements in industrial energy efficiency" and "gas-guzzling vehicles slaked by affordable gasoline."[86] Thus, at this conference, the United States, which emits 20 percent of the world's greenhouse gases, refused to join with other industrialized countries that had met their targets, to set further emission-reduction timetables. In addition, very little aid was offered to Third World countries to help them address pollution.

Women, however, and especially indigenous or aboriginal women, continue to be on the frontlines of ecological struggle. For example, women of the Mirrar people in Northern Australia are struggling against the open-pit mining of uranium, which despoils their water and threatens the home of their ancestral spirit. With the help of other environmental activists, they have brought their case to federal court in Sydney and to the UN Educational, Scientific, and Cultural Organization (UNESCO) in Paris. The latter designated their land as a world heritage site in 1992.[87] Meanwhile, the Indian women of Chiapas in Southern Mexico have been significant participants in the Zapatista rebellion that ignited on the day NAFTA was enacted in 1994. To them, NAFTA represents a "death sentence" to their culture and their communal agricultural land, which they are losing to privatization and the end of agricultural subsidies.[88] At the time the rebellion began, 75 percent of the population of Mexico supported the goals of the uprising[89] and protested in solidarity with the Zapatistas (see Figure 5.10).

These ecological struggles, and countless others across the Americas and the Pacific where indigenous peoples still survive, are drawing links between the destruction of their environments and the undermining of women in these societies that global capitalism and Western modernist ideologies have wrought. We also note, however, that Western ecofeminist and non-Western indigenous strategies that evoke symbols of "Mother Earth" or speak of the "earth as inviolate" can be problematic insofar as they celebrate "the primitive" in a way that denies development not only to the South generally but also to women, who have the least access to land, technologies, and resources worldwide. The ecofeminist strategy that maintains the connection of women to nature in order to argue that women and nature should be equally inviolate—safe from rape, abuse, and use as cheap resources—is particularly flawed. It makes women so coterminous with nature that it provides a rationale for continuing to keep them out of decision-making about the use of nature by

FIGURE 5.10 Demonstrating for Indigenous Rights. Mexican workers demonstrate in Tijuana on May Day in 1995 in solidarity with the Zapatista rebellion in Chiapas by accusing the Mexican armed forces of "killing our brothers, raping our sisters, and poisoning water and food in Chiapas" and calling on the Mexican government to "take care with reforms of Article 123," which is the article in the Mexican constitution that protects workers' rights. Courtesy David Bacon, Impact Visuals.

humans. Here, women's strategic gender interests, which lead to calls for low-technology strategies to protect women and nature, conflict with their practical gender interests in gaining access to the resources necessary for meeting the basic needs of their families. Western ecofeminist demands for low technology and "protection" of nature/women also conflict with the strategic gender interest in women's participation as equals in modern, high-technology, currently male-dominated institutions that control or "manage" resources.

Finally, it is important for all women's ecology movements to resist the idea that women are the most "natural" stewards of the environment. Certainly not all women are environmentalists. Middle- and upper-class women in the North and South, by being major consumers, are particularly profligate destroyers of natural resources. Moreover, poor and working-class women often lack the tools and skills necessary to be effective stewards. These contradictions once again remind us that there is no simple formula for righting gender wrongs. Ending the gendered division of resources is contingent on ending the assumption that masculinism equals resource ownership and exploitation. It is dependent, too, on feminism's relinquishing of the principle that stewardship is the property and responsibility of women only.

CONCLUSION

The pursuit of practical gender interests often leads activists to discover strategic gender interests, which, in turn, drive the participation of women (and men) in non-, anti-, and transstate social movements. The issues raised and actions undertaken have important implications for both how we understand world politics and how we choose to shape our future.

That women's political movements of all types are complicit, to a greater or lesser degree, in gendering processes leads us to some ruminations in our final chapter on what it will take to "ungender" world politics. There, we hope to integrate our findings and our arguments and leave the reader with some sense of the enormous, but also necessary, transformational project to ungender world politics.

NOTES

1. See Laura Macdonald, "Globalizing Civil Society: Interpreting International NGOs in Central America," *Millennium* 23 (1994): 227–285.

2. United Nations Department of Public Information, Charts for the Fourth World Conference on Women, September 4–15, 1995, Beijing, China, Action for Equality, Development and Peace. (Recall Figure 3.3 in the present volume.)

3. Jan Jindy Pettman, *Worlding Women: A Feminist International Politics* (London: Routledge, 1996), p. 34.

4. Anannya Bhattacharjee, "The Public/Private Mirage: Mapping Homes and Undomesticating Violence Work in the South Asian Immigrant Community," in M. Jacqui Alexander and Chandra Talpade Mohanty, eds., *Feminist Genealogies, Colonial Legacies, Democratic Futures* (New York: Routledge, 1997), pp. 317–318.

5. Inderpal Grewal and Caren Kaplan, "Introduction: Transnational Feminist Practices and Questions of Postmodernity," in Inderpal Grewal and Caren Kaplan, eds., *Scattered Hegemonies* (Minneapolis: University of Minnesota Press, 1994), p. 19.

6. Ibid., pp. 19–20.

7. Postmodernist feminist perspectives on IR are treated at length in V. Spike Peterson, "Transgressing Boundaries: Theories of Knowledge, Gender, and International Relations," *Millennium* (Summer 1992): 183–206; and in Christine Sylvester, *Feminist Theory and International Relations in a Postmodern Era* (Cambridge, Eng.: Cambridge University Press, 1994).

8. See J. K. Gibson-Graham, *The End of Capitalism (as we knew it): A Feminist Critique of Political Economy* (Cambridge, Mass.: Blackwell Publishers, 1996), ch. 6.

9. See Maxine Molyneux, "Mobilization Without Emancipation? Women's Interests, the State, and Revolution in Nicaragua," *Feminist Studies* 11 (Summer 1985): 227–254.

10. Ibid., p. 233.

11. Molyneux's strategic objectives include: "the abolition of the sexual division of labor, the alleviation of the burden of domestic labor and childcare, the removal of institutionalized forms of discrimination, the attainment of political equality, the establishment of freedom of choice over childbearing, and the adoption of adequate measures against male violence and control over women" (ibid., pp. 232–233).

12. Sallie Westwood and Sarah A. Radcliffe, "Gender, Racism and the Politics of Identities in Latin America," in Sarah A. Radcliffe and Sallie Westwood, eds., *Viva: Women and Popular Protest in Latin America* (London: Routledge, 1993), p. 20. Postmodernist feminists go further by questioning the use of the term *interests*. They argue, and we agree, that *interests* are socially constructed and arise from women's and men's social locations, not from their natures.

13. Marianne H. Marchand, "Latin American Women Speak on Development: Are We Listening Yet?" in Marianne H. Marchand and Jane L. Parpart, eds., *Feminism, Postmodernism, Development* (London: Routledge, 1995), p. 64.

14. Jennifer Schirmer, "The Seeking of Truth and the Gendering of Consciousness: The Comadres of El Salvador and the Conavigua Widows of Guatemala," in Radcliffe and Westwood, eds., *Viva*, p. 61; emphasis in original.

15. See Sandi E. Cooper, "Women's Participation in European Peace Movements: The Struggle to Prevent World War I," in Ruth Roach Pierson, ed., *Women and Peace: Theoretical, Historical, and Practical Perspectives* (London: Croom Helm, 1987), pp. 51–75.

16. Ibid., pp. 63–65.

17. Ursula Herrmann, "Social Democratic Women in Germany and the Struggle for Peace Before and During the First World War," in Pierson, ed., *Women and Peace*, pp. 91–92.

18. See Lela B. Costin, "Feminism, Pacifism, Internationalism and the 1915 International Congress of Women," in Judith Stiehm, ed., *Women and Men's Wars* (Oxford: Pergamon Press, 1983), pp. 301–316.

19. See Yvonne Aleksandra Bennett, "Vera Brittain and the Peace Pledge Union: Women and Peace," in Pierson, ed., *Women and Peace*, pp. 192–213.

20. See Ruth Roach Pierson, *"They're Still Women After All": The Second World War and Canadian Womanhood* (Toronto: McClelland and Stewart, 1986); and Maureen Honey, *Creating Rosie the Riveter: Class, Gender, and Propaganda During World War II* (Amherst: University of Massachusetts Press, 1984).

21. See D'Ann Campbell, *Women at War with America* (Cambridge, Mass.: Harvard University Press, 1985).

22. Karen Beck Skold, "'The Job He Left Behind': American Women in the Shipyards During World War II," in Carol R. Berkin and Clara M. Lovett, eds., *Women, War, and Revolution* (New York: Holmes and Meier, 1980), p. 69.

23. James J. Kenneally, "Women in the United States and Trade Unionism," in Norbert C. Soldon, ed., *The World of Women's Trade Unionism* (Westport, Conn.: Greenwood Press, 1985), p. 80.

24. Campbell, *Women at War*, p. 216.

25. Carolyn Strange, "Mothers on the March: Maternalism in Women's Protest for Peace in North America and Western Europe, 1900–1985," in Guida West and Rhoda Lois Blumberg, eds., *Women and Social Protest* (New York: Oxford University Press, 1990), p. 215.

26. Ibid., p. 216.

27. Berenice Carroll, "Women Take Action! Women's Direct Action and Social Change, *Women's Studies International Forum* 12, no. 1 (1989): 17.

28. See Anne Sisson Runyan, "Feminism, Peace, and International Politics: An Examination of Women Organizing Internationally for Peace and Security," Ph.D. Dissertation, American University, Washington, D.C., 1988.

29. See ibid.

30. Kathleen Binge, "For Organizing the Campaign for a World Free of Landmines: Jody Williams," *Ms.*, January/February 1998, p. 50.

31. See Simona Sharoni, *Gender and the Israeli-Palestinian Conflict* (Syracuse, N.Y.: Syracuse University Press, 1995), ch. 7.

32. Cynthia Enloe, *The Morning After: Sexual Politics at the End of the Cold War* (Berkeley: University of California Press, 1993), p. 2.

33. See Katharine H. S. Moon, *Sex Among Allies: Military Prostitution in U.S.-Korea Relations* (New York: Columbia University Press, 1997).

34. Yuri Kageyama, "Sex Slaves Win Lawsuit," *Dayton Daily News*, April 28, 1998, p. 5A.

35. See Laura Flanders, "Rwanda's Living Casualties," *Ms.*, March/April 1998, pp. 27–30.

36. See, for example, Lynne Segal, *Is the Future Female?* (New York: Peter Bedwick Books, 1987); Jean Bethke Elshtain, *Women and War* (New York: Basic Books, 1987); and Christine Sylvester, "Some Dangers in Merging Feminist and Peace Projects," *Alternatives* 12 (October 1987): 493–510.

37. See, for example, Mary Ann Tetreault, ed., *Women and Revolution in Africa, Asia, and the New World* (Columbia: University of South Carolina Press, 1994); Berkin and Lovett, eds., *Women, War, and Revolution;* Miranda Davies, comp., *Third World—Second Sex: Women's Struggles and National Liberation* (London: Zed Books, 1983); Linda Labao, "Women in Revolutionary Movements: Changing Patterns of Latin American Guerrilla Struggle," in West and Blumberg, eds., *Women and Social Protest*, pp. 180–204; and Lois West, ed., *Feminist Nationalism* (New York: Routledge, 1987).

38. Margaret Randall, *Sandino's Daughters: Testimonies of Nicaraguan Women in the Struggle* (Vancouver/Toronto: New Star Books, 1981), p. 10.

39. Ibid., p. 16.

40. Ibid., p. 66.

41. Jane Deighton, Rossana Horsley, Sarah Stewart, and Cathy Cain, *Sweet Ramparts: Women in Revolutionary Nicaragua* (London: War on Want and the Nicaraguan Solidarity Campaign, 1983), p. 50.

42. Ibid., p. 55.

43. Davies, comp., *Third World—Second Sex*, p. 105.

44. Ibid.

45. Ibid., p. 119.

46. Ibid.

47. See Margaret E. Leahy, *Development Strategies and the Status of Women: A Comparative Study of the United States, Mexico, the Soviet Union, and Cuba* (Boulder: Lynne Rienner Publishers, 1986).

48. Donna Vukelich and Estelle Schneider, "Women's Rights Under Threat in Nicaragua," *Ms.*, March/April 1998, p. 31.

49. Nanette Funk, "Introduction: Gender Politics and Post-Communism," in Nanette Funk and Magda Mueller, eds., *Gender Politics and Post-Communism* (New York: Routledge, 1993), p. 2.

50. Cynthia Enloe, *Bananas, Beaches & Bases: Making Feminist Sense of International Politics* (Berkeley: University of California Press, 1989), p. 63. The literature on gendered nationalism is now extensive. For an excellent overview, see Nira Yuval-Davis, *Gender and Nation* (London: Sage Publishing, 1997); for a discussion in relation to foreign policy, see V. Spike Peterson, "The Politics of Identity and Gendered Nationalism," in Laura Neack, Patrick J. Haney, and Jeane A. K. Hey, eds., *Foreign Policy Analysis* (Englewood Cliffs, N.J.: Prentice-Hall, 1995), pp. 167–186.

51. See, for example, Minoll Reeves, *Female Warriors of Allah: Women and the Islamic Revolution* (New York: E. P. Dutton, 1989).

52. Pettman, *Worlding Women*, p. 48.

53. See Benedict Anderson, *Imagined Communities: Reflections on the Origin and Spread of Nationalism*, 2nd ed. (London: Verso, 1991).

54. Pettman, *Worlding Women*, p. 48.

55. Ibid., p. 62.

56. Cynthia A. Bouton, "Gendered Behavior in Subsistence Riots," *Journal of Social History* 23, no. 4 (Summer 1990); Carroll, "Women Take Action!" pp. 3–24.

57. Bouton, "Gendered Behavior," p. 743.

58. Carroll, "Women Take Action!" p. 8.

59. Ibid.

60. Jackie Pope, "Women in the Welfare Rights Struggle: The Brooklyn Welfare Action Council," in West and Blumberg, eds., *Women and Social Protest*, p. 66.

61. Ruth Leger Sivard, *Women . . . A World Survey* (Washington, D.C.: World Priorities, Inc., 1995), p. 11; the figure of $8,000,000,000,000 is given on page 5.

62. Debbie Taylor, "Women: An Analysis," in Debbie Taylor, ed., *Women: A World Report* (New York: Oxford University Press, 1985), p. 81.

63. Ibid., p. 26.

64. Susan Bullock, *Women and Work* (London: Zed Books, 1994), p. 14.

65. Carol Lees, quoted in Marilyn Waring, "A Woman's Reckoning: Update on Unwaged Labor," *Ms.*, July/August 1991, p. 15.

66. Carroll, "Women Take Action!"

67. Enloe, *Bananas, Beaches & Bases*, pp. 144–146. See also Sheila Rowbotham and Swasti Mitter, eds., *Dignity and Daily Bread: New Forms of Economic Organizing Among Poor Women in the Third World and the First* (New York: Routledge, 1994).

68. Lynn M. Kwiatkowski and Lois A. West, "Feminist Struggles for Feminist Nationalism in the Philippines," in West, ed., *Feminist Nationalism*, p. 163.

69. See ISIS: Women's International Information and Communication Service, *Women in Development* (Philadelphia: New Society Publishers, 1984).

70. See Rachel Kamel, *The Global Factory: Analysis and Action for a New Economic Era* (Philadelphia: American Friends Service Committee, 1990).

71. See Gita Sen and Caren Grown, *Development, Crises, and Alternative Visions: Third World Women's Perspectives* (New York: Monthly Review Press, 1987).

72. Jeanne Vickers, *Women and the World Economic Crisis* (London: Zed Books, 1991), p. 112.

73. Ibid.

74. Women's Global Alliance for Development Alternatives, "Women Reclaim the Market," Draft Report prepared by WIDE, Brussels, August 1995, p. 2.

75. Joanne Kerr, "Expert Group Meeting on Women and Global Economic Restructuring," June 20–22, 1994, Ottawa, Canada. Final Report prepared by North—South Institute, Ottawa, July 1994.

76. Valentine M. Moghadam, *Women, Work and Economic Reform in the Middle East and North Africa* (Boulder: Lynne Rienner Publishers, 1998), p. 234.

77. Annabel Rodda, *Women and the Environment* (London: Zed Books, 1991), p. 110.

78. Ibid., p. 111.

79. Ibid., p. 116.

80. Quoted in Leonie Caldecott and Stephanie Leland, eds., *Reclaim the Earth: Women Speak Out for Life on Earth* (London: Women's Press, 1983), p. 6.

81. Ibid., p. 7.

82. See Joni Seager, *Earth Follies: Coming to Feminist Terms with the Global Environmental Crisis* (New York: Routledge, 1993), ch. 7.

83. Rosi Braidotti, Eva Charkiewicz, Sabine Hausler, and Saskia Wieringa, *Women, the Environment and Sustainable Development* (London: Zed Books, 1996), p. 75.

84. Ibid., p. 82.

85. Ibid., pp. 102–103.

86. John H. Cushman, Jr., "Pollution Politics: Clinton's Choice," *New York Times*, June 27, 1997, p. A7.

87. Clyde H. Farnsworth, "Where the Sacred Serpent Rests, a Mine Intrudes," *New York Times*, July 18, 1997, p. A4.

88. Christina Gabriel and Laura Macdonald, "NAFTA, Women, and Organising in Canada and Mexico: Forging a 'Feminist Internationality,'" *Millennium* 23 (1994): 546–547.

89. Noam Chomsky, *World Orders Old and New* (New York: Columbia University Press, 1996), p. 171.

SIX

□ □ □

Ungendering World Politics

World politics has long been practiced and studied as if it were "ungendered"—that is, either gender neutral or devoid of gender issues. We have argued that world politics is, in fact, a highly gendered enterprise that privileges the interests of one gender over the other. In Chapter 5, we differentiated and drew linkages between women's practical and strategic gender interests. In this chapter, we differentiate and draw linkages between reformist strategies, which focus on changing the *position of women* in order to increase their visibility, representation, and efficacy in world politics, and more transformative strategies, which call attention to the *power of gender* in reformulating world politics. In doing so, we argue that both strategies are necessary to ungender world politics in the interests of all the world's inhabitants.

UNGENDERING POWER AND POLITICS

To ungender power and politics we must alter the gendered division of power that established and has continued to reproduce masculinist politics. The latter privileges an androcentric definition of power—as power-over—and discriminates against women as political actors. As Chapter 3 illustrated, women are un- or underrepresented in elite decision-making power in state governments and international organizations. And women who do hold such positions are either depicted as exceptional or rendered largely invisible as significant actors in world politics. Moreover, when a few "exceptional" women do gain power, particularly as heads of state, they often adopt masculinist leadership styles and eschew gender-sensitive or feminist policy-making.

These observations highlight a two-way interaction between the underrepresentation of women in conventional power structures and the

213

invisibility of gender issues in world politics: too few women and too little awareness of gender hierarchy. Therefore, we need to have more women in leadership positions and greater attention paid to the role of gender in shaping world politics. The former changes the position of women in international affairs, whereas the latter alters the power of gender as a hierarchical-ordering principle. Similarly, for large numbers of women to hold positions of conventional power, the power of gender to produce the inequalities that keep women out of conventional power structures must be challenged. In short, the task of ungendering power is twofold—adding women to the existing world politics power structures *and* transforming those very power structures, ideologically and materially.

At the least, adding more women to existing power structures will put so-called women's issues on policy-making agendas. Evidence for this comes from a recent study in the United States indicating that female legislators tend to focus and work together more than male legislators on such issues as violence against women, abortion rights, health care, and child care.[1] Indeed, women's unprecedented successes in the 1992 U.S. election were attributable in part to their ability to address domestic and equity problems that became key political issues in the post–Cold War context. Unfortunately, a neoconservative backlash quickly produced a very different U.S. Congress and agenda in 1994, leading to attacks on abortion rights and affirmative action, "welfare reform" that significantly reduced benefits for poor and immigrant women and children (and men), increased military spending, and decreased foreign aid.

Nevertheless, the evidence from the short-lived 103rd U.S. Congress suggests that increasing women's representational power makes a significant difference in political decision-making by shifting the focus away from short-term gains for the few and toward long-term benefits for the many. This kind of policy-making is required in a world where economic, social, and environmental security rival military security on the world politics agenda of governments and in the minds of citizens. Moreover, as female policy-makers examine these issues from a fresh perspective, they call attention to the disproportionate impact of such problems on women.

In line with this view, increasing the numbers of women in formal political positions at all levels serves women's practical gender interests. First, greater attention would be drawn to issues related to women's reproductive roles and work. Second, there would be increased demand for gender-differentiated research to document how such national and global problems as militarization, globalization, and environmental degradation disadvantage women particularly. Third, this type of gender-differentiated research would serve as a basis for changing policy to transfer more public resources to women and other overburdened groups. This would entail reducing subsidies for military and economic practices that impoverish and/or endanger the lives of women and their families. Instead, more public funds would be directed toward providing adequate food and shelter, clean and accessible water, safe and affordable energy sources, adequate health- and child-care services, and sufficient income-generating or employment opportunities in environmentally safe workplaces.

This redistribution of funds and resources to meet women's practical gender interests in fulfilling their reproductive tasks is a necessary (but not sufficient) condition for achieving gender justice. It is also necessary for reducing women's vulnerability to military conflicts and economic crises. Moreover, distributive gender justice reduces the likelihood of military conflicts because there would be fewer resources put into war preparation (and thus more respect for international law); it reduces the likelihood of economic crises insofar as resources would be less concentrated at the top.

Increasing women's access to public power and resources also serves their strategic gender interests by empowering women to meet their own needs and control their own futures. However, for substantial numbers of women to gain public power and shape the transfer of public resources, a second, more transformative strategy for ungendering power must be pursued along with the reformist strategy of adding women to the ranks of power-wielders. This involves undermining the *power of gender* to produce inequalities of all kinds. To do so requires that we think about power in a way that denaturalizes, deglorifies, and delegitimates power-over— coercive power—as it is exercised at all levels, from the interpersonal to the interstate. This rethinking would necessarily alter how we identify power-over as a desirable, masculine attribute.

Whereas international law has long recognized that the use of force is legitimate only as a last resort, we argue that coercion in general is necessitated only by a hierarchically divided and therefore unjust world order. The use of or threat of coercion to maintain social hierarchies involves the concentration and expenditure of a great deal of power. This power—and the resources it drains—could be employed for more productive and less destructive purposes. In Cynthia Enloe's words, IR commentators

> have put power at the center of their analyses—often to the exclusion of culture and ideas—but they have under-estimated the amount and varieties of power at work. It has taken power to deprive women of land titles and leave them little choice but to sexually service soldiers and banana workers. It has taken power to keep women out of their countries' diplomatic corps and out of the upper reaches of the World Bank. It has taken power to keep questions of inequity between local men and women off the agendas of many nationalist movements in industrialized as well as agrarian societies. It has taken power to construct popular culture—films, advertisements, books, fairs, fashions—which reinforces, not subverts, global hierarchies.[2]

When we recognize how much coercive power it takes to run this inequitable system, we begin to see why feminists argue that the deployment of coercive power is ultimately destructive of those who rule as well as those who are ruled. Disabling people—especially women—by depriving them of even the most basic needs so that the few can accumulate wealth and weaponry destroys genuinely popular support for states, international organizations, and their leaders. In the absence of popular support and consent as the sources of legitimacy for those in power, coercion is the *only* mechanism available to insecure rulers, who must rely on dividing, impoverishing, and degrading people and the planet to maintain their power. Therefore, we must question not only the validity but also the efficacy of "power-over" as *the* mechanism for organizing world politics or solving world problems.

An alternative to coercive power is the more feminist concept of empowerment, or enabling power. If this model is used, world order looks less like a pyramid, where few are on the top and many are on the bottom, and more like a rotating circle in which no one is always at the top and no one is always at the bottom. Instead, all participate in complex webs of interdependence. Interests, rather than being defined in opposition to each other, are developed through relationships with others. Conflicts are resolved not by force or its threat but in nonviolent interaction and mutual learning.

This model is derived in part from feminist theorizing about the high degree of reciprocity and interconnectedness typifying most social relations even though they take place in contexts of contingency and ambiguity. The model denies neither the need for autonomy nor the complexities of social interaction, but it does deny that a depiction of only hostile and competitive forces at work in the world is accurate or adequate. Christine Sylvester described this model as **relational autonomy** and contrasted it with the masculinist ideal of **reactive autonomy** (valuing independence over interdependence and order over justice), which permeates the practice of international relations:

> In liberal theory, the cast of masculine reactive autonomy appears in stories of abstract social contracts entered into, seemingly, by "orphans who have reared themselves, whose desires are situated within and reflect nothing but independently generated movement." Realist international relations theory follows this mold, even as it focuses on those anarchic spaces that elude social contract; for it depicts states as primitive "individuals" separated from history and others by loner rights of sovereignty—backed up, for good measure, by military hardware—and involved in international conventions and institutions only on a voluntary basis.[3]

The reactive autonomy model in effect erases most social reality, especially the webbing that constructs meaning and order. Reactive autonomy assumes that cooperative relations are virtually impossible without coercion. In contrast, relational autonomy assumes that cooperation typifies human relations when they are relatively equal and is destroyed in the presence of inequality and coercion. By adopting the lens of reactive autonomy, IR practitioners—even without intending to—reproduce expectations of hostile and competitive behavior, which, in turn, generate uncooperative and defensive responses. This is how we find ourselves caught in self-perpetuating, vicious cycles such as arms races. For the model of relational autonomy to flourish, we must not only alter our lenses but also make profound changes in our individual and collective practices.

Moving toward a relational autonomy model for world politics would move us toward ungendering world politics more deeply than we could simply by adding women to existing power structures. However, this transformation cannot take the form of a simple reversal that merely privileges feminine "care" over masculine "coercion." In such a reversal, not only gender dichotomies but also features of the feminine concept of care that oppress women would remain in place. Specifically, because caring has historically been a demand imposed upon subordinated groups and is in this sense inextricable from relations of inequality, a care model may offer insights on, but not solutions to, oppressive social relations. Caring that exclusively takes the form of sacrificing self or group interests is just another framing of inequality. Emphasizing relational autonomy as a model of international relations would assist women in terms of their practical gender interests, but that is not sufficient. We also need to facilitate women's autonomy (sometimes of the reactive sort) so that women's strategic gender interests can be met. Full equality, not only *between* men and women but also *among* women and *among* men cannot be achieved until men have an equal responsibility for reproductive or relational work and women have an equal say in how the world is organized.

Ungendering power by increasing women's political representation *and* reconceiving power as relational autonomy requires a variety of material changes in the organization of world politics. Most important, there must be proportional representation of women in the governments of all countries and in international organizations. As indicated earlier, there is growing evidence that women do bring a relational autonomy perspective to governing, especially if there are significant numbers of women and if they have commitments to principles of equality. Ideally, proportional representation would mean approximately equal percentages not only of women and men at all levels but also of women (and men) in terms of nationality, race, ethnicity, class, sexual orientation, and so on.

In order for women in power to be truly representative of all women, the paths to power must change. Given the global problems now confronting us, a legal career, military service, or neoliberal economic credentials cannot remain the major prerequisites for public service. Why are human relations skills not deemed crucial for practitioners of international relations? Local grass-roots organizing challenges multiple aspects of the global divisions of power, violence, labor, and resources. Why are these skills not considered far more important qualifications for global leadership? In a world of reactive autonomy that shores up global hierarchies, these skills and experiences are seen as trivial, useless, and even dangerous. But trivial, useless, and dangerous for whom and for what? One could hazard that those who are most threatened by such leadership would be those interested in maintaining a world of reactive autonomy. However, those committed to creating a world of relational autonomy where global divisions and inequalities are challenged might find such leadership qualities essential.

As we make the transition, however, from reactive autonomy to relational autonomy, women will need more resources and new laws behind them to seek public office. Some political parties, particularly of the social-democratic and green party variety, have adopted rules ensuring that up to 50 percent of the candidates put forward are women, who are then given equal access to party funds and machinery. Similar quotas and practices should be adopted by all political parties in the world. This measure could be enforced by making a state's UN membership contingent on such measures to create proportional representation. For this to be credible, however, the United Nations, the biggest men's club in the world, must alter its own top-down image by implementing a quota system—for women *and* Third World representation.

To ungender world politics more completely, we require more than quota systems for women leaders. It is also vital that *all* states ratify the UN conventions relevant to the status of women. Box 6.1 identifies a number of such conventions that still lack ratification by many UN member states. Most significant among these is the Convention on the Elimination of All Forms of Discrimination Against Women (CEDAW), which was adopted in 1979, in the middle of the UN Decade for Women, and ratified by 131 countries by 1995. Glaringly, the United States is the only industrialized country that has still failed to ratify it. Equally important, the Forward Looking Strategies for the Advancement of Women (FLS) was adopted by 157 governments on July 27, 1985, in Nairobi, at the end of the Decade for Women.[4]

The Decade for Women had three interrelated and mutually reinforcing objectives: equality, development, and peace. Three subthemes—employment, health, and education—represented the concrete basis for achieving the decade's triple objectives. Attaining the multiple goals of the decade and the FLS entails a sharing of responsibility by women and men and society as a whole. It also requires that women play a central role as intellectuals, policy-makers, decision-makers, planners, and contributors to and beneficiaries of development.[5] The Fourth World Conference on Women, held in Beijing, China, in 1995 as a follow-up to the Decade for Women, was designed to renew international commitments to the goals of the FLS in the face of overwhelming evidence of continued discrimination against, worsening poverty among, and increasing attacks on the human rights of women the world over. The task of this conference was to produce a Platform for Action[6] that would create institutional and financial mechanisms at national, regional, and international levels for addressing twelve areas of concern (see Figure 6.1). Over 30,000 women and men representing 150 countries and 3,000 NGOs attended the NGO Forum at Beijing to pressure governments to support the Platform for Action, which was adopted unanimously by 189 countries on September 15, 1995.

The Beijing conference was the most recent culmination of UN conferences since 1972 that have taken women's issues seriously (see Box 6.2). The Decade for Women served to mobilize women internationally to become major NGO actors and lobbyists at all UN conferences since 1985. Although significant advances have been made especially in the 1990s, such as extending the concept of human rights to encompass women's rights (including sexual rights) in Vienna and gaining a broad definition of women's reproductive rights (which includes the right to choose to mother or not) in Cairo, a neoliberal and neoconservative backlash became visible in Beijing. On the one hand, religious fundamentalist representatives objected to the use of the term *gender* in the Platform for Action, arguing that it challenged the idea of "natural" roles for women as wives and mothers (and "natural" roles for men as breadwinners). On the other hand, neoliberal IFI representatives turned feminist demands for integrating women and gender analysis into development (in order to change development priorities and practices) into arguments that called for integrating women into development for the purposes of increasing the economic efficiency of current capitalist development models.[7] What we observe are masculinist interests allied against feminist goals. And these contemporary expressions of masculinism are consistent with the historical unwillingness of states and international organizations "to undertake the radical restructuring of their economies and societies that would be necessary to bring about the changes that many women's movements" have demanded since the nineteenth century.[8] In combination, these masculinist interests explain why states are loathe to obligate themselves, despite signing declarations and conventions, to provide the funds and infrastructures to produce and enforce legislation that would not only end the formal and informal discrimination against women in all sectors but also change development practices, reverse militarization, and ensure equal representation of women in all decision-making bodies.

220

```
┌─────────────────────────────────────────────────────────────────┐
```

BOX 6.1   INTERNATIONAL INSTRUMENTS
RELEVANT TO WOMEN

1. UNITED NATIONS

A. General instruments

Charter of the United Nations, 1945
Universal Declaration of Human Rights, 1948
International Covenant on Economic, Social and Cultural Rights, 1966
International Covenant on Civil and Political Rights and Optional
   Protocol, 1966
Supplementary Convention on the Abolition of Slavery, the Slave Trade,
   and Institutions and Practices Similar to Slavery, 1956
International Convention on the Elimination of All Forms of Racial
   Discrimination, 1965
Declaration on Social Progress and Development, 1969
World Population Plan of Action, 1974
Programme of Action on the Establishment of a New International
   Economic Order, 1974
Charter of Economic Rights and Duties of States, 1974
International Development Strategy for the third United Nations Devel-
   opment Decade, 1980
International Development Strategy for the Fourth United Nations Devel-
   opment Decade, 1990

B. Instruments relating specifically to the status of women

Convention for the Suppression of the Traffic in Persons and of the
   Exploitation of the Prostitution of Others, 1949
Convention on the Political Rights of Women, 1952
Convention on the Nationality of Married Women, 1957
Convention and Recommendation on Consent to Marriage, Minimum
   Age for Marriage and Registration of Marriages, 1962 and 1965
Declaration on the Elimination of Discrimination against Women, 1967
Programme of concerted international action for the Advancement of
   Women, 1970
Declaration of Mexico: World Plan of Action, 1975
Convention on the Elimination of All Forms of Discrimination Against
   Women, 1979
Nairobi Forward-looking Strategies for the Advancement of Women, 1985

2. SPECIALIZED AGENCY INSTRUMENTS

A. International Labour Organization

Convention concerning the employment of women on underground work
in mines of all kinds, No. 45, 1935

Convention concerning night work of women employed in industry (revised), No. 89, 1948

Convention concerning equal remuneration for men and women workers for work of equal value, No. 100 (1951); and Recommendation No. 90 (1951)

Convention concerning minimum standards of social security, No. 102, 1952

Convention concerning maternity protection (revised) No. 103 (1952); and Recommendation No. 111, (1958)

Convention concerning discrimination in respect of employment and occupation, No. 111, 1958; and Recommendation No. 111, 1958

Recommendation concerning the employment of women with family responsibilities, No. 123, 1965

Convention concerning Equal Opportunities and Equal Treatment for Men & Women Workers: Workers with Family Responsibilities No. 156, 1981

B. United Nations Educational, Scientific and Cultural Organization (UNESCO)

Convention against Discrimination in Education, 1960

Protocol instituting a Conciliation and Good Offices Commission to be responsible for seeking a settlement of any disputes which may arise between States Parties to the Convention against Discrimination in Education, 1962

Source: Hilkka Pietila and Jeanne Vickers, *Making Women Matter: The Role of the United Nations,* 2nd ed. (London: Zed Books, 1994), Annex 6.

Because this would involve restructuring the nature and priorities of states, international organizations, and corporations, neither full ratification nor any serious enforcement after ratification is likely until there are sufficient women (and men) in power who are committed to this kind of restructuring. In this sense, transformational change is linked to women's proportional representation in state and UN bodies.

If and when more women gain power through quota mechanisms and eventually reach parity in power structures, the question arises as to how female leaders will remain accountable not only to women in their own countries but also to women in other countries who may be negatively affected by the domestic policies of foreign governments. A mechanism for ensuring that one woman's "liberation" does not translate into another's oppression would be the ratification and enforcement on both the national

ANATOMY OF THE PLATFORM FOR ACTION

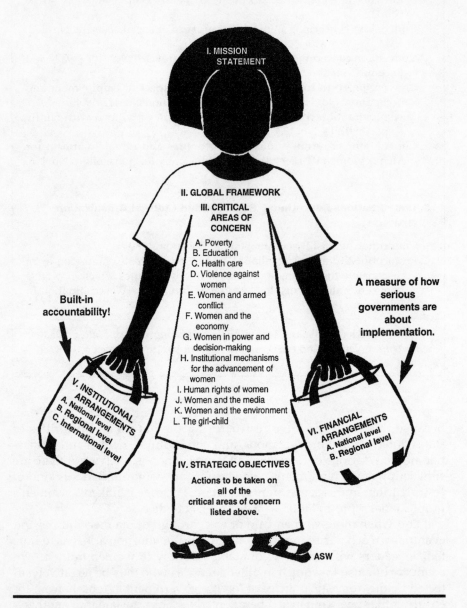

FIGURE 6.1   The Beijing Platform for Action. Courtesy of the International Tribune Centre, Inc. Illustrator: Anne S. Walker.

BOX 6.2 WORLD CONFERENCES
RELEVANT TO WOMEN SINCE 1972

1. UN Conference on the Human Environment, Stockholm — 5–16 June 1972
2. UN World Population Conference, Bucharest — 19–30 Aug. 1974
3. World Food Conference, Rome — 5–16 Nov. 1974
4. World Conference of the International Women's Year, Mexico City — 19 June–2 July 1975
5. HABITAT: UN Conference on Human Settlements — 31 May–11 June 1976
6. Tripartite World Conference on Employment, Income Distribution, Social Progress & International Division of Labour, Geneva — June 1976
7. Conference on Economic Co-operation Among Developing Countries, Mexico — 13–22 Sept. 1976
8. UN Water Conference, Mar del Plata — 14–25 March 1977
9. UN Conference on Desertification, Nairobi — 29 Aug.–9 Sept. 1977
10. World Conference to Combat Racism and Racial Discrimination, Geneva — 14–25 Aug. 1978
11. UN Conference on Technical Co-operation Among Developing Countries, Buenos Aires — 30 Aug.–12 Sept. 1978
12. Primary Health Care Conference, Alma Ata — Sept. 1978
13. World Conference on Agrarian Reform and Rural Development, Rome — 12–20 July 1979
14. UN Conference on Science and Technology for Development, Vienna — 20–31 Aug. 1979
15. World Conference of the UN Decade for Women, Copenhagen — 14–30 July 1980
16. UN Conference on New and Renewable Sources of Energy, Nairobi — 10–21 Aug. 1981
17. UN Conference on the Least Developed Countries, Paris — 1–14 Sept. 1981
18. World Conference to Review and Appraise the Achievements of the UN Decade for Women, Nairobi — 15–26 July 1985
19. International Conference on Relationship Between Disarmament and Development, New York — 24 Aug.–11 Sept. 1987
20. UN Conference on Environment and Development, Brazil — 3–14 June 1992
21. World Conference on Human Rights, Vienna — 14–25 June 1993
22. International Conference on Population and Development, Cairo — 5–13 Sept. 1994
23. World Summit for Social Development, Copenhagen — 6–12 March 1995
24. The Fourth World Conference on Women, Beijing — 4–15 Sept. 1995

Source: Hilkka Peitila and Jeanne Vickers, *Making Women Matter: The Role of the United Nations,* 2nd ed. (London: Zed Books, 1994), Annex 4.

and global levels of such documents as CEDAW, FLS, and the Platform for Action. Indeed, relational autonomy cannot be practiced in one state alone, and women's strategic gender interests will not be served so long as women are treated as second-class citizens anywhere. Ungendering national politics entails globalizing relational autonomy in ways that challenge not only the divisions of sex, race/ethnicity, class, and sexuality but also the repressions associated with global capitalism, nationalist and religious fundamentalisms, and militarized statism. This will produce as-yet-unimagined political communities that do not rely on coercive power for their unity or inequality for their continuity.

As two sides of the same coin, rethinking world politics requires rethinking gendered "givens." For women to reach parity in power structures, we must revalue women as leaders, which challenges conventional gender dichotomies. For men to endorse the model of relational autonomy, we must revise divisions of labor that largely exclude men from nurturing activities. For world politics to change, we must relate the gender politics of everyday life and personal experience to their consequences for systemic processes and global crises.

UNGENDERING VIOLENCE

As we pointed out in Chapter 4, women have rarely been the beneficiaries of world politics organized around military security. Women make up a very small portion of the world's armed services, and they and their children tend to suffer most from military priorities that reduce "butter" in order to increase "guns." However, assuming that military security will remain a dominant dimension of world politics for the near future, one reformist strategy to make women "count" in military security policy-making is to increase the presence of women in the world's militaries. As we indicated in Chapter 4, the odds are against reaching female-male parity in the armed services of even the most "democratic," advanced industrial nations. Nevertheless, as long as state militaries continue to control a great deal of national and global wealth and resources, provide paths to power for government leaders, and offer avenues for employment and benefits for unskilled and semiskilled workers, pressure will continue for greater access to and opportunities in the military for women.

Again, the United Nations could be instrumental in encouraging states to increase their proportion of female soldiers. Since the Persian Gulf war, in which women in the U.S. military were extremely visible, more and more military actions in the form of peacekeeping operations are being coordinated by the United Nations. Whether in Somalia, Haiti, or Bosnia, UN-sponsored peacekeepers have been involved more in disaster relief, humanitarian aid activities, and nonpartisan police operations than in what is normally associated with military action. Under such conditions, the United Nations could argue that all contributing countries should send a much larger percentage of women in their complement of troops. This would not only signal a commitment to nondiscrimination that the UN supposedly upholds, but it would also provide more military personnel with the skills necessary for actual peacekeeping (and peacebuilding) work.

Unfortunately, as we noted in Chapter 4, the United States in particular has eschewed meaningful participation in and funding for UN peacekeeping operations, especially since the so-called quagmire in Somalia. It prefers to engage in "peace enforcement" activities, either unilaterally or through a joint military command such as NATO, to achieve short-term political objectives. As Francine D'Amico puts it:

> The United States seeks to enlist its allies in what one officer called "these quick-fuck operations." This multilateral strategy resembles a gang bang/gang rape. Allies serve as both accomplice and audience to these feats of military prowess, (re)confirming for one another their power and political status, conceptualized as masculinity. These "quick fucks" and "spitting (or pissing) contests" appear understandable in terms of the need to reinvigorate what Cynthia Enloe called "militarized masculinity."[9]

Refusal to put its troops under UN command for peacekeeping operations, current witchhunts to weed out gays and lesbians in its military ranks, and recent proposals to separate women and men in basic training are all part of an effort to "remasculinize" the U.S. military.[10] The latter is also behind the resistance to vigorously prosecuting and stamping out sexual assault and harassment of women in the military. According to Richard Rayner, one military expert recently exclaimed, "'Demasculinize an army and of course rape will stop. But is that what we want? Men who have that inadequacy join the armed forces. If you take that motivation away, you're in trouble.'"[11] As Rayner observes, this supports radical or antimilitarist feminist arguments "for not having an army at all."[12] But it also supports the strategy called for by liberal or equality feminists to increase women's numbers in the military in order to demasculinize it in terms of its makeup and purposes. Thus, greater numbers of women in military positions could serve not only reformist equity goals but also transformational processes, both of which are in women's strategic gender interests.

Increasing the presence of women in state- and UN-sponsored militaries also serves women's practical gender interests to the degree that more women will have access to the considerable resources of militaries. Partaking of a (larger) piece of the military pie would mean less poverty for some women and increased wages and health and social security benefits for other women. It would also mean that more women would have access to training in a variety of male-dominated fields, enhancing their job opportunities when and if they return to civilian life. However, as we also indicated in Chapter 4, military preparation and action have sorely compromised women's practical gender interests by extracting health, welfare, and environmental resources from the civilian economy. Beyond impoverishing many women and children through this resource extraction, militarism and wars have contributed to a culture of violence against women, rendering them unsafe in their homes and on the street. Systemic violence—sexual harassment, battering, rape, and torture—is the persistent price that women pay for the maintenance of large militaries and the accompanying militarization of national life.

In short, the increase in economic security that some women could achieve if there were a greater presence of women in the military must be measured against the continued economic and physical insecurities experienced by women outside of (and partly as a result of) the armed forces. Indeed, even women inside the military face the physical insecurities of sexual harassment and rape as well as, of course, the possibility of dying in combat along with female noncombatants. Accordingly, increasing the presence of women in the military does not greatly benefit the practical gender interests of most women and only minimally serves their strategic gender interests if it does not lead to a transformation of military purposes. Allowing women to join militaries and take combat roles does strike a major blow against the stereotype of femininity and the discrimination that women face in the context of the gendered division of violence. However, it does not necessarily challenge the masculine side of the gendered division of violence, and it does not necessarily contribute to gender equality outside or even inside the military. Finally, increasing the presence of women in militaries does not necessarily call into question the utility and inevitability of violence itself.

Thus, like ungendering power, ungendering violence is a twofold process. Increasing the numbers of women in militaries does yield some benefits for some women in the short term and could ultimately demasculinize and thus reorient what militaries do. But the reigning power of gender violently divides the human community into unequal and opposed beings who must resort to violence to settle disputes, usually without significantly reducing existing inequalities. As a consequence, merely increasing the presence of women without also analyzing the power of gender will leave most women's practical and strategic gender interests unmet. Such an analysis must take issue with gendered dichotomies in world politics that arise from the gendered division of violence. These include distinctions between domestic and international violence, between structural and direct violence, and between "us" and "them."

The assumption that violence is largely the result of anarchic international relations—in contrast to supposedly "peaceful" domestic communities—obscures the question of the amount of and the way in which violence is deployed from the local to the global level. For example, domestic violence—the euphemism for the wide range of physical and emotional abuse suffered mostly by wives and children in families—is widespread throughout the world.[13] Hence, it makes little sense to argue that the level and frequency of violent conflict is what separates international relations from domestic relations. It makes more sense to see domestic and international violence as intimately connected (see Figure 6.2) Through this lens, international violence is revealed more as an extension of domestic masculinist socialization designed to produce aggressive "men" (including some females). In addition, military security policies and practices can be seen, in part, as the pursuit of masculinist reactive autonomy that can tolerate no interdependent relations.

Similarly, the definition of peace simply as the absence of the direct violence of war obscures the deep, structural inequalities that both give rise

DOMESTIC VIOLENCE.

FIGURE 6.2 The Link Between Domestic and International Violence. Domestic violence is a crime against women's international human rights. Reprinted by special permission of Kirk Anderson.

to and are the result of violence. Sustaining sexism, racism, classism, heterosexism, and gendered nationalism has heretofore been vital to sustaining militarism and the "us" and "them" mentality that goes along with it. Thus, any serious attempt to end war must involve significant alterations in local, national, and global hierarchies.

One promising strategy that would greatly assist women's practical and strategic gender interests is being implemented by feminists in human rights groups. The Women's Project of Human Rights Watch, for example, has been monitoring the amount of domestic violence occurring in states around the world since the early 1990s. Through this project, Human Rights Watch is holding "countries responsible for 'complicity' in the actions of private individuals—like husbands—who violate women's human rights."[14] Minimally, this strategy could facilitate the passage and enforcement of domestic violence legislation in all states. But it could also promote critiques of a military "security" that generates a great deal of economic, social, and physical insecurity for women and put into question the right of states to manipulate **sovereignty** (claims to self-determination and nonintervention) to hide and avoid dealing with the abuses of women within their borders. In this regard, Saskia Sassen recently identified one positive consequence of globalization: As state sovereignty is eroded, there is greater political space for women to expand definitions of human rights (as they did in Vienna) and to make legal claims on the basis of international human rights conventions that posit "the individual as . . . an object of law and a site for rights regardless of whether a citizen or an alien."[15] As this approach—and international human rights laws more generally—gain in credibility and consequence, it is unlikely that the use of force can continue to be a justifiable prerogative of states.

In short, ungendering violence may require increasing the numbers of women in military positions, insofar as this disrupts women's "victim" or "protected beautiful soul" status. But more important, transformative changes require undermining the power of gender to victimize vast numbers of women—and all who are vulnerable to structural violence—in the name of military security.

UNGENDERING LABOR

According to the statistics provided in Chapters 2 and 4, women are major participants in the world's labor force, constituting almost half the paid workers in many countries and continuing to enter the workforce in unprecedented numbers worldwide. Yet, as we also pointed out, women tend to be positioned in low-wage jobs in formal and informal labor markets, so the feminization of poverty is increasing despite the growing number of women workers and breadwinners. In order for women to re-alize their practical gender interest in making a living wage, the presence of women must be increased in particular sectors of the labor market—male-dominated sectors that tend to offer the highest pay and best bene-fits—and the presence of men must be increased in the caring professions such as nursing and teaching.

As we noted in Chapter 3, women are relatively absent at the top of cor-porate hierarchies. In fact, they are less represented there than in govern-ments. This is not surprising, given that TNCs rival and even surpass states as powers in the global political economy. Transnational capital de-pends on women's cheap labor to exert its power. Because there have been so few women at the top of TNC and finance hierarchies, there is lit-tle way of telling if female executives would make a difference—that is, would be less willing than men to exploit other women to make a profit. However, there is some evidence that women employ a management style that is more interpersonal, less hierarchical, less individualistic, and more group oriented than men's.[16] Female managers are also more sensi-tive to the dual demands of work and family that affect women far more than men. It thus seems likely that women, in sufficient numbers, might be more supportive of corporate and national day-care policies.

Unfortunately, a 1997 study conducted in Canada found that although male chief executive officers (CEOs) felt that women "have good interper-sonal skills, are team players and are good communicators," their justifica-tion for not promoting women was their fear that women's family respon-sibilities would make them insufficiently flexible to work and travel at a moment's notice. Women executives who were victims of this "glass ceil-ing" reported that, despite all the rhetoric about corporations valuing coop-erative management styles in a global economy, women are in fact forced to abandon these values and conform to more traditionally masculine, hierar-chical behaviors.[17] Charlotte Hooper notes that in a globalized economy, male corporate elites are claiming to be more feminized—that is, more con-cerned with parenting, flexible work schedules, and cooperative manage-ment styles—which ultimately means that they do not need women and must only *appear* more sensitive without "losing their class and gender privileges."[18] Tellingly, the ILO found in a 1998 survey of 152 countries that the United States, where global corporate cultures are concentrated, is one of only six countries that has no national policy on paid maternity leave.[19]

Even if increasing women's presence at the top of corporate hierarchies might translate into more humane and gender-sensitive work policies, the fact remains that few women and few men can actually be at the top of pyramidal hierarchies. Increasing the number of women in higher-pay-ing, male-dominated occupations may increase some women's wages and status. But that would not necessarily lead to challenging the global gendered dichotomy between productive and reproductive labor, which renders the latter "nonwork." Nor would it necessarily lead to questioning what is produced, why, and under what circumstances. These more fundamental problems lie at the heart of the international gendered division of labor and disadvantage women in the global political economy. To get at these problems and completely ungender labor, we need transformative strategies.

To begin with, we must continue efforts to include women's reproductive labor and their work in the informal and extralegal labor force in the **United Nations System of National Accounts (UNSNA),** which is an accounting of everything of value in and to markets in every country. These activities were previously deemed "externalities" in national accounting systems. Including statistics on such activities to determine GDP and guide policy-making would significantly reorient the way that states generate wealth because the costs of generating that wealth would seem much greater. As Marilyn Waring puts it:

> Can you imagine a nation's annual budget becoming a realistic description of the well-being of the community and its environment, a reflection of real wealth and different values? The budget would answer all of the following: Who does what work and where—paid and unpaid? What is the position of the nation's children and the aged? Who is not housed adequately? Who has the poorest health? What changes have occurred in water and air quality levels and why? What is the nature, cause, and region of pollution, and what are the health costs? What national resources have been harvested or conserved? Who relieves the state of the burden of care and dependency of others? What is the scope of subsistence production, and what are the nutritional results? At what price does the nation currently value war?[20]

By making visible the costs of current economic priorities as well as who (women) and what (the environment) bear the brunt of these costs, states and corporations would find it harder to justify a great deal of what they claim is wealth-generating activity. Indeed, a state budget reflecting such statistics would reveal that only a few are benefiting from the wealth that many workers are producing. In fact, such a budget would demystify the current assumption that reproductive work and informal labor is of little or no value. It would show that the formal sector of so-called productive work is dependent on the reproductive and informal sectors rather than the reverse. Keeping the reproductive and informal sectors undervalued is "functional" only for those few at the top who reap greater profits as a result of this under- or devaluation.

Although valuing women's reproductive work and informal labor would better protect and enhance women's practical gender interests, additional strategies will be needed to fully meet women's strategic gender interests. These include legislation in every country to institute equal pay for equal or comparable work (which would aid in "degendering" jobs); national child-care policies as well as legislative and educational programs to encourage shared parenting and an ethic of responsibility for all the nation's and the world's children; and the guarantee of full reproductive rights to every woman in every country to ensure that women can participate equally in the workforce, whether or not they *choose* to have children.

It will also be necessary to undermine the gendered dichotomy of "traditional" versus "modern" that pervades the thinking and practices of international development agencies. The power of gender creates an association between "women's work" and "primitive" economic and technological practices found in traditional societies—an association that acts to marginalize women in modernization processes. But it also acts to devalue the quite complex, self-sufficient, and ecologically sustainable economic activities and technological developments in which many women engage in traditional societies. Undermining this association and the devaluation of both women and traditional cultures requires questioning the kind of progress that men and modernity have brought to us.

The recommendations put forward by the expert group on women and global economic restructuring in Ottawa in 1994 that we outlined in Chapter 5 are also crucial to undermining the gendered divisions of labor, poverty, and wealth. These recommendations were forwarded on to Beijing through the NGO Forum held concurrently with the Economic Commission for Europe (ECE) preparatory meeting for the Beijing conference held in Vienna in 1994. These and similar recommendations arising out of women's, labor, environmentalist, and sustainable development movements also figured prominently in NGO declarations at the World Summit for Social Development in Copenhagen in 1995. What continues to be a focal point for feminist activism at local, national, and international levels is the transnational feminist call for states (and regional supra-states) to regulate and tax global capital and reinvigorate social welfare policies as well as worker and environmental protections; for IFIs to cancel Third World debts and support women-centered sustainable development; for TNCs to be made accountable to governments, citizens, workers, the poor, and women generally; and for NGOs to be fully representative of women and their multiple concerns in the struggle to build transnational networks to resist and redirect global restructuring. These movements are connecting across borders, nationalities, races, classes, and sexualities to demand economic, political, cultural, and social justice for women and all living things (see Figure 6.3).

Individual women, too (particularly middle- and upper-class women in advanced industrial societies), have a responsibility to change and curb their consumption patterns. These women benefit—in the form of cheap

232

FIGURE 6.3   Transnational Feminist Activism. Shown here are images from the Beijing meeting where women from all over the world connected with one another to make linkages among local, national, and global gender issues. Courtesy of the International Women's Tribune Centre, Inc. Photographer: Anne S. Walker.

consumer goods—from the cheap labor of primarily poor, Third World women. However, they do so at the expense of creating international solidarity among women to struggle against the global gendered division of labor. Ultimately, ungendering labor will involve increasing not only the presence of women in male-dominated occupations and institutions at all levels but also the presence of all women and supportive men in struggles against the power of gender to divide, devalue, impoverish, and unequalize women (and many men).

UNGENDERING RESOURCES

As enumerated in Chapter 4, the sum of the effects of the gendered divisions of power, violence, and labor denies women any significant access to or control over the world's resources. Women have lost land rights to men, states, and corporations the world over and have been generally kept out of the decision-making within families, states, and corporations about how to use resources and for what purposes.

Instead of having an equal say in what and how resources are to be used, women are treated as resources themselves. Noting that "added resources" give added power to "states to do things that they could not have done previously," Christine Sylvester argues that "women are nonrecognized resources for realist states, occupying positions ranking with oil, geography, industrial capacity, and military preparedness as contributions to power."[21] In fact, all states (and corporations) appropriate women's bodies and labor to extend their resource base and thus their power within and outside state borders. Yet this fact is concealed by the gendered division of resources. However, when a gender-sensitive lens is used to view world politics, the positions of women in a state's and a corporation's resource base are revealed, permitting women to specify strategies of resistance against this appropriation of their bodies and labor.

Those most likely to see that states, corporations, and international organizations turn women into resources to expand state and corporate power are women themselves. Therefore, it is crucial that the presence of women be increased in a variety of decision-making bodies, from the local to the global level, that determine which resources are expendable in order to create other resources. In Chapter 5 we described transnational feminist ecology movements that are demanding the equal representation of women in all environmental policy-making bodies on the assumption that women can see more clearly than men how women as well as the environment are reduced to resources for the enhancement of state and corporate power (see Figure 6.4). We also highlighted how local indigenous women's ecology movements are exposing the relationship between

FIGURE 6.4   Women's Input. Women who work the land need to be the decision-makers if there is to be sustainable development. Courtesy of the International Tribune Centre, Inc. Illustrator: Anne S. Walker.

international trade liberalization and the destruction of the land, liveli-hood, and cultures of indigenous peoples. Indeed, such movements reveal how deeply the global is implicated in the local and how critical women's local activism is for connecting the political, economic, cultural, and envi-ronmental features and consequences of globalization processes.[22]

Making women and nature expendable by sacrificing them on the altar of elite male power, in all its forms, serves neither the practical nor the strategic gender interests of women. It is in women's practical and strate-gic gender interests to have the presence of women as state resources exposed and to increase the presence of women in decision-making bod-ies that control resource use and allocation. However, in order for women to cease being used as resources themselves and to avoid abusing re-sources that come into their hands, the human community—perhaps led by individuals with ecofeminist analyses and sensibilities—will have to develop a different relationship with "nature." That is, we must under-mine the global gendered dichotomy of culture (or man) versus nature that leads to the growth imperative (at any cost) in the world economy.

Although globalization processes are undermining even the small and insufficient steps called for in the Earth Charter that was adopted at the UNCED conference in 1992,[23] and although the Women's Action Agenda 21 that was brought forward to Beijing still remains largely unheeded, the struggle goes on to challenge the power of gender that permits corporate and state elites to rest their networks of transnational production and capital and their military conflicts on the back of nature as well as on the backs of women. We must begin to see nature as part of, not distanced from or beneath, "our" world community. Using an ecofeminist lens, we are more likely to respect the ecosystems of which we, as humans, are only a part. However, we must resist constructions of "Mother Earth," which in turn construct us as children who "cannot be held responsible for our actions."[24] We also must resist the idea that we are one with nature or that nature is some kind of idyllic netherworld to which we can escape, free from our responsibilities to grapple with human, state, and global corporate destruction of the environment—manipulations that have altered everything we associate with the natural world, including our bodies.[25] Finally, we must be careful not to celebrate "the natural" in ways that support oppressive and repressive claims about what is "natural" for or in the "natures" of women or men.

Respect for nature as a partner in, not a slave to, the world community must be accompanied by respect for the needs of women and Third World peoples to enjoy a much greater share of the world's resources. At the same time, it is incumbent on those who struggle for equity in parenting, work, consuming, soldiering, officeholding, decision-making, and property-owning to concern themselves with transforming these activities in ways that are not ecologically harmful.

CONCLUSION

Looking at world politics through a gender-sensitive lens affords a different view of "reality." What we see is in many ways harsher than the realist image of warring states, because we also see the underside of neoliberal celebrations of the triumph of capitalism and the spread of globalization. Indeed, whereas conventional IR lenses show us an iceberg as it emerges from the sea, feminist lenses take us below the surface to see the deep inequalities that shape international hierarchies and erupt into international conflict on the surface. They also allow us to see the hidden hierarchies on which global elites on the tip of the iceberg depend to accumulate wealth and power.

If we were interested only in the surface problems that women face as a result of international hierarchies and conflict, we would recommend that women be given more resources—more land, food, clean water, health care, education, jobs, child care, reproductive rights, money, and formal political power. However, transferring resources to meet women's practical gender interests represents only a small part of what needs to be done. We must also deal with what forms the iceberg largely below the surface. As argued in this text, the production of gender dichotomies and inequalities significantly contributes to the chilly climate that freezes international hierarchies in place. These hierarchies generate the conflicts and crises of world politics.

The global gender dichotomy of masculine-feminine fuels the production of other dichotomies that shape world politics: from war-peace and us-them to modern-traditional, production-reproduction, and culture-nature. The value of the "feminine" sides of these dichotomies is consistently denigrated, whereas the value of the "masculine" side is over-inflated. Clearly, gender divisions of power, violence, labor, and resources present an oppressive image. Although a gender-sensitive lens reveals the pervasiveness of gender hierarchy, it also offers hope. Through this lens, those with the most conventional power in world politics appear surprisingly dependent because their power-over relies on sustaining the dichotomies that reproduce gender and other inequalities. According to this view, those in power are remarkably insecure and their power remarkably unstable. If we expose how world politics depends on artificial notions of masculinity and femininity, we can see that "this seemingly overwhelming world system may be more fragile and open to radical change than we have been led to imagine."[26]

A great deal must change before world politics is ungendered. Toward that end we have identified a number of policy options, but these are only a beginning. Ungendering world politics requires a serious rethinking of what it means to be human and how we might organize ourselves in more cooperative, mutually respectful ways. We would have to reject gendered dichotomies: male versus female, us versus them, culture versus nature. Ungendering world politics also requires a reconceptualization of politics and a shift from power-over to power-to. We would have to recognize power in its multiple forms and be willing to imagine other worlds. Overall, these changes are less a matter of top-down policy than of individually and collectively remaking human society by reconstructing our identities, beliefs, expectations, and institutions. This is the most difficult and complex of human projects, but history shows that we are capable of such revolutionary transformations (see Figure 6.5).

In one sense, we have no choice. Contemporary global processes force us to develop new understandings of who "we," as humans, are and how "we," as global citizens and planetary stewards, must act. In another sense, we willingly seek systemic transformations because we desire more than the absence of war and the presence of commodities: We demand the actualization of justice. And whatever our commitments to justice, we cannot pursue them if we remain blind to gender hierarchy and the (re)production of other hierarchies that it fuels. There is no single enemy to fight or simple strategy to follow—but there is much that we can do.

FIGURE 6.5   Revolutionary Transformations. This sign at a 1995 demonstration against fundamentalist assaults on women's reproductive rights in Washington, D.C., reminds us that "Feminists Are the Majority" given the historical and ongoing struggles of women around the world to achieve equity and justice. Courtesy of Jerome Friar, Impact Visuals.

By acting in concert around particular issues in particular contexts to advance practical and strategic gender interests all over the world, women *and* men alter existing power structures. Although the goals of particular struggles may vary, the most important point is that each struggle contributes to a global climate that nourishes equity and social justice. Such a climate is necessary for melting the iceberg of international hierarchies that deprives many women, men, and children of resources they need and deprives the planet of the care it requires to support those lives. Every effort makes a difference, and many individual and collective efforts are required, for nothing less than the elimination of structural violence will ungender world politics.

NOTES

1. In 1995 the Center for American Women and Politics at Rutgers University found that women in the 103rd Congress (in which there were record numbers of women during 1993–1995) passed thirty bills on women's issues in its first year

compared to five or fewer in any previous year. See Michelle Meadows, "Measuring the Distance," *American Association of University Women Outlook*, Summer 1998, p. 8.

2. Cynthia Enloe, *Bananas, Beaches & Bases: Making Feminist Sense of International Politics* (Berkeley: University of California Press, 1989), pp. 197–198.

3. Christine Sylvester, "Feminists and Realists View Autonomy and Obligation in International Relations," in V. Spike Peterson, ed., *Gendered States: Feminist (Re)Visions of International Relations Theory* (Boulder: Lynne Rienner Publishers, 1992), p. 157.

4. For the full text of CEDAW, see Hilkka Pietila and Jeanne Vickers, *Making Women Matter: The Role of the United Nations,* 2nd ed. (London: Zed Books, 1994). For the full text of the FLS, see Arvonne S. Fraser, *The U.N. Decade for Women: Documents and Dialogue* (Boulder: Westview Press, 1987). See also Deborah Stienstra, *Women's Movements and International Organizations* (New York: St. Martin's Press, 1994), for an analysis of the Nairobi conference and the women's international activism that led up to it.

5. See United Nations, *The World's Women: 1970–1990 Trends and Statistics* (New York: United Nations, 1991); and Women, Public Policy, and Development Project of the Hubert H. Humphrey Institute of Public Affairs, *Forward Looking Strategies for the Advancement of Women to the Year 2000* (Minneapolis: University of Minnesota, 1985).

6. For the full text of this agreement, see United Nations, *The Beijing Declaration and the Platform for Action* (New York: United Nations Department of Public Information, 1996).

7. See Sally Bader and Anne Marie Goetz, "Who Needs [Sex] When You Can Have [Gender]? Conflicting Discourses on Gender at Beijing," *Feminist Review* 56 (Summer 1997): 3–25.

8. Stienstra, *Women's Movements and International Organizations,* p. 157.

9. Francine D'Amico, "Policing the U.S. Military's Race and Gender Lines," in Laurie Weinstein and Christie C. White, eds., *Wives & Warriors: Women and the Military in the United States and Canada* (Westport, Conn.: Bergin & Garvey, 1997), p. 203.

10. Ibid., p. 203. See also Susan Jeffords, *The Remasculinization of America: Gender in the Vietnam War* (Bloomington: Indiana University Press, 1989).

11. Richard Rayner, "The Warrior Besieged," *New York Times Magazine,* June 22, 1997, p. 29.

12. Ibid.

13. See Lori Heise, "Crimes of Gender," *Worldwatch,* March-April, 1989, pp. 12–21; Marilyn French, *The War Against Women* (New York: Simon & Schuster, 1992); and Charlotte Bunch and Niamh Reilly, *Demanding Accountability* (New York: UNIFEM, 1994).

14. Gayle Kirshenbaum, "Why Aren't Human Rights Women's Rights?" *Ms.,* July/August 1991, p. 12. For overviews, see Julia Peters and Andrea Wolper, eds., *Women's Rights, Human Rights* (New York: Routledge, 1995); and Rebecca Cook, ed., *Human Rights of Women* (Philadelphia: University of Pennsylvania Press, 1994). On human rights as heterosexist, see V. Spike Peterson and Laura Parisi, "Are Women Human? It's Not an Academic Question," in Tony Evans, ed., *Human Rights Fifty Years On: A Radical Reappraisal* (New York: St. Martin's Press, 1998).

15. Saskia Sassen, "Towards a Feminist Analytics of the Global Economy," *Indiana Journal of Global Legal Studies* 4 (Fall 1996): 35.

16. See, for example, Patricia Lunneborg, *Women Changing Work* (New York: Bergin & Garvey, 1990).

17. Margot Gibb-Clark, "Inexperience Held Against Women," *Globe and Mail*, December 10, 1997, pp. A1, A4.

18. Charlotte Hooper, "Masculinist Practices and Gender Politics: The Operation of Multiple Masculinities in International Relations," in Marysia Zalewski and Jane Parpart, eds., *The "Man" Question in International Relations* (Boulder: Westview Press, 1998), p. 37.

19. Elizabeth Olson, "U.N. Surveys Paid Leave for Mothers," *New York Times*, February 16, 1998, p. A5.

20. Marilyn Waring, *If Women Counted* (San Francisco: Harper, 1988), p. 314.

21. Sylvester, "Feminists and Realists View Autonomy and Obligation in International Relations," p. 169.

22. See Amrita Basu, *The Challenge of Local Feminisms* (Boulder: Westview Press, 1995); and Cathy Cohen, Kathleen Jones, and Joan Tronto, eds., *Women Transforming Politics* (New York: New York University Press, 1997).

23. See Rosi Braidotti, Eva Charkiewicz, Sabine Hausler, and Saskia Wieringa, *Women, the Environment and Sustainable Development* (London: Zed Books, 1996), pp. 126–131.

24. Joni Seager, *Earth Follies: Coming to Feminist Terms with the Global Environmental Crisis* (New York: Routledge, 1993), p. 219.

25. See Anne Sisson Runyan, "The 'State' of Nature: A Garden Unfit for Women and Other Living Things," in Peterson, ed., *Gendered States*, pp. 123–140; Donna Haraway, "Structured Knowledges: The Science Question in Feminism and the Privilege of Partial Perspective," *Feminist Studies* 14 (1988): 575–599; Linda Vance, "Ecofeminism and Wilderness," *NWSA Journal* 9 (Fall 1997): 60–76; and Jane Bennett and William Chaloupka, eds., *In the Nature of Things* (Minneapolis: University of Minnesota Press, 1993).

26. Enloe, *Bananas, Beaches & Bases*, p. 17.

□ □ □

Discussion Questions

CHAPTER 1

1. How does the metaphor of a lens permit us to see world politics—or other topics—from varying perspectives? Think about and identify different lenses that you, your parents (or children), your teachers, and particular authors use.

2. How are the terms *global*, *gender*, and *issues* used in this text? How are they related, and what is their relevance to world politics?

3. What do the *position of women* and the *power of gender* refer to? How are they related, and what is their relevance to world politics? Apply a gender-sensitive lens to an institution with which you are familiar (e.g., school, church, organization) and give examples of the position(s) of women and the power of gender.

4. Why is gender hierarchy an issue now? In what ways is it relevant to the study of world politics? How is it relevant in your own life? What activities do you engage in that reinforce or resist gender hierarchy?

5. Review another book or article on the subject of gender and international relations to see how others relate gender issues to world politics.

CHAPTER 2

1. What are some patterns that differentiate theoretical lenses? How do positivists and postpositivists differ in their understanding of language and how it is political? In what ways are the feminist lenses we describe related and differentiated?

2. How is gender distinguished from sex? To what does gender hierarchy refer, and how is it related to other social inequalities? What are stereotypes, dichotomies, and ideology? How do they interact in the construction of gender hierarchy? Provide examples from your own life of

241

how stereotypes, dichotomies, and ideologies interact. (Consider your gender, race, class, sexual, and national identities in relation to your family history, educational opportunities, career decisions, etc.) How does privilege shape your life and social relationships? How are privilege and responsibility related?

3. If gender is so pervasive, why is it so invisible? What are the ways in which gender is obscured in the study of world politics? Compare reading assignments within this or with another course: How visible is gender? How are argumentations altered by recognition of gender biases and issues?

4. How are gendered divisions of power, violence, labor, and resources related to issues of world politics, world security, global political economy, and global ecology? Provide examples that demonstrate how these divisions in one country are related to divisions in another country.

5. How does the study of gender and the examination of gender dichotomies inform our understanding of world politics? What do they enable us to "see" that was "invisible" in conventional accounts of international relations?

CHAPTER 3

1. What does the gendered division of power mean? In what ways does it privilege men and masculinist ideologies?

2. In which decision-making bodies are women the least represented? In what parts of the world are women most represented in terms of formal political power? What patterns are there in terms of where women and men are positioned as state actors? In what sense is the relative absence of women from senior positions in business and religions institutions a political issue?

3. How are women in power rendered invisible, insignificant, or viewed as "honorary males"? Collect news accounts of a female head of state in the past or present and identify the images/stereotypes that are used to describe her and her actions.

4. How do gender socialization, situational constraints, and structural obstacles shape the proportion of women and men as state actors and position women and men in different locations of state power?

5. What are typical paths to power for women? For men? How do women and men in office differ in terms of gender issues? What variables affect how much attention political actors pay to gender issues? Choose a current woman leader and track how she rose to power, what issues she has been associated with, and what she has done for women's rights.

CHAPTER 4

1. Find a traditional definition of power in conventional international relations (IR) literature and explore how this concept of power is gendered. What are the world political consequences of this definition for women? For men?

2. Compare a traditional IR description of militarism with a gender-sensitive analysis of it. How does a gender-sensitive analysis affect our understanding and pursuit of "security" in international relations?

3. Look for traditional IR explanations (liberal, realist, Marxist) of the global political economy and explore the ways in which women and gender relations are absent from or rendered invisible by these accounts. In what ways would making women and gender dynamics visible in discussions of the international political economy and globalization alter our understanding of how states and transnational corporations amass wealth, how international trade works, and why Western development strategies don't work?

4. Choose an environmental problem and explore how the sources and proposed solutions to the problem may be gendered. What does such an inquiry tell you about the causes of and the (lack of) solutions to global ecological crises?

5. Find an example in the United States and in one other country of how global gendered divisions of violence, labor, and resources interact to reduce women's power and influence in international politics.

CHAPTER 5

1. How do different feminist perspectives approach the issue of women and militarization or women and globalization? How do these different perspectives challenge and/or reinforce gender dichotomies? What are the differences and relationships between "practical" and "strategic" gender interests?

2. How have practical gender interests motivated women to protest war? What strategic gender interests do women have in promoting peace? What might be a feminist definition of peace? How might different feminist perspectives/movements analyze and respond to a specific conflict, such as the Persian Gulf war or the war in Bosnia? Look for a women's peace organization/movement website and determine what feminist perspectives are represented in the information it presents.

3. How have socialist and democratizing revolutions served women's practical gender interests? Why have socialist and democratizing revolutionary movements failed to meet women's strategic gender interests?

Can "national liberation" produce "women's liberation"? Find an Eastern European or Russian feminist organization website that discusses what changes in civil society are needed to transform the nation, the state, and the market.

4. What factors unique to women's roles and responsibilities in the family and the world economy hinder and/or facilitate women's organizing against economic exploitation? How might transnational movements against economic exploitation be strengthened by paying attention to women's practical and strategic gender interests? Look for feminist websites that address the issue of globalization and cross-border organizing strategies for resisting and redirecting it.

5. How is women's activism in environmental movements connected to women's practical and strategic gender interests? How might women's environmentalist movements intersect with other women's movements? On what bases can women (and supportive men) form transnational coalitions to simultaneously confront the gendered divisions of power, violence, labor, and resources? Can you find any contemporary examples of such coalitions on the web?

CHAPTER 6

1. How is changing the *position of women* in all aspects of world politics related to women's practical gender interests? To women's strategic interests?

2. How does the *power of gender* operate to keep women and other underrepresented groups as well as the issues they raise subordinated in world politics? How is undermining the power of gender related to women's strategic gender interests? Why is it important to attend to the power of gender when we analyze world politics?

3. What might a world based on the model of relational autonomy look like? How would it be different from the world of reactive autonomy for women? For men?

4. What strategies would you recommend to ungender violence, labor, and resources in world politics? How would you interrelate these projects? Review websites from the Beijing conference to learn what proposals were made by IGOs and NGOs to ungender world politics.

5. Do you think it is important to ungender world politics? Why or why not?

6. As an exercise, participate in the feminist-IR computer network FEMISA for a brief period. (To subscribe, see the information provided in "List Serves and Websites.") What are the issues being discussed? How do they relate to your own studies and to international understanding?

□ □ □

Suggested Readings

Afshar, Haleh. 1996. *Women and Politics in the Third World*. London: Routledge.

Alexander, M. Jacqui, and Chandra Talpade Mohanty. 1997. *Feminist Genealogies, Colonial Legacies, Democratic Futures*. New York: Routledge.

Amnesty International. 1990. *Women in the Front Line: Human Rights Violations Against Women*. New York: Amnesty International Publications.

Bakker, Isabella, ed. 1994. *The Strategic Silence: Gender and Economic Policy*. London: Zed Books.

Bandarage, Asoka. 1997. *Women, Population, and Global Crisis*. London: Zed Books.

Basu, Amrita, ed. 1995. *The Challenge of Local Feminisms*. Boulder: Westview Press.

Beckman, Peter R., and Francine D'Amico, eds. 1994. *Women, Gender, and World Politics: Perspectives, Policies, and Prospects*. Westport, Conn.: Bergin & Garvey.

Bem, Sandra Lipsitz. 1993. *The Lenses of Gender*. New Haven: Yale University Press.

Bennett, Jane, and William Chaloupka, eds. 1993. *In the Nature of Things*. Minneapolis: University of Minnesota.

Berry, Ellen E., ed. 1995. *Postcommunism and the Body Politic*. New York: New York University Press.

Bock, Gisela, and Susan James, eds. 1992. *Beyond Equality and Difference: Citizenship, Feminist Politics, and Female Subjectivity*. New York: Routledge.

Boris, Eileen, and Elisabeth Prugl, eds. 1996. *Homeworkers in Global Perspective*. London: Routledge.

Braidotti, Rosi, Eva Charkiewicz, Sabine Hausler, and Saskia Wieringa. 1996. *Women, the Environment and Sustainable Development*. London: Zed Books.

Brecher, Jeremy, and Tim Costello. 1994. *Global Village or Global Pillage*. Boston: South End Press.

Brecher, Jeremy, John Brown Childs, and Jill Cutler, eds. 1993. *Global Visions: Beyond the New World Order*. Boston: South End Press.

Breuer, William B. 1997. *War and American Women: Heroism, Deeds, and Controversy*. Westport, Conn.: Praeger.

Brittan, Arthur. 1989. *Masculinity and Power*. New York: Blackwell.

Brod, Harry, and Michael Kaufman, eds. 1994. *Theorizing Masculinities*. Thousand Oaks, Calif.: Sage Publishing.

Brown, Wendy. 1988. *Manhood and Politics*. Totowa, N.J.: Rowman and Littlefield.

Bullock, Susan. 1994. *Women and Work*. London: Zed Books.

Bunch, Charlotte, and Niamh Reilly. 1994. *Demanding Accountability*. New York: UNIFEM.

Chomsky, Noam. 1996. *World Orders Old and New.* New York: Columbia University Press.

Cohen, Cathy J., Kathleen B. Jones, and Joan C. Tronto, eds. 1997. *Women Transforming Politics: An Alternative Reader.* New York: New York University Press.

Connell, R. W. 1987. *Gender and Power.* Cambridge, Eng.: Polity Press.

Cooke, Miriam, and Angela Wollacott, eds. 1993. *Gendering War Talk.* Princeton: Princeton University Press.

Coole, Diana. 1993. *Women in Political Theory: From Ancient Misogyny to Contemporary Feminism,* 2nd ed. New York: Harvester Wheatsheaf.

D'Amico, Francine, and Peter R. Beckman, eds. 1995. *Women and World Politics.* Westport, Conn.: Bergin & Garvey.

DeLamotte, Eugenia C., Natania Meeker, and Jean F. O'Barr, eds. 1997. *Women Imagine Change: A Global Anthology of Women's Resistance from 600 BCE to Present.* New York: Routledge.

Einhorn, Barbara. 1993. *Cinderella Goes to Market: Citizenship, Gender and the Women's Movement in East Central Europe.* New York: Verso.

Eisenstein, Zillah. 1994. *The Color of Gender: Reimagining Democracy.* Berkeley: University of California Press.

Eisler, Riane, David Loye, and Kari Norgaard. 1995. *Women, Men, and the Global Quality of Life.* Pacific Grove, Calif.: Center for Partnership Studies.

Elman, Amy, ed. 1996. *Sexual Politics and the European Union.* Providence, R.I.: Berghahn Books.

Elshtain, Jean Bethke. 1987. *Women and War.* New York: Basic Books.

Elshtain, Jean Bethke, and Sheila Tobias. 1990. *Women, Militarism, and War.* Savage, Md.: Rowman and Littlefield.

Enloe, Cynthia. 1983. *Does Khaki Become You? The Militarization of Women's Lives.* Boston: South End Press.

———. 1989. *Bananas, Beaches & Bases: Making Feminist Sense of International Politics.* Berkeley: University of California Press.

———. 1993. *The Morning After: Sexual Politics at the End of the Cold War.* Berkeley: University of California Press.

Faludi, Susan. 1991. *Backlash: The Undeclared War Against American Women.* New York: Crown Publishers.

Flammang, Joyce. 1997. *Women's Political Voice: How Women Are Transforming the Practice and Study of Politics.* Philadelphia: Temple University Press.

French, Marilyn. 1992. *The War Against Women.* New York: Simon & Schuster.

Funk, Nanette, and Magda Mueller, eds. 1993. *Gender Politics and Post-Communism.* New York: Routledge.

Garlick, Barbara, Suzanne Dixon, and Pauline Allen, eds. 1992. *Stereotypes of Women in Power: Historical Perspectives and Revisionist Views.* New York: Greenwood Press.

Genovese, Michael A., ed. 1993. *Women as National Leaders: The Political Performance of Women as Heads of State.* Newbury Park, Calif.: Sage Publishing.

George, Jim. 1994. *Discourses of Global Politics.* Boulder: Lynne Rienner Publishers.

Ghorayshi, Parvin, and Claire Belanger, eds. 1996. *Women, Work, and Gender Relations in Developing Countries: A Global Perspective.* Westport, Conn.: Greenwood.

Gibson-Graham, J. K. 1996. *The End of Capitalism (as we knew it): A Feminist Critique of Political Economy*. Cambridge, Mass.: Blackwell Publishers.

Gonick, Lev S., and Edward Weisband, eds. 1992. *Teaching World Politics: Contending Pedagogies for a New World Order*. Boulder: Westview Press.

Grant, Rebecca, and Kathleen Newland, eds. 1991. *Gender and International Relations*. Bloomington/Indianapolis: Indiana University Press.

Grewal, Inderpal, and Caren Kaplan, eds. 1994. *Scattered Hegemonies*. Minneapolis: University of Minnesota Press.

Haraway, Donna. 1991. *Simians, Cyborgs, and Women: The Reinvention of Nature*. New York: Routledge.

————. 1997. *Modest_Witness@Second Millennium. FemaleMan©_Meets_Onco-Mouse™: Feminism and Technoscience*. New York: Routledge.

Harding, Sandra. 1991. *Whose Science? Whose Knowledge? Thinking from Women's Lives*. Ithaca: Cornell University Press.

Hekman, Susan. 1990. *Gender and Knowledge*. Cambridge, Eng.: Polity Press.

Heyzer, Noleen, ed. 1995. *A Commitment to the World's Women*. New York: UNIFEM.

Hoskyns, Catherine. 1996. *Integrating Gender: Women, Law and Politics in the European Union*. London: Verso.

Johnson, Allan G. 1997. *The Gender Knot: Unraveling Our Patriarchal Legacy*. Philadelphia: Temple University Press.

Karl, Marilee. 1995. *Women and Empowerment: Participation and Decision Making*. London: Zed Books.

Kofman, Eleonore, and Gillian Youngs. 1996. *Globalization: Theory and Practice*. London: Pinter.

Korten, David C. 1996. *When Corporations Rule the World*. West Hartford, Conn.: Kumarian Press.

Lentin, Ronit, ed. 1997. *Gender and Catastrophe*. London: Zed Books.

Lips, Hilary. 1991. *Women, Men, and Power*. Mountain View, Calif.: Mayfield.

Longeneker, Marlene, ed. 1997. Special Issue on Women, Ecology, and the Environment. *NWSA Journal* 9 (Fall).

Lorber, Judith. 1998. *Gender Inequality: Feminist Theories and Politics*. Los Angeles: Roxbury Publishing Company.

Lorber, Judith, and Susan A. Farrell, eds. 1991. *The Social Construction of Gender*. Newbury Park, Calif.: Sage Publishing.

Marchand, Marianne H., and Jane L. Parpart, eds. 1995. *Feminism, Postmodernism, Development*. London: Routledge.

Marchand, Marianne H., and Anne Sisson Runyan, eds. (forthcoming). *Gender and Global Restructuring: Shifting Sites and Sightings*. London: Routledge.

Martin, Hans-Peter, and Harald Schumann. 1997. *The Global Trap: Globalization and the Assault on Prosperity and Democracy*. New York: St. Martin's Press.

Massey, Doreen. 1994. *Space, Place and Gender*. Cambridge, Eng.: Polity Press.

McClintock, Anne. 1995. *Imperial Leather: Race, Gender and Sexuality in the Colonial Contest*. New York: Routledge.

McClintock, Anne, Aamir Mufti, and Ella Sohat, eds. 1997. *Dangerous Liaisons: Gender, Nation, and Postcolonial Perspectives*. Minneapolis: University of Minnesota Press.

Messner, Michael A. 1997. *Politics of Masculinities: Men in Movements.* Thousand Oaks, Calif.: Sage Publishing.

Meyer, Mary K., and Elisabeth Prugl, eds. (forthcoming). *Gender Politics in Global Governance.* Boulder: Rowman & Littlefield.

Midgley, Claire, ed. 1998. *Gender and Imperialism.* Manchester, Eng.: Manchester University Press.

Mies, Maria, Veronika Bennholdt-Thomsen, and Claudia von Werlhof. 1988. *Women: The Last Colony.* London: Zed Books.

Mies, Maria, and Vandana Shiva. 1993. *Ecofeminism.* London: Zed Books.

Miles, Angela. 1995. *Integrative Feminisms: Building Global Visions, 1960–1990.* New York: Routledge.

Mittelman, James H., ed. 1996. *Globalization: Critical Reflections.* Boulder: Lynne Rienner Publishers.

Moghadam, Valentine M. 1998. *Women, Work and Economic Reform in the Middle East and North Africa.* Boulder: Lynne Rienner Publishers.

Moghadam, Valentine M., ed. 1994. *Identity Politics and Women: Cultural Reassertions and Feminisms in International Perspective.* Boulder: Westview Press.

Mohanty, Chandra Talpade, Anne Russo, and Lourdes Torres, eds. 1991. *Third World Women and the Politics of Feminism.* Bloomington: Indiana University Press.

Momsen, Janet H., and Vivian Kinnaird, eds. 1993. *Different Places, Different Voices: Gender and Development in Africa, Asia and Latin America.* London: Routledge.

Moon, Katharine H. S. 1997. *Sex Among Allies: Military Prostitution in U.S.-Korea Relations.* New York: Columbia University Press.

Neft, Naomi, and Ann D. Levine. 1997. *Where Women Stand: An International Report on the Status of Women in 140 Countries, 1997–1998.* New York: Random House.

Nelson, Barbara J., and Najma Chowdhury. 1994. *Women and Politics Worldwide.* New Haven: Yale University Press.

Neufield, Mark A. 1995. *The Restructuring of International Relations Theory.* Cambridge, Eng.: Cambridge University Press.

Nicholson, Linda J., ed., 1990. *Feminism/Postmodernism.* New York: Routledge.

Okin, Susan Moller. 1989. *Justice, Gender and the Family.* New York: Basic Books.

Peterson, V. Spike, ed. 1992. *Gendered States: Feminist (Re)Visions of International Relations Theory.* Boulder: Lynne Rienner Publishers.

Pettman, Jan Jindy. 1996. *Worlding Women: A Feminist International Politics.* London: Routledge.

Pettman, Ralph. 1991. *International Politics: Balance of Power, Balance of Productivity, Balance of Ideologies.* Boulder: Lynne Rienner Publishers.

———. 1996. *Understanding International Political Economy.* Boulder: Lynne Rienner Publishers.

Pierson, Ruth Roach. 1987. *Women and Peace: Theoretical, Historical, and Practical Perspectives.* London: Croom Helm.

Pietila, Hilkka, and Jeanne Vickers. 1994. *Making Women Matter: The Role of the United Nations,* 2nd ed. London: Zed Books.

Plumwood, Val. 1993. *Feminism and the Mastery of Nature.* London: Routledge.

Radcliffe, Sarah A., and Sallie Westwood, eds. 1993. *Viva: Women and Popular Protest in Latin America.* London: Routledge.

Rodda, Annabel. 1991. *Women and the Environment.* London: Zed Books.

Rowbotham, Sheila, and Swasti Mitter, eds. 1994. *Dignity and Daily Bread: New Forms of Economic Organizing Among Poor Women in the Third World and the First.* New York: Routledge.

Runyan, Anne Sisson, and V. Spike Peterson. 1991. "The Radical Future of Realism: Feminist Subversions of International Relations Theory." *Alternatives* 16, pp. 67–106.

Sassen, Saskia. 1991. *The Global City.* Princeton: Princeton University Press.

Scott, Joan W., Cora Kaplan, and Debra Keates, eds. 1997. *Transitions, Environments, Translations: Feminisms in International Politics.* New York: Routledge.

Seager, Joni. 1993. *Earth Follies: Coming to Feminist Terms with the Global Environmental Crisis.* New York: Routledge.

———. 1997. *The State of Women in the World Atlas.* New York: Penguin Books.

Sharoni, Simona. 1995. *Gender and the Israeli-Palestinian Conflict.* Syracuse, N.Y.: Syracuse University Press.

Sivard, Ruth Leger. 1995. *Women . . . A World Survey.* Washington, D.C.: World Priorities, Inc.

———. 1996. *World Military and Social Expenditures 1996.* Washington, D.C.: World Priorities, Inc.

Sparr, Pamela. 1994. *Mortgaging Women's Lives: Feminist Critiques of Structural Adjustment.* London: Zed Books.

Staudt, Kathleen. 1998. *Policy, Politics and Gender: Women Gaining Ground.* West Hartford, Conn.: Kumarian Press.

Steans, Jill. 1998. *Gender and International Relations.* Cambridge, Eng.: Polity Press.

Stienstra, Deborah. 1994. *Women's Movements and International Organizations.* New York: St. Martin's Press.

Sylvester, Christine. 1994. *Feminist Theory and International Relations in a Postmodern Era.* Cambridge, Eng.: Cambridge University Press.

Sylvester, Christine, ed. 1993. "Special Issue: Feminists Write International Relations. *Alternatives* 18 (Winter).

Teske, Robin L., and Mary Ann Tetreault, eds. (forthcoming). *Feminist Approaches to Social Movements, Community, and Power,* vols. 1 and 2. Columbia: University of South Carolina Press.

Tetreault, Mary Ann, ed. 1994. *Women and Revolution in Africa, Asia and the New World.* Columbia: University of South Carolina Press.

Tickner, J. Ann. 1993. *Gender in International Relations.* New York: Columbia University Press.

Tong, Rosemarie. 1998. *Feminist Thought: A More Comprehensive Introduction.* Boulder: Westview Press.

Tuana, Nancy. 1993. *The Less Noble Sex: Scientific, Religious, and Philosophical Conceptions of Woman's Nature.* Bloomington: Indiana University Press.

Turpin, Jennifer, and Lester R. Kurtz, eds. 1996. *The Web of Violence: From Interpersonal to Global.* Urbana: University of Illinois Press.

Turpin, Jennifer, and Lois Ann Lorentzen, eds. 1996. *The Gendered World Order.* New York: Routledge.

United Nations (UN). 1995. *The World's Women 1995: Trends and Statistics.* New York: United Nations.

———. 1996. *The Beijing Declaration and the Platform of Action.* New York: United Nations Department of Public Information.

United Nations Development Program (UNDP). 1997. *Human Development Report 1997.* New York: Oxford University Press.

Vickers, Jeanne. 1991. *Women and the World Economic Crisis.* London: Zed Books.

———. 1993. *Women and War.* London: Zed Books.

Walby, Sylvia. 1997. *Gender Transformations.* New York: Routledge.

Waters, Malcolm. 1995. *Globalization.* London: Routledge.

Waylen, Georgina. 1996. *Gender in Third World Politics.* Boulder: Lynne Rienner Publishing.

Weinstein, Laurie, and Christie C. White, eds. 1997. *Wives & Warriors: Women and the Military in the United States and Canada.* Westport, Conn.: Bergin & Garvey.

West, Guida, and Rhoda Lois Blumberg, eds. 1990. *Women and Social Protest.* New York: Oxford University Press.

West, Lois. 1997. *Feminist Nationalism.* New York: Routledge.

Whitworth, Sandra. 1994. *Feminism and International Relations.* London: Macmillan.

World Commission on Environment and Development. 1987. *Our Common Future.* Oxford: Oxford University Press.

Young, Gay, Vidyamali Samarisinghe, and Ken Kusterer, eds. 1993. *Women at the Center: Development Issues and Practices for the 1990s.* West Hartford, Conn.: Kumarian Press.

Young, Iris Marion. 1990. *Justice and the Politics of Difference.* Princeton: Princeton University Press.

———. 1998. *Intersecting Voices: Dilemmas of Gender, Political Philosophy, and Policy.* Princeton: Princeton University Press.

Yuval-Davis, Nira. 1997. *Gender and Nation.* London: Sage Publishing.

Zalewski, Marysia, and Jane Parpart, eds. 1998. *The "Man" Question in International Relations.* Boulder: Westview.

□ □ □

List Serves and Websites

LIST SERVES

Feminist International Relations

send message: sub femisa yourname
  to: listserve@csf.colorado

Third World Women

send message: subscribe third world women
  to: majordomo@jefferson.village.virginia.edu

WEBSITES

Information on Websites

Bowles-Adarkwa, Linda, and Ann Kennedy. 1997. "Global Priorities for Women:
  A Bibliography of Resources and Research Strategies." *Women's Studies International Forum* 20: 165–178.
Fallon, Helen. 1998. *WOW Women on the Web: A Guide to Gender-Related Resources on the Internet*. Dublin: Women's Education, Research and Resource Center.
Penn, Shana. 1997. *The Women's Guide to the Wired World*. New York: The Feminist Press.
A Women's Guide to the Best Web Sites: http://www.yin.org
FeMiNa—"Yahoo for Women" search engine: http://www.femina.com/

General

Women's Web World (Feminist Majority Foundation): http://www.feminist.org/
WomensNet: http://www.igc.apc.org/womensnet/
The World's Women On-Line: http://wwol.inre.asu.edu/intro.html
UN Development Fund for Women (UNIFEM): http://www.unifem.undp.org
Women's International Center: http://www.wic.org
Women Leaders On-Line: Women Organizing for Change: http://wlo.org
Women's Wire: http://www.women.com

National Organization for Women (NOW): http://www.now.org/
Global Issues resources: http://www.igc.apc.org/women/activist/global.html
Women of the World, Reproductive Law and Policy: http://www.echonyc.com/~
jmkm/wotw/
Black Girl International: http://www.blackgirl.org/
Global Fund for Women: http://www.igc.apc.org/gfw/
Women, Islam, and Resistance: http://www.iran-e-azad.org/
One World: http://www.oneworld.org/
Global Survival Network: http://www.globalsurvival.net

Men/Masculinity

The Men's Issues Page: http://www.vix.com/pub/men/index.html

Beijing Conference on Women

Once and Future Action Network post-Beijing Newsletter: http://www.ifias.ca/
gsd/ofan/3index.html

Development/Environment

Women's Environment and Development Organization: http://www.wedo.org
UN Development Fund for Women (UNIFEM): http://www.unifem.undp.org
Women in Development Committee Home Page: http://www.pitt.edu/~women

Health Issues

World Health Organization: http://www.who.org/

Sexual Violence

Trafficking and Prostitution (Migration Information Programme): http://www.
iom.ch/ doc/MIP_TRAFWMN.htm
RAINN (Rape, Abuse, & Incest National Network): http://www.rainn.org/

Third World Women

Solid Africa's Economic Empowerment for Women: http://humanism.org/
SolidAfrica/empow.htm
South Asian Women's NETwork: http://www.umiacs.umd.edu:80/users/
sawweb/sawnet
Women's Issues in Third World Countries: http://women3rdworld.miningco.
com/mbody.htm

Women in Post-Communist Countries

Network of East-West Women: http://www.neww.org

Women and Politics

Women of the World Homepage: http://www.astrawow.com/wow/index.html
Center for the American Woman and Politics: http://www.rci.rutgers.edu/~
cawp
Center for Women's Global Leadership: http://www.feminist.com/cfwgl.htm

Women's History

Women's History: http://frank.mtsu.edu/~kmiddlet/history/women.html
Women in World History: http://home.earthlink.net/~womenwhist/

Women and the Military

Women's Military Organization: http://www.militarywoman.org
H-Minerva (Women and the Military): http://h-net2.msu.edu/~minerva/

Women's Rights

NARAL (National Abortion and Reproductive Rights Action League): http://
www.naral.org/
Convention on the Elimination of Discrimination Against Women (CEDAW):
http://www.un.org/womenwatch/daw/cedaw/
Human Rights Watch: http://www.hrw.org/
International Women's Rights Action Watch: http://www.igc.apc.org/iwraw

□ □ □

Glossary

An **androcentric** (male-centered or male-as-norm) orientation treats men's ways of being and knowing as the norm or standard for *all* people (men and women), thus obscuring or denying alternative vantage points.

Civil society can refer either to all private-sector actors (corporations, organizations, families, and individuals) that are in tension with and seek autonomy from the state or, more specifically, to social movements that resist both state oppression and capitalist market exploitation. Political struggles within the family and the community to counter sexism, racism, classism, heterosexism, and nationalism are required to produce progressive, as opposed to reactionary, social movements.

Colonization or **colonialism** is a practice that dates back to the early 1500s, when European powers conquered and then ruled peoples throughout the Americas, Africa, and Asia for the purposes of extracting wealth and resources, through the use of slave labor, to enrich European monarchies and, later, to fuel European industrial development. Although most direct colonial rule ended after World War II, it was replaced by neo-colonialism or imperialism, through which Western powers continued to indirectly control the economies and policies of politically independent Third World states.

The **debt crisis,** which began in the 1980s, was set in motion by the oil crisis in the 1970s, when oil-producing nations deposited their windfall profits into the Western banking system. Western banks, in turn, encouraged many Third World countries to borrow money at low interest rates for development purposes. The worldwide recession during the late 1970s and early 1980s led to a reduction in the price of commodities that Third World countries typically export and a rise in interest rates. This combination of factors made it impossible for Third World borrowers to pay back their loans, threatening the stability of the Western banking system.

Dependent development or **underdevelopment** occurs when countries in the South are expected to provide cheap raw materials and agricultural commodities to meet the needs of industries and consumers in the North, resulting in the impoverishment of the South and the enrichment of the North, upon which the South becomes dependent for food and manufactured goods.

Development is usually measured by a country's GDP and its degree of industrialization, urbanization, technological advancement, export capability, and consumer orientation. Based on these economic measurements, developed countries are mostly those in the North (or the First World) and developing countries are mostly those in the South (or the Third World). Human development, as opposed to the narrow category of economic development, is measured very differently. Such things as the amount of inequality, the levels at which basic needs are met, and the status of the natural environment determine progress or regress in human development.

Dichotomy refers to a binary, oppositional contrast that privileges the first term over the second and obscures the historical and therefore changing meaning of the terms. Dichotomies are habitual ways of organizing thought; they permeate language and hence affect decision-making and action. They are political insofar as they naturalize an opposition between masculine and feminine and fuel either-or thinking, which distorts our understanding of social reality.

Double workday refers to the dual labor that women typically perform in the home and in the workplace. Many women in the Third World experience a triple day—doing reproductive labor in the home, working for wages in the formal or informal economy, and growing subsistence crops to feed their families when their wages do not cover the price of food.

Empowerment, which means "enabling power" or "power-to," is in contrast to "power-over." It is about enhancing the capacity of people to live and work together productively and effectively rather than coercively dividing and controlling people in a way that reduces their abilities to act individually or collectively.

The **feminine principle** refers to the basis on which many nonindustrialized people have related to the land as a source of sustenance that can be used, but not abused. Central to this understanding is a reverence for the land as a mother and a recognition of women's stewardship of the land.

Feminism is an orientation that views gender as a fundamental ordering principle in today's world, that values women's diverse ways of being and knowing, and that promotes the transformation of gender and related hierarchies. There are many feminist lenses that are not mutually exclusive but, rather, differ in terms of what problems they emphasize and explanations they favor, including liberal, radical, cultural, socialist, postcolonial, postmodern, and ecofeminism.

The **feminization of labor** has at least three dimensions: preference for women workers as cheap labor in the global economy; the degradation of work, reduction in incomes, and decline of labor unions in the formal sector brought on by trade liberalization; and the growth of financial and service sectors at the expense of the manufacturing sector.

The **feminization of poverty** refers to the exceptionally high numbers of women within the ranks of the poor. It conspires with the racialization of poverty to ensure that Third World and visible minority women are the poorest of the poor.

Flexibilized or **casualized labor** refers to temporary, part-time, or contract work that provides no job security, little or no benefits, and few regulatory protections with respect to wages and health and safety.

Food-fuel-water crises refer to the processes of deforestation and desertification that result from "man-made" development practices and military operations that threaten the ability of people in subsistence economies to meet their daily needs for food, water, and shelter.

Free trade zones (FTZs), also known as export-processing zones (EPZs) (or *maquiladoras* in the case of Mexico), are special areas created by governments, especially in the Third World, to attract TNCs to assemble products for export in order to circumvent trade barriers. Host governments promise cheap labor, minimal environmental and workplace regulation, and tax incentives.

Nationalist and/or religious **fundamentalisms** seek to regain and reassert "authentic" national identities, cultural traditions, and belief systems in response to cultural homogenization processes and erosions of national self-determination associated with globalization.

Gender is not a physiological concept but a social one that refers to sets of culturally defined character traits labeled "masculinity" and "femininity."

Gender hierarchy describes a system of power that privileges men and that which is associated with masculinity over women and that which is associated with femininity. This "privileging" includes men's appropriation of women's productive and reproductive labor, men's control over women's bodies and regulation of women's activities, and the promotion of masculinism to "naturalize" (depoliticize) this hierarchy.

Gendered nationalism refers to the construction of a national identity and solidarity based on masculinist notions of self-determination and autonomy—a construction that occurs at the expense of women's self-definitions and solidarity. Historically, gendered symbols, identities, and divisions of power, labor, and resources have been central features of nationalism.

A **gender-sensitive lens** enables us to see the extent and structure of gender hierarchy by examining both how social constructions of masculinity and femininity shape our ways of thinking and knowing and how women's and men's lives are patterned differently as a consequence of gendered practices.

Genocidal rape refers to a systematic program of raping women and girls to humiliate (or feminize) the enemy and to dilute it as a (biological) nation through the impregnation of the enemy's women. This war crime has occurred most recently in Bosnia and Rwanda.

Globalization, or global restructuring, refers to the internationalization of the capitalist economy in which states, markets, and civil society are restructured to facilitate the flow of global capital. Globalization is an economic, political, cultural, social, organizational, and technological process that disrupts familiar categories and patterns at the same time that it intensifies old and new forms of domination.

The **green revolution** refers to an attempt to combat hunger and famine in the Third World by increasing its crop yields through the introduction of highly mechanized, large-scale farming techniques.

The **gross domestic product (GDP)** is the total final output of goods and services produced by a nation within its borders. It is distinguished from the gross national product (GNP), which includes income produced abroad.

Heterosexism refers to beliefs, practices, and institutions that impose heterosexuality as the only "normal" and therefore legitimate expression of sexual desire, intimacy, and family life. It fuels a rigid gender dichotomy that denigrates feminization and fosters homophobia, which, in turn, demonizes and even criminalizes nonheterosexual relations.

Ideology refers to a system of beliefs and expectations about human nature and social life that seems to justify the status quo by "naturalizing" (depoliticizing) existing arrangements.

The **informal sector,** or informal work, encompasses a wide range of legal and extralegal economic activities that lie largely outside national accounting and state regulatory protection and are typically performed in the contexts of self-employment, family businesses, clandestine activities, and insecure wage work not covered by formal agreements between workers and employers.

Internal security refers to the steps taken typically by military regimes to quell revolts by their own people against their authority.

The **interstate system** is composed of (formally) equal, sovereign states that are not controlled by a supranational authority and thus are presumed to exist in a state of anarchy where power politics reigns. States, however, do cooperate in various ways through international regimes or organizations, constituting regional and global systems that regulate to some degree the behavior of states.

Masculinism is the ideology that justifies and "naturalizes" gender hierarchy by not questioning the elevation of ways of being and knowing associated with men and masculinity over those associated with women and femininity.

Militarization refers to processes by which characteristically military practices are extended into the civilian arena—as when businesses become dependent on military contracts, clothing fashions celebrate military styles, or toys and games embody military activities.

The **military-industrial complex** refers to the close association between government defense establishments and corporate defense contractors. This association can lead to a permanent war economy in which productive resources are disproportionately channeled into the creation of weapons of mass destruction.

Modernization refers to Western or Eurocentric development strategies designed to increase a Third World country's GDP by stimulating industrialization and urbanization to produce an export-led economy. Critics of this kind of economic development argue that it is pursued at the expense of human development because it does not focus on meeting basic human needs.

Politics is about differential access to resources, both material and symbolic, and how such power relations and structures are created, sustained, and reconfigured.

Power-over systems are those that rely on coercion deployed from the top down in order to control those on the bottom of social, economic, and political hierarchies in the name of order and stability.

Power politics is a realist concept in IR. It holds that, in the absence of a supranational authority, states will pursue their own self-interests by amassing and deploying military and economic resources in order to gain power over other states or at least maintain a balance of power among competing states.

Practical gender interests arise from women's immediate needs in local contexts, and addressing them typically requires a change in particular gender-based conditions. However, when they are linked to women's strategic gender interests, they can involve a transformation of gender hierarchy.

Privatization occurs when activities that previously were funded and controlled by the state (such as education, health care, social security, and even some forms of law enforcement and national defense) are given over to private corporations to be conducted for profit. Privatization is associated with the erosion of the welfare state and public accountability, turning public citizens into private consumers and reducing political (and moral) issues to matters of economic efficiency.

Productive labor or **production** usually implies work done for wages in the so-called public sector of the formal economy to produce surplus (nonsubsistence) goods and services that can be sold on the open market.

Proportional representation (PR) is an electoral system that allots parliamentary seats according to the proportion of votes received for a slate of candidates (e.g., in Norway), in contrast to single-member legislative districts, where only the candidate with the most votes is seated (e.g., in the United States).

The **public-private** separation or dichotomy refers to the (artificial) distinction between the home (the private or reproductive sphere) to which women are assigned and the workplace (the public or productive sphere) to which men are assigned.

Reactive autonomy refers to an ideology that values independence over interdependence, separation over connection, and order over justice. It is most associated with realist thinking in IR.

Recolonization refers to both the intensification of colonization of the South and the extension of colonizing practices into the North brought about under the banner of globalization.

Relational autonomy refers to an ideology that values interdependence over independence, connection over separation, and justice over order. It is most associated with feminist thinking in IR.

Reproductive labor or **reproduction** commonly implies activities (rarely referred to as work) undertaken in the so-called private sphere (the home) that are necessary to meet the daily needs of household members and to perpetuate human life. These activities include childbearing, child care, elder care, housework, subsistence food production, and food preparation, and they are typically performed by women.

Sex refers to the binary categorization of persons as male or female based on chromosomal and/or anatomical characteristics.

Sexism refers to the systematic and systemic discrimination against and denigration of women and girls in all aspects of life. Encompassing **sexist** behavior, ideologies, and structures, it reproduces masculinism and arises from assumptions that females are "naturally" the weaker, inferior, or second sex.

Socialization is the process by which individuals learn the rules, roles, and relationships deemed appropriate within their culture; people "fit in" to the extent that they adopt and internalize these prescribed patterns of thought and behavior.

Sovereignty refers to a state's right to self-determination and noninterference by other states. In this sense, it is an example of reactive autonomy.

Stereotypes are overgeneralized and rigid preconceptions of traits and behaviors attributed to a particular social group; such fixed images filter people's perceptions and shape their expectations.

Strategic gender interests arise from women's awareness that their immediate problems in local contexts are often the result of larger (national, global, structural) systems of domination. When women move along the continuum from practical to strategic gender interests, they increasingly call for more fundamental transformations, including the elimination of gender hierarchy.

Structural adjustment programs (SAPs) are austerity programs imposed by the International Monetary Fund on Third World debtor countries amidst the debt crisis. These programs essentially require that debtor countries reduce government expenditure on social services and step up production for export to make more foreign exchange to pay back their loans.

Structural violence, which is differentiated from but related to direct physical violence, arises from social, economic, and political structures that increase the vulnerability of various groupings of people (women, minorities, children, the aged, the disabled, gays and lesbians, etc.) to many forms of harm (poverty, hunger, infant mortality, disease, isolation, etc.).

Terrorism usually refers to semi-random acts of violence perpetrated against innocent civilians by nonstate or antistate groups to bring (media and state) attention to their grievances, legitimate or illegitimate. However, states themselves have also been known to engage in terrorism through the deployment of death squads or even nuclear weapons that hold ordinary people hostage to the threat of nuclear annihilation.

The **United Nations System of National Accounts (UNSNA)** is supposedly an accounting of everything of value in or to the market in every country, but it fails to consider such things as the value of reproductive labor and the costs of environmental degradation.

Index

Women's International League for
Peace and Freedom, 181(figure),
182
Women's issues
failure of the media and academe to
respond to, 67(n18)
women politicians and, 96–97
Women's movements
civil society and, 163–165
gender interests and, 177–179
grass-roots, 174–175
liberal feminism, 168
postcolonial feminism, 172–175
postmodern feminism, 175–177
radical feminism, 168–170
socialist feminism, 170–172
Women's Pentagon Action (U.S.), 183,
203
Women's Project of Human Rights
Watch, 228
Women's suffrage, 91–92
Women Strike for Peace (U.S.), 182
Women's work, 9, 57
effects on women's political
participation, 85–87
as family care, 85–86
gender ideology and, 42
gender stereotyping and, 88–89
See also Domestic labor;
Reproductive labor
"Women" trees, 161(n128)
Women warriors, 116
Women Warriors: A History (Jones), 116
Women Workers Movement
(Philippines), 197
Work. See Labor
World Bank, 104, 135, 136

World politics
care model for, 217
civil society and, 163–165
gendered divisions of, 51,
53–61
gender issues in, immediacy of,
14–15
gender-sensitive lens in, 10, 12–13,
33, 236–237
interrelations with international
relations studies, 3–5
position of women in, 11–12
power of gender in, 12–13
reformist and transformative
strategies in, 213
role of the military in, 119
theoretical perspectives in, 1–2,
21–29
ungendering, 237–238
See also International relations
World Summit for Social
Development, 199
World Trade Organization, 75–76, 104,
143
World War I, peace movements and,
181–182
World War II, war effort, women in,
182

Yellen, Janet, 76

Zambia, economic protests in, 195
Zapatista revolution, 187(figure),
205(figure), 206
Zepezauer, Mark, 67(n22)
Zimbabwe, nationalist movement in,
189–190